PERGAMON GENERAL PSYCHOLOGY SERIES

Editors: Arnold P. Goldstein, *Syracuse University*
Leonard Krasner, *SUNY, Stony Brook*

The Psychology of Nonviolence

PGPS-48

The Psychology of Nonviolence

LEROY H. PELTON

PERGAMON PRESS INC.

New York · Toronto · Oxford · Sydney

PERGAMON PRESS INC.
Maxwell House, Fairview Park, Elmsford, N.Y. 10523

PERGAMON OF CANADA LTD.
207 Queen's Quay West, Toronto 117, Ontario

PERGAMON PRESS LTD.
Headington Hill Hall, Oxford

PERGAMON PRESS (AUST.) PTY. LTD.
Rushcutters Bay, Sydney, N.S.W.

Copyright © 1974. Pergamon Press Inc.
Library of Congress Cataloging in Publication Data

Pelton, Leroy H
    The psychology of nonviolence.

    (Pergamon general psychology series, PGPS-48)
    1. Nonviolence. I. Title. [DNLM: 1. Violence.
HM278 P393p 1974]
HM278.P44 1974   301.6'32'019   74-2167
ISBN 0-08-018099-X
ISBN 0-08-018098-1 (pbk.)

Printed in the United States of America

In memory of my father,
Myer Pelton
(1900–1964)

Contents

The Author

Leroy H. Pelton (Ph.D., Wayne State University) is Assistant Professor of Psychology at Susquehanna University in Selinsgrove, Pennsylvania. He received his M.A. from the New School for Social Research. In addition to his teaching duties, Dr. Pelton is active as a researcher of cognitive processes, perception, and social psychology. He is a member of the Society for the Psychological Study of Social Issues and he has written journal articles in the areas of perception and cognition.

Preface

How can we achieve a world of peace and justice? This question, together with my belief that the philosophy of nonviolence holds a promising answer that is in need of further exploration, has motivated the writing of this book. My purpose is to study the meaning of nonviolence—its philosophy, strategy, and implications—from a psychological perspective.

This book represents an instance of the explicit injection of values into social science. Any theory is derived from certain untested and even untestable premises; in psychology these premises often take the form of broad assumptions about the nature of man. The philosophy of nonviolence can be construed as a theory of conflict resolution that has been derived from certain moral premises as well. Those who are critical of a scientific work for being "value-laden" are obliged to consider whether the injection of values into science constitutes any violation of science itself and, if so, in what way.

The questions that a scientist asks, and those that he devises experiments to test, already partially determine the answers that will be obtained and the generalizations that will be drawn. Science is in many ways a subjective enterprise. (For some social psychology of the history of science see Burtt [1932] and Kuhn [1962].) I believe that it is far worse for a social scientist to feign objectivity than to openly display his subjectivity.

What qualifies this book as being scientific is only that it reports scientific evidence, often based on experiments performed as closely in conformance with the rules of experimentation as the subject matter would permit. But the questions that are asked and the interpretations of the evidence that are made have little to do with the rules of experimentation; here as anywhere in social science, they are influenced by the inclinations and values of the investigator. The fact of the presence of these influences often seems to draw criticism only when the issues involved are of a socially controversial nature, as are the ones that will concern us here.

Since in this book I attempt to apply modern social psychological evidence to the study of the philosophy and strategy of nonviolence, a word should be said about the role of experimental research in social-psychological theorizing. The conditions surrounding a particular social phenomenon are frequently so complex that it is often difficult to say with certainty when experimental findings apply to particular situations in the world outside of the laboratory and when they do not. Nonetheless, if we were to view most experimental social-psychological research as serving the function of guiding our thinking about social phenomena rather than as being a source of direct generalizations to the world outside of the laboratory, such research could help to increase the sophistication of our thinking and theorizing about social phenomena. Kelman (1968, p. 159) has expounded this view by saying that the contributions that experimental research can make to social-psychological knowledge "take the form of providing *unique inputs into systematic thinking about social-psychological processes*, rather than of establishing laws about social behavior." While somewhat partial to Kelman's view to begin with, my writing of this book has led me to a deeper appreciation of it.

Moral considerations can be another important input or guide for the thinking of the psychologist who is concerned not only with describing the experience and behavior of man but with exploring his potentiality. If such a subjective inclination as sun-worship could guide Kepler to important discoveries about the universe (Burtt, 1932, pp. 44 ff.), social scientists might be guided by moral premises to important insights pertaining to the improvement of the quality of human interaction. Nonviolence suggests a strategy of conflict resolution derived from moral premises. Psychological evidence can aid us in examining and refining its practicality. Incidentally, the application of psychology to nonviolence is not a one-way affair, for my consideration of nonviolence from a psychological perspective has also led me to entertain certain questions about current trends in experimental psychology.

Mankind may well be on the brink of destroying itself. In this century of great technological advancement, millions upon millions of people have already been slaughtered, and world peace is nowhere in sight. It is often said that our next advancement must be in our understanding of ourselves. We have reached the moon, so the argument goes, but we have not yet discovered how to live with each other. People everywhere long for a just and enduring world peace, for a world of brotherly love.

Is the field of psychology irrelevant to such concerns? I feel the obligation to apply my psychological knowledge to the problems of peace and social justice. Who shall judge that I should not? Earlier in this century, physical scientists left the moral issues to others. But who are the "moral experts"—politicians, lawyers, business executives? Who? Should the psychologist decline to raise the moral issues himself, and then cry later as some physicists have done? I am a psychologist *and* I am a human being—a man born into a world of war and violence, now raising children who live in a world still unchanged in that respect. I am as entitled as anyone to speak on morality, and I will not divorce my morality from my psychology.

Because of the unconventional nature of this book, I am especially grateful to those individuals who have believed in the worth of my project (notwithstanding its strange character) and who have advised and encouraged me.

Professor Edward L. Walker provided me with many thoughtful and constructive comments and criticisms on each chapter as the writing progressed. He was especially concerned with my achieving a satisfactory level of integration of the philosophy of nonviolence and psychological evidence. His suggestions aided me greatly in this regard. However, on this and other matters I did not always follow his advice as diligently as I might have, and I must bear sole responsibility for any shortcomings in the attempted integration as well as for any fallacies that may be unwittingly promulgated in this book. Dr. Walker's contribution includes his constant encouragement, for which I am very grateful.

I wish to thank Professor Lee Sechrest for his encouragement during the crucial early stages of this book.

Professor Marshall Segall was instrumental in assuring the publication of this book. I was gratified by his quick grasp of the essence of what I was attempting to do, and refreshed by his faith in the product.

My friendship with Mrs. Gloria Cecchetti began when I happened to hire her to type the final draft of my manuscript, a task that she performed excellently. Much to my surprise, she soon became so involved with the manuscript that she took upon herself the role of copy editor. Before long, she was not only correcting grammatical errors but aiding me in the improvement of word usage. Best of all, her great faith in my work carried me over periods of depression.

The original sources of inspiration for this work are numerous, and some will become evident from a reading of the text. Here I wish to mention that I was inspired, in part, by the sincere and selfless efforts of the people of the Capital Area Peace Center in Albany, New York, especially at the height of American involvement in the Vietnam War, who contributed to the attempts of the peace movement to end that war. One member of the Center in those days, Richard Evans, a young nonviolent activist, especially inspired me by the calm moral courage with which he refused to cooperate with the draft system and prepared himself to accept the consequences.

Finally, a note of appreciation is due to Professor Charles M. Solley, my former advisor in graduate school at Wayne State University. Although he had no knowledge of my writing of this book, his influence on my thinking in psychology has been considerable. The study of perceptual and cognitive constructs as an approach to psychology is one that Dr. Solley stimulated me to consider, as did my prior readings in Gestalt psychology, and is one that is evident throughout this book.

I will contribute my royalties from this book in equal parts to the following organizations: War Resisters League, Fellowship of Reconciliation, SANE (A Citizens' Organization for a Sane World), American Friends Service Committee, Southern Christian Leadership Conference, and the Martin Luther King, Jr. Memorial Center in Atlanta, Georgia.

Therefore I suggest that the philosophy and strategy of nonviolence become immediately a subject for study and for serious experimentation in every field of human conflict, by no means excluding the relations between nations.

MARTIN LUTHER KING, JR.

CHAPTER 1

Violence and Nonviolence

It is said that on the last day of his life Gandhi was asked how, with nonviolence, he would meet the atom bomb. He answered:

> I will not go into shelter. I will come out in the open and let the pilot see I have not a trace of ill will against him. The pilot will not see our faces from his great height, I know. But the longing in our hearts—that he will come to no harm—would reach up to him and his eyes would be opened.

If the answer does not seem satisfactory, we must consider the absurdity of the question. The moment of nuclear disaster lies beyond a time for any answer other than its own terrible verdict on the supreme failure of mankind to find peaceable means of resolving conflict.

Gandhi could have tactfully replied that he would not have been so foolish as to have waited until the bombs were overhead before he initiated nonviolent action. Surely the earlier a conflict is dealt with the better chance there is of resolution, and the conflict that eventuated in nuclear warfare must have been developing for quite some time.

Likewise, social scientists must not wait until the bombs are overhead before they attempt to examine possible humane approaches to the resolution of conflict and to the attainment of a peaceful and just world. As Bondurant (1965, p. xv) has said:

> The problem of human conflict is perhaps the most fundamental problem of all time. In this age when the physical sciences have outstripped the more slowly advancing social sciences, it is one of undeniable urgency, and one which already attracts social scientists in many disciplines.

This book is primarily concerned with an experimental social-psychological approach to the study of nonviolence. The perspective of

1

nonviolence is adopted at the outset in order to explore its possibilities for the waging and resolution of social conflict.

Both violent and nonviolent means have their apparent drawbacks—the one because it leads to the destruction of human life, and the other because of its seeming inability, or lack of power, to deal adequately with severe conflict and injustice or to stop violence. But in a world in which social conflicts constantly arise, time is running out for us to explore peaceable means for resolving conflict.

When we are faced with self-destruction, idealism becomes the only practicality. By carefully examining the ideal of nonviolence, we have nothing to lose and the prospect of lasting peace to gain. Perhaps we will find nonviolence challenging, possible, and not so unpromising after careful study as at first glance; perhaps "we will be able to hew out of the mountain of despair a stone of hope."

It is the specter of the nuclear destruction of mankind that is often raised to induce us to seek ways in which we might put an end to war. But, while not belittling the nuclear threat that hangs over all of us, we should remind ourselves that the massive slaughter of human beings proceeds without the use of nuclear weapons—that, for example, about 600,000 people were killed during the American Civil War without such weapons; that in World War II, according to some estimates, more people were killed by the fire-bombing of Dresden than by the atom-bombing of Hiroshima; and that the long and unspeakable horror of Vietnam has evolved without the "benefit" of nuclear weaponry.

If we believe in the sanctity of human life, if we agree with Martin Luther King, Jr. (1967, p. 72) that "when we say 'Thou shalt not kill,' we're really saying that human life is too sacred to be taken on the battlefields of the world," then we must find an alternative to war and violence.

Tragically, nothing has changed, in a sense. Those of my generation were born into a world of war and continue to live in a world of daily violence and war. There are men who detect injustice in our world, and they think that they will root it out through war, violence, and terror. Others seek to protect what they believe is rightfully theirs, and out of fear lash out violently and oppressively. How strange it is that everyone today, even two parties to the same conflict, thinks that *he* is the one who is fighting for peace, justice, and freedom. Men still go to war with so much self-righteousness, with such a noble sense of justice and determination for peace. They seem blind to the possibility presented by history that war cannot end war, that violence cannot bring enduring world peace, that a means that in itself perpetrates injustice cannot eventuate in just ends. It is as if our world is made up of individuals in whom reflective conscious awareness (that highest and strangest of mental qualities) has undergone a stunted development, so that they seem to lack the capacity to step outside their situation and view their folly from a temporary, uninvolved vantage point, to step back and view the horror and irony of the ever-repeating pattern of war and violence. Perhaps they fail to see that a new way might be needed.

Martin Luther King, Jr. (1968, p. 213) said:

> One day we must come to see that peace is not merely a distant goal that we seek but a means by which we arrive at that goal. We must pursue peaceful ends through peaceful means. How much longer must we play at deadly war games before we heed the plaintive pleas of the unnumbered dead and maimed of past wars?

Gandhi subtitled his autobiography *The Story of My Experiments with Truth*. Throughout his life he accepted the extraordinary challenge of nonviolence and experimented with it in the world of action. Perhaps the full exploration of an idea sometimes requires that we commit ourselves to it and, while looking at the world through its perspective, take it to its limits and beyond. It is in this sense that we can best understand Gandhi's willingness to entertain a direct reply to the question of how he would meet the bomb. And it is in this spirit that I wish to explore nonviolence here. Inspired and instructed by the history of nonviolent action and by the writings of others on the concept from various points of departure (such as the disciplines of sociology and political science), I will attempt to bring modern psychology to bear upon the philosophy of non-violence. Some reflection on the nature of violence will facilitate this endeavor.

VIOLENCE

Psychologists have used the term aggression more frequently than violence but have experienced difficulty in agreeing upon a definition of it. We might define aggression as action that is intended to hurt others.

However, the man who attempts to rob a store intends to obtain money; although he might prefer not to shoot the owner, he may do so if the owner offers resistance. A nation goes to war in order to obtain certain objectives, but it can often be said that the ultimate goal is not to kill people. The national leaders might have gladly achieved their goals without killing anyone if only they knew how. Furthermore, the soldier who obeys orders to shoot at the enemy might prefer not to kill anyone. He might have the same ultimate goals as his leaders, or he might merely tell you that he has to do what he is told.

Perhaps it can be said that at the moment of pulling the trigger the thief has the short-run intention of injuring the store owner in order to stop his interference, even though his long-run intention is to obtain money; that the national leaders who have long-run intentions of reaching certain ultimate goals nonetheless have the short-run intention of injuring others in order to obtain those goals; and that the soldier, at the moment of shooting, has the momentary intention of injuring someone.

However, in order to encompass the above examples while avoiding confusion, it might be better to define aggression as action that is initiated with some *expectation* (Kaufmann, 1970) that it will injure another person.

But there is another difficulty with the term aggression. In common usage it possesses the connotation illustrated by contrasting it with defense—i.e., it carries the meaning of an *unprovoked* attack. (As will be indicated later, what constitutes "no provocation" is often unclear, and whether one will call a given action aggressive or defensive is often more dependent upon which side one favors that anything else.) In order to avoid this connotation, I will use the term violence rather than aggression. To those who wish to concern themselves with the problems of "who started" and of fixing blame in a conflict situation, I leave the popular connotation of the word aggression. In this book I will be more concerned with the problem of human beings inflicting physical injury on each other and killing each other, no matter what the circumstances. I will define violence as action that is initiated with some expectation that it will physically injure another living being.

Violence has certainly been defined more broadly at times. Some people refer to violence to inanimate objects or to property, and some would include "psychological" injury. It is often surprising to learn what types of acts some people would call violent. A recent survey showed that some people regard burglary, student protests, sit-ins, and "not letting people have their civil rights" as violence, while some do not regard the shooting of looters or the beating of students by police as violence (Blumenthal, 1972). (Indeed, whether a given act is considered to be violent, much less aggressive, often seems to depend upon what side one favors.) Violence seems to be regarded by some as almost synonymous with injustice—as when they speak of bad schools and inadequate housing as forms of violence.

While being concerned about all such matters as those mentioned above, and certainly with injustice, I will use my admittedly extremely narrow definition of violence in order to distinguish (especially) the killing and maiming of people from other forms of injustice.

However, on top of all the other difficulties of definition, I must implore the reader to allow me one technical misuse of the English language: the word nonviolence will not be used to merely connote the absence of violence. Given my stubbornness about using a particularly narrow definition of violence (which, by the way, other writers on nonviolence do not share), but even without it, the necessity for this linguistic error will soon become clear. Briefly, nonviolence is used here as the name of a particular philosophy of action.

Psychologists have agreed that frustration can induce violent action, although their definitions of frustration have varied. While frustration might be defined as the blockage of or interference with one's movement or activity toward a goal, we might require that the individual at least be cognizant of this interference in order for us to say that he has been frustrated. Furthermore, the frustration may or may not involve emotion. An engineer might calmly face the obstacles involved in designing a bridge without getting emotionally upset. An individual might seek out a difficult crossword puzzle or golf course. A tennis player might not want to play against anyone not as good as he. Far from experiencing negative emotions, these people might enjoy confronting obstacles although, of course, the engineer, puzzle enthusiast, golfer, and tennis player *may* at times become upset during their activity and experience what we might call emotional frustration and anger.

Violence often begets violence, as seemingly attested to by mankind's long history of violence and retaliation. Illustrative of this are the findings of an experiment in which male university students were given either one or seven electric shocks, supposedly as a form of evaluation of some work they had been asked to do, and then were given the opportunity to shock the person who had shocked them. Those who had received seven shocks responded with more and longer shocks than those who had originally received just one (Berkowitz and LePage, 1967). It was also found that the presence of a rifle or revolver on the table next to the shock key increased the number of shocks given by the students who had originally received seven shocks (the weapons effect).

However, whether or not the arousal of anger is necessary for such reciprocation of violence has been called into doubt by a recent investigation (Page and Scheidt, 1971).

There is another way in which violence may beget violence, a way that might be quite important in our modern world of mass media. The possible role of observed violence in stimulating violence on the part of the observer has received much attention in the field of psychology.

In one study, nursery school children between the ages of three and six years witnessed an adult (the "model") punching and kicking a large inflated Bobo doll and striking it in the head with a mallet. The children were then frustrated by not being allowed to continue playing with some attractive toys after they had just become involved with them. When then placed with a Bobo doll, the children were found to exhibit much "violence" resembling that of the model's behavior they had viewed previously.[1] They were more "violent" than similarly frustrated children who had watched a model who had ignored the Bobo doll (Bandura, Ross, and Ross, 1961).

In a later study, these same investigators (Bandura, Ross, and Ross, 1963) showed that a similar filmed sequence of modeled "violence" against the Bobo doll, as well as "violence" displayed by filmed cartoon models, facilitated later "violence" in nursery school children after they had been subjected to a frustrating experience. Those children who had witnessed the "violent" human or cartoon models were much more "violent" than children in a control group who had been frustrated but did not view the filmed "violence."

To demonstrate that the stimulating effects of observed violence are not limited to children, Walters, Thomas, and Acker (1962) showed male hospital attendants the knife-fight scene from the motion picture *Rebel Without a Cause*. Male attendants in a control group watched an educational film that did not contain violent content. Each man was then required to run a purported conditioning experiment in which the subject (a confederate of the investigators) was to be punished for errors by having the man deliver shock to him. The men in the group who had previously watched the fight punished errors with more intense shock than did members of the control group.

Since frustration was not induced in this experiment, the findings indicate that a person need not be in an angered state in order for observed violence to have its effect. Hartmann (1969), using adolescent delinquents as his subjects, also found that those who had seen a film with violent content later administered more punitive shock to their "partners" for errors on a presumed learning task, regardless of anger arousal, than those who had watched a similar film without the violent content.

Because of the propensity of people to try to justify their use of violence to others, sometimes by depicting their victim as "deserving" of it, the following findings are interesting. In a study by Berkowitz (1965), two groups of college students who had been angered (by being insulted) were shown the prize-fight scene from the motion picture *Champion*, in which the protagonist is severely beaten. Prior to seeing the film, one group heard the protagonist described as a cynical and heartless opportunist, while the other group heard him described in a manner that was likely to arouse sympathy for him. Afterward, in a situation in which the subjects had the opportunity to shock the confederate who had previously angered them, a greater number of shocks were delivered by the subjects who had heard the protagonist described as a villain than by those who had heard the more sympathetic description. Observation of the more "justified" violence more strongly facilitated violence in the angered students than did observation of the less "justified" violence.

However, although only a fraction of the evidence that seems to support the notion that observed violence has a stimulating effect on violent behavior has been reported above, there is still much room for doubt as to how pervasive this relationship is. In an experimental field study lasting over a period of weeks, Feshbach and Singer (1971) did not find television violence to have any facilitative effect upon the violent behavior of boys (although other field studies have).

Furthermore, Page and Scheidt (1971) have provided evidence that suggests that Berkowitz and LePage's weapons effect (noted above) might not be due to the weapons per se. Many subjects might have been aware of the purpose of the experiment and might have acted in accordance with what they thought was "expected" of them. If this was the case, it is not unlikely that such cooperation with "demand characteristics" (Orne, 1962) of the experiment (i.e., with cues that convey a hypothesis to the subject) was operating in many of the laboratory experiments involving the observation of violence.

Moreover, in investigations pertaining to human beings, asking the question of how an "input" such as filmed violence relates to an "output" such as violent behavior (and concentrating on those two gross variables while relatively ignoring the intervening cognitive processes) can lead to overly simplistic conclusions about violent behavior as well as to suggestions of inadequate remedies. Should we not be more concerned with what the individual can do with what he sees—how he interprets and thinks about it—and explore the possibilities in this domain? For example, if a child has generated and strongly internalized a value that prohibits violence in any situation, I doubt whether watching television violence many hours a day for the next year would make him become violent. What he sees would be interpreted in the context of his value, for man is not a robot. Environmental stimuli do not necessarily "trigger" certain responses in a blind, mechanical, and reflexive manner.

Prior experience and learning do not always determine behavior in the sense that they lock or clamp behavior into a particular form. Prior experience and learning do not always operate as rigid constraints upon our behavior. If this were the case, there would be nothing new or creative ensuing from man's behavior. On the contrary, man acts upon his prior experience with thinking and reasoning. Prior experience feeds his thinking and reasoning processes. It is not the experience that is the master, but these processes. In fact, it can be said that it is not behavior that is learned, but concepts, and it is these concepts that man often works with before he behaves.

I do not deny that there might be a relation between observed violence and violent behavior. And I am not saying that situational variables are unimportant. I merely wish to point out that even when we can make statements about gross stimulus-response relationships, we should often regard such statements as descriptive of current trends in behavior rather than view the relationships as fundamental. In order to discover the potential of man to overcome situational determinants of his behavior, we must examine his cognitive processes.

Be that as it may, I would suggest that the violence that has caused the overwhelming proportion of the countless millions of violent deaths in this century alone can best be accounted for neither by momentary feelings of emotional frustration and anger nor by the observation of violence. To understand organized violence and war, we must look elsewhere. I do not claim that emotional frustration, anger, and the observation of violence are unimportant. If they account for one death, they are important. Moreover, I do not claim that they are not involved in war and organized violence; on the contrary, I believe that their possible roles in such activity should be given much consideration. Yet it would seem that *violence is often rationally planned and obediently executed.*[2]

Social conflict can be viewed as a problem for its participants, whether they be nations, groups, or individuals. Each of the two participants can be said to have certain goals it wants to achieve, while believing that the other participant is setting obstacles in its path. The problem is how to overcome those obstacles and achieve the goal. One "solution" to this problem that has been decided upon time and again throughout history when no others could be found has involved the use of violence.

Surely we can say that such a decision to employ violence is partially determined by frustration, in the sense that the decision maker has understood that his movement toward a certain goal has been blocked. But emotional frustration and an intense feeling of anger need not be significantly involved. When one is faced with a problem that he finds no other means of confronting except by violence, his lack of anger will matter little. National leaders, for example, do not usually declare war on the spur of an angry moment. The decision to go to war might have been the outcome of months of deliberation, involving many people in discussion and deep reflective thought. (Of course, the build-up of American participation in the Vietnam War involved numerous decisions made over a period of years; a look at the famous Pentagon Papers is instructive in this regard. Also, for one view on the dynamics of group decision-making among national policy makers, see Janis [1971].)

There is the possibility that the observation and knowledge of violence in the past may play a role here. The decision makers might look to what they consider to have been the successful use of violence by others, and they may be influenced by this in their decision. And, once the choice of violence is made, they will of course be interested in learning from anyone they can how to best use violence, what weapons to select, etc. In this sense it can be said that they rely on past models.

But what is of overriding significance is that they did not see any other way to try to solve their problem. Calm, rationally planned and initiated violence is the violence that has destroyed the most human life, not the reflexive violence that stems from immediate anger or that is triggered by stimuli in a blind and mechanical way. It is often observed that national leaders express great reluctance on the eve of war. They wanted to solve the problem in another way, they claim, but could not find an alternative. It may well be that it is their ignorance of alternatives to war that often drives men toward war.

It is for these reasons that I would suggest that Clark's (1971) proposal that we give "psychotechnical medication" to our national leaders in order to "reduce or block the possibility of their using power destructively" is inadequate. Clark suggests a "biochemical intervention which could stabilize and make dominant the moral and ethical propensities of man and subordinate, if not eliminate, his negative and primitive behavior tendencies." But, whereas drugs might prevent the individual violence of an occasional impulsively violent criminal, the violence of war is not only rationally and calmly planned but might be determined more by the "uniquely human moral and ethical characteristics of love, kindness, and empathy," which Clark seeks to enhance, than by the "animalistic, barbaric, and primitive propensities in man." After all, with few possible exceptions in the animal kingdom, it is only man that engages in organized violence. Do not our leaders take us to war out of love for their country? During war, do not many people display great kindness toward each other, and do not some sacrifice greatly for the sake of their countrymen? (Watson [1966, p. 497] has pointed out that war involves a stupendous organized bureaucratic enterprise in which more men are involved in cooperative activity than in direct violence against the enemy, and that, far from relishing the anticipation of some sort of satisfaction from violent behavior, men often have to be drafted into armies by their nations.) But wait: these rhetorical questions are too glib. Surely the expansion of our spheres of love and empathy to include all of humanity would help, as would an understanding of how to put love into action. But, as we shall see, it is rational thought that can aid us in these matters. Thus, the *same* processes that underlie the decision to use violence are the ones that can lead us to alternatives to violence, and it is unlikely that drugs can help us to solve, without violence, the problems we face in social conflicts.

Once organized violence is rationally planned, it must be obediently carried out. Surely the internalization of such attitudes as that one's cause is just, that violence is necessary to uphold it, and that the enemy is evil—along with feelings of anger and hostility toward the enemy—might contribute to the making of a good soldier. The role of such factors will be discussed later, but they are beyond the minimal requirements of soldiery. For those who face the call of "duty" to fight for one's country, what is crucial is not the hours of television violence that one might or might not have watched as a child but the inclination to obey legitimate authority. The potential of obedience to generate violence was demonstrated in a dramatic manner by Milgram (1963).

In this study, each subject was led to believe that he was participating in an experiment designed to investigate the effects of punishment on learning. He was to deliver an electric shock to the learner (hereafter referred to as the victim) every time the latter made an erroneous response on a word-pair learning task. After having witnessed the victim being strapped down in a chair and an electrode being attached to his wrist, the subject was seated in front of a simulated shock generator in an adjacent room. He was faced with an impressive instrument panel consisting of 30 levers, with labels above them ranging from "slight shock" through "moderate," "strong," "very strong," "intense," and "extreme intensity shock," to "danger: severe shock." The last two switches were labeled XXX. The voltage designation ranged from 15 to 450 volts in steps of 15 volts. Unknown to the subject, the imposing-looking machine was not capable of generating any shock to the victim, who was actually an accomplice of the experimenter. However, before beginning, the subject was given a painful sample shock of 45 volts. The painfulness of higher-level shocks was left to his imagination, although he had been informed that, while they could be extremely painful, no permanent tissue damage could result from them. He was then told that he was to deliver the 15-volt shock to the victim after the latter made an error, *and he was to move to the next highest shock level after each succeeding erroneous response.*

During this procedure, the victim was silent up until the time that the subject delivered the 300-volt shock. At that point, the victim pounded on the wall and thereafter did not even signal his answers anymore. The subject was then instructed by the experimenter to treat no response as a wrong answer and to continue with the procedure. If the subject went on to deliver the 315-volt shock, he again heard pounding on the wall, but thereafter the victim fell silent. If, at any time during this procedure, the subject turned to the experimenter for advice or to indicate his reluctance to continue, the experimenter had ready a number of prods, which he spoke in a firm voice, ranging from "Please continue" to the stern command: "You have no other choice, you *must* go on."

It is important to note that while the subjects in this study (male adults) were told to deliver what they believed to be extremely painful shock, there was no tangible threat hanging over their heads; they must have known that the experimenter had no power to punish them in any way for not complying, and they could have refused to continue at any time. What was being studied here was obedience to legitimate authority—in this particular case, to a social scientist who was the authority within the laboratory setting.

None of the 40 subjects observed in this particular study defied the experimenter before administering what he believed to be an intense shock of 300 volts. Some subjects refused to continue at some point after that, but 26 subjects (or 65%) obeyed until the end, and pressed the lever marked 450 volts, which was two steps beyond the designation "danger: severe shock."

It should not be supposed that this remarkable display of obedience in harming another person came easily to many of the subjects; there were indications that they suffered severe inner conflict and tension. As Milgram (1965b) said:

> A conflict develops between the deeply ingrained disposition not to harm others and the equally compelling tendency to obey others who are in authority.

Some subjects indicated a reluctance to go on at various points during the ordeal, and many were observed to sweat and tremble and exhibit other signs of nervousness; but they obeyed nonetheless. Strange nervous laughter was observed in a number of subjects.

There were other variations of this procedure (Milgram, 1965b), each involving different subjects. In one, the victim let out a light grunt when the 75-, 90-, and 105-volt shocks were administered. He reacted to the 120-volt shock by shouting to the experimenter that the shocks were becoming painful. Painful groans were heard at the next shock level and at higher levels the protests became increasingly frantic. The victim at one point yelled to the experimenter to get him out of there and said that he refused to go on. At 180 volts he cried out that he could not stand the pain and screamed out in agony at higher shock levels. Still, a similar proportion of subjects (62.5%) as in the first study were obedient to authority until the bitter end. In another variation, subjects still shocked the victim upon command even when he cried out that he had heart trouble.

In Munich, Mantell (1971) replicated Milgram's study, observing West German men. Groans, sobbing, screams, and protests were heard up until 375 volts, and thereafter the victim fell silent. The results were again similar, with 85% of the subjects going all the way.

Milgram (1965b) found that when there were no protests of any kind from the victim, virtually all subjects obeyed completely.

In yet another variation by Milgram, when the victim was seated next to the subject instead of being in another room, 40% were completely obedient. Even when, in order to administer shocks to the victim, the subject had to forcibly place the victim's hand onto a shock-plate amidst his protests (and was so ordered by the experimenter), 30% of the subjects obeyed until the end.

In regard to this finding—that the more removed the victim is from a person the more likely that person would be to inflict pain upon command—it should be remembered that in a world of modern weaponry much violence is committed from a distance, with little chance of direct contact with the suffering of the victim.

In commenting on his personal observations of the subjects in his obedience studies—who numbered about one thousand, resided in southern Connecticut, and represented a wide variety of occupations— Milgram (1965b) asserted:

> With numbing regularity good people were seen to knuckle under the demands of authority and perform actions that were callous and severe. Men who are in everyday life responsible and decent were seduced by the trappings of authority, by the control of their perceptions, and by the uncritical acceptance of the experimenter's definition of the situation, into performing harsh acts.

Obedience, of course, can serve good as well as evil. And, as Milgram (1963) has commented, "the very life of society is predicated on its existence." Yet the fact is that obedience was necessary for, and did contribute to, much of the massive slaughter of our time.

The possibility that in the above studies the subjects could believe that they were helping the experimenter to achieve a worthy goal—the advancement of scientific knowledge—does not set them apart from other instances of destructive obedience. Those who give commands often hint at some worthy end.

In a recent survey, it was found that when asked what they would do "if ordered to shoot all inhabitants of a Vietnamese village suspected of aiding the enemy, including old men, women and children," 51% of Americans who were sampled said that they would follow orders and shoot (Kelman and Lawrence, 1972).

The slaughter of the Six Million Jews was hardly due to the existence of an entire nation of vicious people with evil intent. The calm, calculated, organized murder of the Jews must have been contributed to by nice, loving, decent people, many of them in offices merely shifting papers from desk to desk. As Milgram (1963) has pointed out:

> Gas chambers were built, death camps were guarded, daily quotas of corpses were produced with the same efficiency as the manufacture of appliances. These inhumane policies may have originated in the mind of a single person, but they could only be carried out on a massive scale if a very large number of persons obeyed orders.

In Milgram's studies, there was no tangible risk or threat involved in disobedience, but obedience was prevalent nonetheless. Although those who participate in destructive obedience may often do so partly because of a belief that their acts serve some ultimate noble end, we must remember that disobedience in Nazi Germany probably *would* have involved *considerable* risk, and people fear the sometimes severe personal consequences of disobedience. It is often not what many of us consider to be the negative qualities of people (such as hatred, bigotry, and viciousness) that bring them to participate in evil; rather, often only what we frequently *praise* people for (such as courage) allows them to *withhold* their contributions to evil—although, of course, courage can serve evil as well as good. The perpetration of massive evil can be facilitated by people who fail to exhibit the courage of dissent or disobedience.

It is, however, always surprising to observe how slight a risk, how small a reward, and how minimal a threat of punishment, and indeed that fear of the most trivial form of social disapproval, is often enough to gain the compliance of people to do what they otherwise would not have done. Yet I do not wish to belittle the fact that in some situations, such as those in which people are ordered to participate in killing, the risks of disobedience are often considerable. Disobedience must entail an ability and willingness to face those risks and to suffer greatly, and this fact must be faced by those who would resist evil.

NONVIOLENCE

Some of the comments made in my discussion of violence might aid us in our understanding of nonviolence. As I have indicated, nonviolence is not meant here as merely the absence of violence. I use the term nonviolence to refer to what is a philosophy and strategy of conflict resolution, a means of fighting injustice, and in a broader sense a way of life, developed and employed by Gandhi in South Africa and India. It is known by the name Satyagraha, which means holding to the truth, or truth force, but in our country it is more commonly referred to as nonviolence.

The interpretation of this philosophy of action to be presented here is derived from other writings on nonviolence and is particularly dependent upon Bondurant's (1965) analysis of Satyagraha; but ultimately it is merely my own.[3]

One of the central concepts of Gandhi's philosophy is *ahimsa*, which literally means non-injury. In a more positive sense, it can be taken to mean love or active goodwill. *Ahimsa* is predicated upon the belief in the sacredness of life, and can be more explicitly interpreted as action based on the refusal to do harm.

I will take the liberty of explicating even more what I believe to be the full sense of *ahimsa* by saying that it is action based on the refusal to do harm and injustice or to allow harm and injustice to exist.[4] Nonviolence not only suggests that we act in a manner that will not harm anyone but that we strive to root out injustice in the world. Nonviolence, then, is action that does not do or allow injustice.

It might be thought that the nonviolent activist (or Satyagrahi—i.e., one who practices Satyagraha, or nonviolence) believes that he knows precisely what constitutes justice, or thinks that he has cornered the market on truth. This is far from the case. It is partly because the nonviolent activist believes that he cannot know absolute truth, and that he can act only on the basis of what he *considers to be* injustice, that he uses nonviolent means. He believes that violence carries an implicit judgment on other men that contains a finality that no man is fit to impose upon others. The perpetrator of violence, through his action, sets himself up as a judge of who is to live and who is to die. But, according to the concept of truth in the philosophy of nonviolence, he is not fit to judge such an issue for he, like all of us, is trapped by his own subjective reality; he acts from one aspect of reality only. Gandhi (1951, p. 3) said that Satyagraha "excludes the use of violence because man is not capable of knowing the absolute truth and, therefore, not competent to punish."

Thus, the concept of truth in the philosophy of nonviolence is that of relative truth. Moreover, the relative truth of the nonviolent activist is judged in terms of the fulfillment of human needs. Such truth would be destroyed through the use of means that violate human needs. Bondurant (1965, p. 25) has said:

> If there is dogma in the Gandhian philosophy, it centers here: that the only test of truth is action based on the refusal to do harm.

A third principle of the philosophy of nonviolence is that of self-suffering. This concept has many implications within the context of nonviolence. The test of love in action is the willingness to sacrifice for the sake of others. But, in addition, it has often been said in the literature on nonviolence that one of the functions of voluntary suffering is to appeal to the conscience of the adversary and to persuade him. It has been claimed that such suffering will "melt the hearts" and elicit the sympathy and understanding of others. Another function of voluntary self-suffering is to dramatize the alleged injustice, or the position of the nonviolent activist, and perhaps it is partly through such dramatization that the above results are expected to be achieved.

There are other implications of this concept. The nonviolent activist will suffer the violence of others rather than respond with violence and thereby inflict suffering on others. There is the belief that such a policy (when combined with other positive action) will ultimately result in the least total loss of life. Then, too, suffering can demonstrate one's sincerity, for only to the extent that a person is sincere about his beliefs would he be willing to undergo suffering on their behalf. Also, the self-suffering that nonviolent action often entails acts as a safeguard that the nonviolent activist will not contribute to the disruption of the status quo of society (which nonviolent action sometimes entails) unless he sincerely believes that an injustice exists. Furthermore, one's ability and willingness to suffer allows one to resist injustice. The refusal to comply with injustice often necessitates suffering. In the face of coercive attempts to get me to act in a manner contrary to my own beliefs, I must endure suffering if I am to remain true to my beliefs. When others seek to control our behavior by punishing us for noncompliance and rewarding us for compliance, we can liberate ourselves from complicity with what we consider to be injustice and free ourselves from the manipulative attempts of others to the extent that we are willing to suffer instead. *Self*-control requires self-discipline and an ability and willingness to suffer and sacrifice. "Just as *ahimsa* carries in the Gandhian ethic the positive meaning of love and goodwill, self-suffering requires the positive attribute of courage" (Bondurant, 1965, p. 28).

—These principles of *ahimsa*, relative truth, and self-suffering underlie and guide nonviolent action and the nonviolent waging of conflict.

— Nonviolence is action-oriented; it does not avoid conflict but seeks to confront and resolve it. It acknowledges, I think, that there are not only actions (such as violence) that are themselves unjust and therefore must be avoided but that sometimes inaction can contribute to injustice. Those of my generation have seen the crimes of silence. The nonviolent activist holds the attitude that we are responsible for other human beings, for they all are our brothers and sisters.

The nonviolent activist proceeds on the basis of what he considers to be injustice. As Bondurant (1965, p. 33) has said:

> Holding to the truth means holding to what the satyagrahi believes to be the truth until he is dissuaded from that position or any part of it. Meanwhile his effort is steadfastly to persuade his opponent.

While the nonviolent activist is not prepared to yield any position he holds to be the truth, he remains open to and invites the persuasive attempts of his adversary, and is prepared to depart—either totally or partially—from his original position if persuaded that he is in error (Bondurant, 1965, pp. 196–197).

The nonviolent activist tries not to depict the conflict in an over-simplified way. He acknowledges the positive points of the adversary's arguments and is quick to admit his own mistakes in the conflict situation or flaws in his own reasoning should he be convinced of them. He never, of course, tries to depict the adversary in a dehumanized manner.

—Nonviolence involves an attempt to appeal to the adversary's conscience and rationality in order to convert him. It seeks to change inner attitudes. The nonviolent activist hopes to see the adversary act in a way that the former considers just, ultimately because the latter also considers it just. There is perhaps the implicit assumption that changed behavior, in order to endure, must eventually stem from changed attitudes.

Nonviolence entails a positive regard for the adversary. He must be treated with dignity and respect at all times. The nonviolent activist respects the human rights of all individuals—of the adversary in a conflict and of the oppressor as well as the oppressed.

The nonviolent activist distinguishes between a man and his role. He understands that the structure of a social situation may cause injustice, while it is not necessary to assume that those who carry out the unjust acts through their roles within that structure are motivated by evil. The structure must be changed and it must be changed nonviolently.

Through the clash of relative truths that is involved in conflict, the nonviolent activist seeks a resolution that will encompass the needs of both parties to the conflict. It is the conviction of the nonviolent activist that this seeking of a wider truth judged in terms of human needs cannot be done through violence, which violates human needs and destroys life. There is the implicit belief that violence itself is a form of injustice.

Nonviolent action does not aim for victory over the adversary. Conflict is not taken as a game in which there is a winner and a loser and in which we attempt to "beat" the other party. On the contrary, the nonviolent activist strives to avoid this game mentality. What is sought is a resolution of the conflict at a higher level of understanding and satisfaction (for both parties) than perhaps either party possessed before the conflict resolution. The resolution that emerges is ideally a new Gestalt, or structure, in which both parties are somewhat transformed. Bondurant (1965, p. 196) has said that the Satyagrahi

> recognizes, and attempts to demonstrate to his opponent that he recognizes, the desirability of a resulting synthesis, and that he is not seeking a one-sided triumph. His effort is to allow for the best restructuring of the situation. He seeks a victory, not over the opponent, but over the situation in the best (in the sense of the total needs of the situation) synthesis possible.

— The nonviolent activist constantly confronts the adversary with openness and sincerity, man to man, in order to dissolve his game mentality. He seeks and invites the adversary's help in restoring justice, for he is not against him, but against injustice. The nonviolent activist wishes the adversary no harm, and actually strives to protect him from harm. He approaches the adversary positively and constructively, without malice, and believes in his sincerity and humanity. He knows that the evil the adversary is capable of, he too is capable of, were he in the adversary's situation and role. Just as confidently, however, the nonviolent activist knows that tendencies of love exist in the adversary just as they do in himself. If he did not believe this about the adversary, he would be implicitly assuming that he is superior to or somehow better than his adversary—perhaps more human than he. The nonviolent activist tries not to indulge in such arrogance.

It should be pointed out that manifestations of love for the adversary should not and need not be insincere or merely outward tactics. Through his reflective consciousness, the nonviolent activist can strive to step back from the conflict situation, even if momentarily, and ponder the similarities of all human beings until he can see his own self mirrored in the adversary.

Nonviolent action operates against injustice, not against people. The nonviolent activist is not against the adversary, but is against his unjust acts. He seeks not only to achieve his own goals but to help the adversary achieve his. Since it is only certain acts that he is against, he can sincerely cooperate with the adversary in acts with which he agrees. In fact, the nonviolent activist might seek out such areas of potential cooperation, perhaps in constructive projects that will benefit everyone. Or perhaps it is within the activist's power to help the adversary himself, but he would not do so in a manner that might humiliate him. The inner attitudes and inclinations of the nonviolent activist are as important as his actions. Furthermore, he does good for its own sake and not merely through ulterior motivation.

Gandhi's nonviolence cannot be characterized as merely a series of outward tactics. Tactics that have been identified with nonviolence have often not been used in a nonviolent way. Nonviolence is a philosophy; it entails a particular outlook on life. The tactics that are used must be consistent with this philosophy and stem from it, and they must be carried out in the context of nonviolent attitudes.

Nonviolence is a philosophy of means. Those who have advocated nonviolence have often assumed that means and ends are inextricably related, that unjust means cannot bring about just ends. Gandhi (1951, p. 10) said:

> The means may be likened to a seed, the end to a tree; and there is just the same inviolable connection between the means and the end as there is between the seed and the tree.

Violence cannot really be said to *resolve* conflict, in that it does not deal with the issues involved. It merely establishes which party, at the moment, has the superior violent force.

Gregg (1966, p. 62) has stated:

> Peace imposed by violence is not psychological peace but a suppressed conflict. It is unstable, for it contains the seeds of its own destruction. The outer condition is not a true reflection of the inner condition. But in peace secured by true nonviolent resistance there is no longer any inner conflict; a new channel is found, in which both the formerly conflicting energies are at work in the same direction and in harmony. Here the outer condition truly reflects the inner condition. This is perhaps one reason why Gandhi called this mode of solving conflict *Satyagraha*—"holding to truth." Such a peace endures.

However, while the practical nature of the relationship between means and ends may be debated, it should be remembered that the philosophy of nonviolence rests upon *moral* premises—ultimately upon the belief in the sanctity of life. Violence is rejected as a means because it directly violates life and is therefore taken to be intrinsically immoral.

Although nonviolence stems from moral grounds, we are, of course, concerned with its practicality in confronting conflict and injustice. The practicality of nonviolence will be explored through much of this book.

GAMES AND CONFLICT

Nonviolent action involves, as we shall see, a combination of firmness and openness. The nonviolent activist confronts violence and injustice in a fearless, firm, and uncompromising manner. In regard to the adversary, however, nonviolent action is always conciliatory and trusting. Although the nonviolent activist is not naive about the risks involved in exhibiting trusting behavior, he is always willing to take such risks.

Trusting behavior does not unequivocally beget cooperation. It can often beget exploitation. This somewhat depressing conclusion, believed by many of us through our personal experience, has been supported in experimentation with what is called the prisoner's dilemma game.

In this game there are two players who have the opportunity to gain points or sometimes imaginary or real money. Each player has two alternatives—e.g., he has the choice of pressing a red or a black button. On each trial (which is considered one game) each player is allowed one turn, and the players do not know each other's choice until after they have both chosen. There are four possible outcomes, and both payoffs of each outcome are known to the players beforehand. One particular payoff matrix (see Fig. 1-1) that qualifies as a prisoner's dilemma game can be described as follows. If both players press black, they each win three points. If both press red, they each win one point. If one presses red while the other presses black, the one who pressed red wins five points and the one who pressed black does not win anything. One can see that red can be described as a competitive response and black as a trusting or cooperative response. If a player presses red, he has the chance of winning many points and of maximizing the difference between his and the other player's gain. Although he simultaneously runs the risk of winning only one point, he has the assurance that whatever the other player presses that other player cannot gain more than he gains. If a player presses black, he stands to win an intermediate number of points, but cannot gain more than the other player and also runs the risk of gaining nothing. Red would appear to be the best defensive strategy in the sense that no matter what the other player chooses at least one point will be gained and the other player cannot gain more. Red would also appear to be the strategy that can potentially net the greatest gain possible and the greatest maximization of difference. However, if each were to choose this "best" strategy, each would wind up with only one point apiece. They would be better off cooperating and gaining three points apiece. But cooperation entails the risk of trust.

Figure 1-2 contains another example of a payoff matrix that can be used in the prisoner's dilemma game. If both players press black, they both win nine points. If both press red, they both lose nine points. If one presses red while the other presses black, the former gains ten points and the latter loses ten points.

In fact, Scodel, et al. (1959), using the matrix displayed in Fig. 1-1, found that the red-red outcome occurred more frequently than any other of the four possible outcomes over a series of 50 trials. The players would have been better off cooperating, but they did not. Minas, et al. (1960), using a different payoff matrix, found that red was chosen 62% of the time. The red-red outcome was the most frequently occurring. Their experiments allowed them to conclude that the player tries to maximize the difference in gain between himself and the other player rather than trying to maximize his individual gain. In other words, he tends to play the

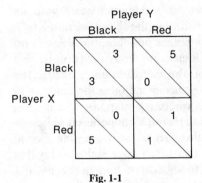

Fig. 1-1

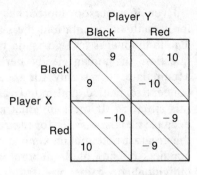

Fig. 1-2

game competitively, even though the instructions to the players do not urge a competitive orientation but rather imply an individualistic approach (to maximize one's own gain).

Thus, the prisoner's dilemma game does seem to be regarded as a competitive "game" in the minds of the subjects. They are likely to take the view that their object is to beat the other player. As for the relevance of this experimental situation to social conflicts outside of the laboratory, it must be conceded that conflict situations often do degenerate into games in which the issues are lost sight of and each side is more intent on "beating" the other side—or on not looking "bad" or appearing to be defeated—than on truly resolving the conflict itself. When the game mentality presides, it will be a long time before cooperation sets in, and this conclusion is reflected in the results of the experimental situation. (Rapoport and Chammah [1965], observing an extraordinarily long series of trials, found that a majority of pairs of players eventually "locked in" to a cooperative pattern, but only after about the 120th trial.)

When Deutsch (1958, 1960), in a prisoner's dilemma game study using the matrix displayed in Fig. 1-2, tried to induce through instructions an individualistic orientation among his subjects (he told them that they should try to maximize their own gain without regard to how well the other person did, and that the other person felt the same way), he found somewhat more cooperative responses being made than when he induced a competitive orientation. Komorita (1965) found that when subjects were specifically instructed not to try to beat the other person but simply to accumulate as many points as possible, the number of cooperative responses was somewhat increased. He concluded that the initial orientation of the subject plays a major role in inducing cooperative behavior.

Even if a person approaches the prisoner's dilemma game with an individualistic orientation, the situation still has the flavor of a "game." The individual is trying to gain the most points possible, but there is no question of human needs here; he does not *need* the points. He accumulates them only for the sake of the game. Human needs, the concept of justice, and moral values have no meaning in the context of this situation. If the individual makes cooperative responses, it is only because he has to *settle* for the gains made through cooperation in lieu of the greatest potential maximization of gains theoretically possible. Social conflicts outside of the laboratory are also often approached with this individualistic game orientation, even though here human needs and moral values do have meaning. Individuals or groups in a conflict may try to maximize certain gains even though they do not need those gains. The gains merely correspond to points in a game. They are made simply because their accumulation might be a sign of "winning" in the game to which the conflict has been reduced.

The game mentality can best be overcome in the prisoner's dilemma game by inducing a cooperative orientation in the players. In one condition of the study previously cited, Deutsch (1958, 1960) instructed each subject to be concerned about the other person's welfare as well as his own, and led the subject to believe that the other person felt the same way. This orientation resulted in approximately 89% cooperative responses, far higher than was found in this study under a competitive or individualistic orientation. Kanouse and Wiest (1967), using a different payoff matrix, also found that a cooperative orientation greatly increased the number of cooperative responses as compared with an individualistic orientation.

The nonviolent activist, however, cannot often depend upon the directives of an authority (such as the experimenters within the context of the above studies) to elicit cooperation. If he is to induce cooperation, he must do so unilaterally. But can he do so solely through exhibiting trusting behavior (making cooperative responses)? As noted at the outset of this discussion, in experimentation with the prisoner's dilemma game trusting behavior has often been found to beget exploitation. I now turn to some studies that clearly demonstrate this finding.

One experimenter went so far as to call a consistently cooperative set of responses over a series of trials the "Gandhi" pattern (Lave, 1965). One "player" was actually a preprogrammed series of all cooperative responses. The subject thought that he was playing with a real person. It was found that when the potential payoff for a competitive response was relatively high, "Gandhi" was exploited. Using a payoff matrix that was

employed in the Scodel, *et al.* (1959) study (see Fig. 1-1), Minas, *et al.*
(1960) found that when a confederate of the experimenters always made
the black response, subjects still predominantly chose red. Solomon
(1960) also found that an unconditionally cooperative strategy does not
fare well. In still another study, Wilson (1969) found that such a strategy
does not induce high levels of cooperation (only slightly more than 50%
cooperative responses were achieved).

Using a different kind of game, but one that also allows for both
competitive and cooperative behavior, Shure, Meeker, and Hansford
(1965) confronted the subject with what they considered to be, in some
respects, a simulated pacifist strategy. In this game, each player can earn
money by completely inserting five-unit "messages" into a six-unit "communication" channel to be used by both players. A player can move only
one unit on each turn and cannot enter a unit that is occupied by the other
player. The game is so structured as to make it monetarily advantageous,
within any given period, to transmit the first "message." Also, if a player
can manage to transmit his first "message" before the other player does,
he acquires a "jolt back action" that enables him, if so inclined, to push
back the other player's units during the next period, thereby allowing him
to transmit first again. But this "jolt back action" is tied to the use of a
presumably painful electric shock in such a way that the player cannot
push back the other's "message" units without delivering a shock to him.
(The other player also has the use of shock available to him, but without
the "jolt back action.") A cooperative arrangement could be tacitly
worked out in this game, and would involve an alternating pattern of one
player passing for several turns while the other player proceeds to occupy
five channel units, thus transmitting his "message" first, and then, in the
next period, the other player passing for several turns to allow the first
player to do the same, and so on.

The "pacifist" (actually a programmed computer, unknown to the
subject) after letting the subject transmit the first "message" (and thereby
allowing him to acquire the "jolt back action") during the first period
would enter his "message" units into the channel at the beginning of the
next period in an attempt to transmit first now. If the subject pushed his
units back, the "pacifist" would again attempt to transmit first in
subsequent periods, thus forcing the subject (if he is to remain uncoopera-
tive) to repeatedly administer shock. The "pacifist" himself, of course,
would never deliver shock.

The subject was pressured by programmed "teammates" to adopt a
dominating strategy. Under such conditions, it was found that the
"pacifist" was often exploited. When the subject was led to believe that

he was playing with a Quaker who was morally committed to nonviolence, the "pacifist" was still frequently exploited. A statement from the "pacifist" about his conciliatory intent, his refusal to use shock, and his intention to enter the channel to pursue his fair share (thus forcing the subject to use shock in order to make unfair gains) helped somewhat but not much. When the "pacifist" gave up even his potential to shock the subject, he was still exploited. The absence of "teammates" did not lead to a much higher overall level of cooperation; the addition of an audience somewhat increased the level of cooperation at certain points, but its overall effectiveness was questionable (Meeker and Shure, 1969).

In the context of yet a different game—one allowing for a relatively wide choice of responses—Deutsch, et al. (1967) tested what they called a "turn the other cheek" strategy. In this game the players make simultaneous moves on each trial (as in the prisoner's dilemma game) by playing one of a number of differently colored pegs. Each peg yields a different outcome for the player, and some of the outcomes depend upon what peg the other player has chosen. For example, a blue peg is a "cooperative" peg in that it earns nine cents for each player if both select blue pegs on the same trial. But it earns only one cent for the one who plays it if the other player does not. A black peg is worth six cents to the one who plays it, regardless of what the other player does on that trial. One player can "attack" by playing an orange peg. In this case, he receives six cents for every red ("attack") peg he had played on previous trials that was in excess of the number of green ("defense") pegs that the other player had selected on previous trials, and the other player loses this same amount. A white peg is an "altruistic" one in that its use gives seven cents to the other player without benefiting the one who selected it. It was found that the "turn the other cheek" strategy, which consisted of playing only the "cooperative" and "altruistic" pegs, tended to be exploited.

In discussing their findings, Deutsch, et al. pointed out that in the experimental game situation the instructions tend to encourage selfish moves. In regard to the "pacifist" strategy of the Shure, et al. (1965) study, as well as their own "turn the other cheek" strategy, they stated that the "pacifist" is "appealing to exterior social values whose relevance has been deliberately minimized by the arrangements and paraphernalia of the experiment" and that such strategies are not likely to be effective "in situations which are depersonalized and provide little to stimulate the awareness of common human bonds." However, it must be said that the availability of electric shock should have served to increase the salience of moral values in the Shure, et al. study.

Regarding the use of "pacifist" strategies in the above experiments, Ofshe (1971) has suggested that the effectiveness of a "pacifist appeal" might really lie in its potential to influence a third party who might be in a position to influence the adversary. In other words, such a strategy might operate by eliciting action from a third party (or audience to a conflict), thus affecting the adversary indirectly rather than directly. The above experiments did not allow for this possibility. (The audience in the Meeker and Shure [1969] study did not have an opportunity to confront the subject during the game.)

I will discuss later in what ways and under what conditions such action as nonviolent protest might operate in this manner. However, the power of nonviolence does not reside solely in making appeals to others. There is a certain firmness in nonviolent action, a power that has not been simulated in the above experiments. The nonviolent activist stands his ground in the face of coercion and refuses to comply with injustice. He refuses to encourage injustice and so he confronts it and does not reward it. These very important characteristics of nonviolent action were not given expression in the strategies discussed above.

Actually, in the Deutsch, et al. experiment, a strategy was tested that might be closer to—given the confines of the game—the nonviolent approach being developed in this book than any of the others mentioned above. (I must emphasize, however, that it is by no means identical with such an approach.) I refer to their "nonpunitive" strategy, which rewarded cooperation and neutralized or nonrewarded attacking or exploitive behavior. If the subject chose a red ("attack") peg on one trial, this strategy entailed responding with a green ("defensive") peg on the next trial, so that the subject could not benefit from "attack." "Counterattacks" were never employed in this strategy (i.e., red and orange pegs were never used). A choice of blue ("cooperative"), black ("individualistic"), or white ("altruistic") pegs by the subject was matched on the next trial. Other moves were responded to with a blue peg on the next trial, and blue was played on the opening trials no matter what the subject chose. To the extent that a power consistent with the moral premises of nonviolence can be found to reward cooperation and to neutralize attempts at exploitation, the "nonpunitive" strategy (given the restricted range of moves allowed in the above games) is much more of a counterpart to the nonviolent approach than the so-called "pacifist" strategies tested in these experiments.

The "nonpunitive" strategy fared relatively well in the above study. It gained higher payoffs for its user than either the "turn the other cheek" strategy or a "deterrent" strategy (which rewarded cooperation and responded to "attacks" with "counterattacks"). The "nonpunitive" strategy led those who played against it to increase the proportion of their cooperative (blue) moves and to decrease the proportion of their individualistic (black) and attack (red and orange) choices. The "nonpunitive" strategy elicited considerably more cooperation than the "deterrent" strategy.

These experiments serve to illustrate important considerations relevant to nonviolence. Trusting behavior often cannot transform the game mentality of the adversary and induce in him a cooperative orientation. Although it would be naive to assume that trusting behavior *by itself* will always elicit cooperation from the adversary, the nonviolent activist extends himself in a trusting manner and risks exploitation nonetheless. Perhaps he can help matters by striving at the outset to avoid polarizing the situation into a game to which the real issues become irrelevant. He might attempt to do this by maintaining a positive regard toward the adversary and by trying to promote the outlook that a situation exists that is perpetuating injustice, and that he wants to join with the adversary, whose *help* he desires in changing the situation. However, in order to be substantially effective in confronting injustice, nonviolent action must consist of more than just a positive regard for the adversary and more than just a trusting and cooperative approach to the adversary.

In order to effectively wage conflict, confront injustice, and bring about social change, we must have *power*. I have already hinted at some of the sources of the power of nonviolence in this chapter.

A nonviolent campaign, while involving a continual readiness to negotiate, can be said to proceed through the stages of persuasion through reason, nonviolent protest, and noncooperation. In discussing these stages in later chapters, I will be exploring the nature and types of nonviolent power. Before doing that, however, in the next two chapters I will more deeply explore the subjective structure of knowledge and the concept of relative truth, the cognitive dynamics of conflict, and the nature of social power in general. A familiarity with these matters might prepare the way for an appreciation of the power of nonviolence.

NOTES

[1]Since the target was an inanimate object, the behavior was not (strictly speaking) violent, according to my definition.

[2]I use the term rational to refer to the process of thinking and reasoning clearly.

[3]The other writings include Shridharani (1939), Diwakar (1946), Gandhi (1961), Miller (1964), Gregg (1966) and Horsburgh (1968), to name just a few.

[4]Here I use the word harm in its broadest sense, not referring only to physical harm.

CHAPTER 2

Cognitive Dynamics

Conflict involves the opposition of forces, either physical or psychological. The opposing forces at the root of social conflict can be needs, wants, values, attitudes and beliefs, or actions that stem from them. Although the waging of conflict requires the use of power, which will be the topic of subsequent chapters, conflict does have its root in issues and does involve disagreement. In order to understand conflict and how to resolve it humanely, we need to understand how two parties can come to hold discrepant views of a situation. The potential grounds of agreement between parties to a conflict must also be explored.

Gandhi recognized that what appears to be truth may vary from one to another. The concept of relative truth, I think, admits of the possible existence of opposing or conflicting views, each of which is in accordance with certain known facts of the situation (perhaps even the same facts as the opposing view) and each of which has been rationally developed from those facts. At the root of conflict there is, of course, the possibility on either side of misperception, delusion, misjudgment, or irrationality. But such factors (and even insincere or evil intentions) are not necessary for the existence or even the development of conflict. Moreover, what is involved in conflict is the clash of *subjective* realities. What is important is what each side *believes* to be the case.

One's knowledge, or conception of truth, involves not only facts but their interpretation. If we are to understand conflict, we must begin with the study of the nature of knowledge acquisition and the structure of human cognition. Perhaps along the way we will find additional moral arguments in support of nonviolence as well as clues for its successful application.

27

How does man gain knowledge of the external world? The world presents an infinite diversity of data to the human mind, which is not capable of assimilating it all. The mind has its limitations. Obviously, it is not a receptacle into which all of the data in its immediate vicinity are sucked up or thrown in through the chute of the senses (as is) and then stored indiscriminately (as is) or even stored in the same order in which it entered. The mind actively processes the data available to it through the senses; it selects, chooses, and organizes. Let us first look at this processing activity at the perceptual level and then at the *higher* cognitive levels.

PERCEPTUAL ORGANIZATION

Why do things look as they do? The Gestalt psychologist, Kurt Koffka (1935, pp. 75ff.), once asked this simply worded question in his analysis of the nature of perception. He rejected the tentative answer that things look as they do because they are what they are, or that, in other words, there is a one-to-one correspondence between a physical object and its percept. Lines can be perceived as curved when they actually form a square, as in Orbison's (1939) illusion (Fig. 2-1).[1] Camouflage can mislead the perceiver by giving rise to perceptual units for him that obscure a particular physical unit. Motion can be perceived where there is none—as, for example, when we look up at the sign surrounding the Allied Chemical Building in Times Square in New York and experience the motion of words where there is only the temporal and spatial succession of stationary patterns of lights going on and off. Furthermore, the same physical stimulus

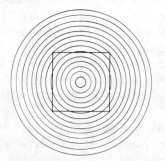

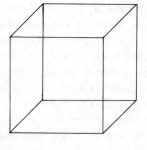

Fig. 2-1   (From Orbison, W. D. Shape as a function of the vector field. *American Journal of Psychology*, 1939, **52**, 31–45. With permission.)

Fig. 2-2

can give rise to more than one percept, as with reversible patterns such as the Necker cube (Fig. 2-2).

How does a physical object give rise to a percept? We are obviously not in direct contact with the object per se, but only with the light energy that is reflected from that object. The object is at a distance from us; it is reflected light energy that impinges upon the receptor cells of the retina, setting off nerve impulses. Koffka referred to these excitations of the retina caused by the reflected light energy as the proximal stimuli. It might seem more plausible to maintain that things look as they do because the proximal stimuli are what they are, since we are in direct contact with those stimuli and not with the things themselves. This postulation that there is a one-to-one correspondence between the percept and the proximal stimuli was also rejected by Koffka. A percept might change while the stimulation remains constant. This can be demonstrated with the Necker cube (Fig. 2-2). If we keep our eyes steadily fixated on the cube, we experience it reversing back and forth from one perspective to another. Since the stimulation at the retina is remaining invariant, something beyond the sensory stimulation itself must be responsible for the alternation of percepts. The same can be demonstrated with the stimulus pattern in Fig. 2-3. It is possible for this pattern to give rise to a percept of the right profile of a face for the reader. The reader can alternately see a left face-profile. The same stimulus pattern can give rise to different perceptual organizations. Processes in the perceiver beyond the sensory stimulation itself must be contributing to the percept. If the reader gazes at Fig. 2-4 continuously for a few minutes, he will find that his perception

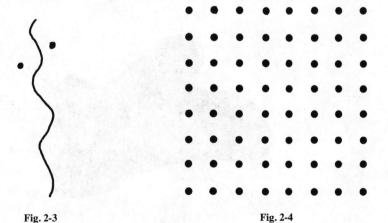

Fig. 2-3   Fig. 2-4

of this fixed pattern of dots does not remain constant. He will successively experience different perceptual organizations of this single stimulus pattern; in other words, reorganizations will occur. Horizontal lines might give way to vertical lines, which in turn might give way to a pattern of squares, etc. There will be a successive and sudden emerging and submerging of figural organizations.

Koffka said that we see, not stimuli, but on account of, because of, stimuli, and he proposed that we must analyze the nature of the organization to which the proximal stimulation gives rise in order to study the question of why things look as they do. Köhler (1929, p. 195) claimed that organization is a function of the nervous system, for "on the retina we have the indifferent mosaic of millions of local stimuli, and nothing else." The manner in which our perceptual world is segregated, in which it is *organized for the perceiver*, must be due to processes beyond the sensory stimulation itself.

The most basic perceptual organization is that of the segregation of figure and ground. We see not a "blooming, buzzing confusion" but figural units segregated from other figural units and from the background on which they appear. Look at Fig. 2-5. The black area tends to be perceived as a figure on a white ground. The contour between the two areas is perceived as belonging to the black area, not the white, giving it shape as a figure, as a "thing," leaving the white area as a relatively formless ground. The ground seems to extend behind the figure, and the figure is experienced as nearer to the observer than the ground. These and other properties of figure-ground perception were first analyzed in a study by Rubin (1921; partial English translation, 1958). Note that these properties

Fig. 2-5

are not in the stimulation itself but arise in perceptual organization. The contour does not belong to any area; it is just there. The black area is no nearer to the observer than the white, and so on. The stimulation gives rise to perceptual organization. The human nervous system, together with the sensory stimulation, determines the resulting perceived organization. As Merleau-Ponty (1962, p. 9) said: "Normal functioning must be understood as a process of integration in which the text of the external world is not so much copied, as composed."

The possibility of perceptual reorganizations are not limited to the special stimulus patterns presented above. As Osgood (1953, p. 220) has said: "We may look upon any sensory pattern as potentially capable of inducing multiple perceptual organizations." There are many possible percepts that might *potentially* "fit" any given sensory retinal representation of an object, although there are many others that cannot under any conditions. So, for example, Fig. 2-2 giving rise to the perception of a circle or sphere is entirely out of the question because the stimulation will not support it. Thus, the sensory stimulation is partially, but not wholly, determinative of the resulting perceived organization. Instead of the Necker cube of Fig. 2-2, one can look steadily at a three-dimensional cube made out of pipe cleaners and see reversals of perspective. This does work somewhat better if one closes one eye or stands far away from the object, the reason being that depth cues (which help the visual system to determine that one part of the object is further away than another) are then reduced.[2] One can, with volitional effort, perceptually reverse the corner of a room so that it is perceived as an out-corner rather than an in-corner, or one can reverse the rim of a coffee cup (see Ulrich and Ammons, 1959).[3] While we may look upon any sensory pattern as *potentially* inducing multiple perceptual organizations, ordinarily, a stimulus pattern gives rise to one percept that is quite stable and does not yield to any other (although if any object is rigidly fixated for an abnormally long period of time, one's percept will eventually change and "break up"). The great stability of our everyday perceptual world can be attributed to the abundance of perceptual cues that strongly support and favor one possible perceptual organization over others. Depth cues help to stabilize a percept, as does the greater integrated stimulus complexity of one potential percept relative to another. For example, if a few sensory elements are added to Fig. 2-3, as in Fig. 2-6, the left face-profile becomes the dominant and most stable percept.

Prior learning also might determine the direction of perceptual organization, as demonstrated in an experiment by Leeper (1935). Fractionated

Fig. 2-6

figures, such as the one in Fig. 2-7, were presented to his subjects. Such figures are often not at first recognized as familiar objects, but are perceptually organized as a cluster of irregularly shaped units. When given knowledge of what familiar object the fractionated figure represented, or the class to which the familar object belonged, the subjects tended thereafter to always perceive the figure as such. Leeper also demonstrated the effect of prior experience on the perceptual organization of the stimulus pattern shown in Fig. 2-8. That pattern can give rise to the perception of either a "wife" or "mother-in-law." Those subjects previously presented with a stimulus pattern that could be perceived only as a "wife" almost always saw the "wife" in Fig. 2-8, while those who were previously presented with one that could be perceived only as a "mother-in-law" almost always perceived that organization of the stimulus pattern of Fig. 2-8.

The Leeper study demonstrates that higher cognitive processes can influence the perceptual process. However, perception is an immediate experience that is largely dependent upon an immediately present pattern of stimulation. In the above study, none of the resulting percepts was inconsistent with the patterns of stimulation that gave rise to them, and the number of potential alternative percepts was extremely limited by the stimulation itself. Some psychologists (e.g., Bruner, 1957) have viewed perception as a cognitive inference process and have sometimes claimed that individual needs, values, and expectancies built up through past

Fig. 2-7   (From Leeper, R. A study of a neglected portion of the field of learning—The development of sensory organization. *Journal of Genetic Psychology*, 1935, **46**, 41–75. With permission from The Journal Press, Provincetown, Mass. and the author.)

Fig. 2-8

experience have a large influence on the perceptual process. But the presumed supporting evidence for such conjectures is largely based upon experiments performed under highly unusual viewing conditions (e.g., the pattern of stimulation is exposed to the subject for an extremely brief duration [less than 2/5 sec.]). Under such conditions, it is obvious that the subject would often have to guess—not perceive—what the object is (based on the fragmentary cues that he does manage to perceive). The limitations on the fluidity of higher cognition into perception are illustrated by the following example. When one looks at the sign surrounding the Allied Chemical Building, one might know full well that movement is not occurring, that there is only the temporal and spatial succession of stationary patterns of lights going on and off, and yet one will still compellingly experience movement. The psychologists who have tried to demonstrate the supposed pervasive role of inference from past experience in perception have sometimes failed to distinguish between what their subjects actually *experience* under given stimulus conditions and what they might be able to report as judgment or previous knowledge.

Perception is a subjective and active process through which the organization of incoming stimulation arises. Many patterns of stimulation ordinarily elicit one and only one percept. These percepts are stable and are the same for all perceivers. Yet they are no less the products of subjective processes. For example, a solid cube-shaped object will always be seen as a cube under normal viewing conditions. But a cube is three-dimensional, while the stimulation it excites on our retina can only be two-dimensional since the retina for all practical intent is a two-dimensional surface. The perceptual depth of the object is somehow organized through the human nervous system. Yet an intersubjective consensus as to the nature of the perceptual experience arises because of the commonality of human nervous systems among all normal perceivers. Other patterns of stimulation leave more freedom and instability to the organizing processes of the nervous system. Even for the patterns of stimulation that easily give rise to multiple perceptual organizations, such as the Necker cube, the type and number of such possible perceptual organizations are restricted and partially dictated by the nature of the pattern of stimulation itself. Moreover, the particular alternative percepts that will arise are often common across all normal (i.e., having physiologically sound nervous and sensory systems) perceivers. I wish to emphasize here that the very vast majority of stimulus patterns that we perceive ordinarily do give rise to one and only one stable percept and that the percept is largely determined and restricted by the stimulus pattern. Stimulation provides the data for perception and, while it does not wholly determine it, the commonality of human nervous systems assures that ordinarily the perceptual organizations to which the stimulation will give rise will be the same for all normal perceivers, even though perception is a subjective organizational process. I will call such percepts that are common across all normal perceivers *perceptual facts*.

Perception, though flexible within limits, is stable within far greater limits and is not very much at the whim and mercy of the higher cognitive processes. If perception were as flexible and as variable between individuals as are the products of higher cognitive processes, there would be little possibility of productive communication and interaction between people. As it is, however, in perceptual facts we have one of the few firm bases for a commonality of knowledge among individuals and between parties to a conflict. But if in the agreement of conflicting parties as to what is perceived we have a common subjective truth, if you will, then in the possible interpretation of those facts we have the basis for the relativity of knowledge (or for relative truth) and for disagreement.[4]

COGNITIVE CONSTRUCTION

When we come to the higher cognitive processes, we find that the subjective cognitive organization of perceptual facts is not as restricted by those facts, not as greatly determined by those facts, as perceptual organization is restricted and determined by stimulation. Cognitive organizations of perceptual facts can be highly variable between individuals and are highly dependent upon the individual learning experiences of people to a much greater extent than perception. Yet even here we should find organizations that are common across almost all individuals, due to the commonality of human nervous systems and of certain learning experiences.

Just as the human perceptual system is not capable of processing the mass of stimulation that is available to it (that can excite the retina) without organization, so the higher cognitive processes cannot deal with the already organized perceptual knowledge without organizing it into higher-level organizations.

Perceived figures and things, movements and events, are not stored in isolation from each other, unrelated and meaningless. They are classified, conceptualized, organized. Man is a construct maker. He relates things to each other and to himself.

In my classroom there are about 50 chairs, all different from each other in many ways, but I subsume them all under the concept chair. To use one concept to include many perceived entities is to use a generalization, a simplification of perceptual reality. The entities are not all exactly the same. Yet a concept emphasizes the similarities and ignores the differences. Differences that are available in my perception are obscured in the concept. Language, of course, helps us to express thousands of concepts.

The process of mental organization does not stop here. We organize our concepts into superordinate concepts. For example, chairs and tables might be subsumed under the concept furniture. We relate our concepts to each other to form beliefs, and we construct relationships between our beliefs to form belief systems.[5]

The individual constructs his world; he is, as Merleau-Ponty (1962) said, a meaning-giving existence. He strives to put meaning into his world, which necessarily means that he organizes it, that he seeks to interrelate aspects of it. In so doing, he simplifies his world, as he must, in order to structure and understand his world. Paradoxically, as he subjectively structures his world for himself—puts meaning into it and strives to understand it—he departs further from the indifferent diversity of perceptual reality. Moreover, great philosophers and scientists throughout history have been guided by the belief that there is an underlying simplicity or unity beneath the diversity of perceptual reality.

Although many of the differences that are available in our perception are lost in higher cognitive organization, they, of course, continue to remain available in our perception. The more perceptual differentiation that is maintained in our mental organization through greater cognitive differentiation, the closer our cognitive organization is to perceptual reality. Yet hierarchical constructs help to make our world stable, mean-ingful, understandable, and predictable. A cognitive system can grow in both directions, increasing differentiation and hierarchic integration (a phrase borrowed from Werner's [1948] principle of organic development) at once. Indeed, construct-making for man is necessary and unavoidable. He could not digest or comprehend all of the information that is potentially available to him through his senses if he did not "work it over," organize it.

From percepts to concepts, to beliefs, to even stereotypes, and the impression we form of another person, to belief systems, and to the hypotheses and theories of scientists—all are constructs which enable us to get a handle on a world that is otherwise an overwhelming confusion. Our constructs allow us to grasp the world around us, to live with less of the anxiety that would be aroused by confusion, and to comprehend our world, making it manageable and predictable.

Belief systems are constructs that are necessarily (over-) simplifica-tions of perceptual reality. Stereotypes are specialized constructs; they are beliefs or belief systems pertaining to groups of people. A stereotype, if related to perceptual reality at all, entails (as do many other constructs) the process of obscuring perceptual differences, inference beyond per-ception, and the generalization of such inferences.

As with other constructs, we can ask how much cognitive differentia-tion an individual acknowledges within a particular stereotype that he holds. How many subcategories does he maintain? We all form broad constructs about nature, issues, and people. Such constructs can be predictive and adaptive. But to the degree that an individual who has formed a construct does not develop or simultaneously maintain differen-tiations within the realm of that construct, I will say that his thinking is prejudicial in regard to that construct. By this definition, prejudicial think-ing is a pervasive aspect of man's cognitive processes. It is never absent and, in regard to any particular construct, it is inversely related to the degree of cognitive differentiation that is maintained. It is not limited to constructs we form about groups of people and it is engaged in by scientists in regard to particular subject matter as well as by bigots and, for that matter, all people in regard to groups of people.

We can ask, as we can in regard to other constructs, whether a particular stereotype is valid. It would seem to me that we are asking whether the construct is in accordance with, or consistent with, the perceptual facts as we know them. Now, constructs can certainly be invalid, but since they are generalizations to begin with, they are often valid in only a statistical-probabilistic sense to begin with. For example, on the basis of random samples of Norwegian and French people given a particular "conformity test," it can be said that Frenchmen are less conforming than Norwegians (Milgram, 1961). This does not mean, of course, that every Frenchman is less conforming than every Norwegian. What we have here is an experimentally demonstrated stereotype that we can say is valid in a statistical sense (if one is willing to accept the criteria of validation used). Yet, to the degree that one does not maintain differentiation within this construct, one is engaging in prejudicial thinking.

In foreshadowing the continuance of this discussion of stereotypes in Chapter 7, I will merely note here that because an individual's actions stem from his subjective conceptions, the question of whether certain stereotypes are valid is, of course, less important in interpersonal relations than are the stereotypes themselves and whether they lead to a positive or negative evaluation of others. Furthermore, although stereotypes can and do change—often due to the incorporation of new perceptual facts, or as they come to be increasingly less predictive and therefore less useful or adaptive—they, like scientific theories, are often maintained by many, with only minor adjustments, long after alternative stereotypes and theories, more predictive and better able to organize the data at hand, have arisen in the minds of others.

Stereotypes pertain to (groups of) people and entail inferences about them. Inference is involved in other constructs as well. The very process of the interpretation of facts often necessitates inference, which can take the form of the attribution of motives and/or characteristics.

This was demonstrated in an interesting laboratory study by Heider and Simmel (1944). These investigators composed an animated cartoon, one frame of which is shown in Fig. 2-9. In the film, the three solid figures—the large triangular unit (T), the small triangular unit (t), and the small circular unit (c)—move in and out and around and within the larger broken rectangular figure, sometimes making contact with each other and with the rectangular figure.

A large majority of the 34 people to whom the film was originally shown and who were asked to report on it interpreted the triangular and circular units as animated beings (usually as human), and most reported a connected story that integrated the entire sequence of action. People who saw the film tended to report that T and t were two men who were fighting over the girl c, that t and c were sweethearts, that T was chasing t, and t and c were fleeing from T, that c was almost captured, and so forth.

Many of the viewers described T as aggressive, mean, or angry, as a

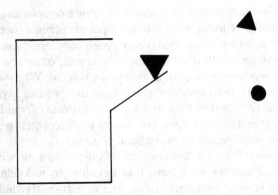

Fig. 2-9 (From Heider, F. and Simmel, M. An experimental study of apparent behavior. *American Journal of Psychology*, 1944, **57**, 243–259. With permission.)

bully or villain. They attributed bravery, courage, independence, and cockiness to *t*. They tended to describe *c* as frightened, meek, and female.

The interpretations of perceived movements and the attribution of motives and qualities are very compelling and even necessary if one is to process the information that the film does provide. In order to incorporate this information, one must organize it, but the organizing process requires inferences that will relate the sequence of percepts to each other in a consistent manner. As Heider and Simmel (1944) state: "Acts of persons have to be viewed in terms of motives in order that the succession of changes becomes a connected sequence."

In the discussion of perception it was pointed out that many patterns of stimulation ordinarily elicit only one percept that is common across perceivers. It has also been pointed out that the subjective organization of perceptual facts is not so restricted by those facts as perceptual organization is restricted by stimulation. There are many perceptual facts that usually do support multiple interpretations, just as in perception there are some patterns of stimulation that ordinarily elicit multiple perceptions. Stimulation determines perception to a greater extent than perceptual facts determine interpretation. Thinking is more flexible than perception. What this means is that disagreement will less often arise over the perceptual facts themselves than over the interpretation of those facts.

In the Heider and Simmel study there appeared to be considerable agreement in regard to the interpretation of percepts. But when the perceptual facts pertain to a conflict each of the parties to the conflict will often be able to interpret those facts in a way that will make them consistent with that party's particular belief system (and thereby impart meaning to those facts); when the belief systems are as divergent as those of the Arabs and Israelis, for example, the interpretations of some events will be quite discrepant.

Since the Six-Day War, Israeli soldiers have been standing on Egyptian land. One can go to certain parts of the U.A.R. and see them there. No one—neither Arabs nor Israelis, nor Russians nor Americans—denies that they are there. Nor does anyone deny that they moved into that land during the Six-Day War. At that time, one could have seen them moving in. These are perceptual facts to which everyone agrees. Those of us who have not seen these events and situations with our own eyes trust the senses and reports of others who have been directly exposed to the appropriate patterns of stimulation. After all, the reports are in agreement. (Of course, in some situations, the perceptual facts might be *lied* about.) One of the points of conflict is not over the perceptual facts (for here we actually have one of the potential grounds of agreement between parties to a conflict) but over the interpretation of those facts. And the interpretation is dependent upon, indeed *is*, the manner in which the facts are incorporated into a prior established belief system. If the two parties happen already to be in conflict, as is the case in the Middle East, the different ways in which these facts are incorporated might sometimes intensify that conflict.

Through the belief system held by many Arabs, the perceived movement and presence of Israeli soldiers on Egyptian land is interpreted as aggression. Note that even such a concept as aggression is not something that is dictated in what is perceived. Only movement and presence are perceived. Interpretations of perceived facts often seem like perceptions to the viewer, which partially accounts for his strong belief in them. Through the belief system held by many Israelis, these same perceptual facts of movement and presence are interpreted as defense.

What allows the Israelis and Arabs to interpret the identical facts in such drastically different ways, and to be so resolute and sincere about their respective interpretations to boot? The relevant beliefs of both sides that give rise to and support the discrepant interpretations are well-known and need not be recounted at great length here. The Israelis believe that they have a right to live on the land they call Israel, that the Arabs wish to drive them out, that they did not create the Arab refugee problem, that the cutting off or blockading of any of Israel's paths of transportation by the Arabs is itself an act of war, that since Israel is so small in both size and population it can only defend itself by quickly moving a battle (even an anticipated one) to Arab soil, and that because Israel is so small and almost surrounded by Arab nations it could be suicide to give up the territory captured in the Six-Day War without a firm peace settlement, and so forth. The Arabs believe that the Arab refugees have a right to live on the land that is now Israel, that the Zionists stole that land, that the Arabs who were living in what was then Palestine were forced to flee, that the Israelis were the aggressors even during the 1948 war, and so forth.

In such an intense and sustained conflict as we have here, it would be difficult, if not sheer folly, to attempt to change either side's interpretation of the perceived facts because each side's interpretation is supported by and rooted in an elaborate, integrated belief system.

A much debated question in regard to what has been called the Palestinian refugee problem is whether, on the eve of the 1948 war, the Arabs who were to become refugees were expelled from Israel by the Jews or whether they fled on their own accord. It is well known that the Arab nations have claimed the former to be the case while the Israelis have claimed that the Arab High Command, through radio broadcasts, had urged the Arabs to flee. It is interesting that Michener (1970) reported that he once considered this question to be so important that he spent two years researching it, but later came to the conclusion that trying to assess who was to blame was unproductive. The important problems are how to alleviate the present suffering of the refugees that has resulted from the conflict and how might the Arabs and Israelis resolve the conflict in a manner that is satisfactory to each party. Thus, Michener also believes that the pursuit of the question of who really is historically entitled to own Palestine—both Jews and Arabs have made historical claims to the land and have each been able to summon up perceptual facts and arguments in support of their views—is equally fruitless.

I would add that because conflict involves the clash of subjective realities, what is important is what each side *believes* to be the case. This is where the conflict is. If a resolution is to be sought, it must somehow deal with the *claims* of both parties and with the present frustrations of human needs that have arisen from that conflict. Since it is highly unlikely that any answers offered by others to the above questions would radically change the belief systems of either side, the questions are irrelevant to the conflict as it now stands.

There is no higher judge we can consult for the "correct" interpretation of the perceptual facts involved in the Mideast conflict. We could consult other human beings who are neither Arabs nor Israelis, but no man is a "neutral" observer. Each has his own subjective belief system with which to interpret the facts. Moreover, in order to resolve conflict we must understand the belief systems that are conflicting. The reality that exists apart from the subjective realities of the parties to the conflict does not exist for them and is not intrinsic to the conflict.

VALUES

One commonality often present among parties to a conflict is in certain of the values they both profess to uphold. Moral values are constructs that pertain to our relationship to other people. We know that children, in their development, tend toward a sense of justice that is interpreted in terms of equality and equity (Piaget, 1965). They also tend toward a mutual cooperation and respect in which morality is recognized as a social agreement for one's own good as well as for others—for a common good.

Turiel (1969) views moral development as "a self-constructive process, culminating in a state in which principles are followed for their own sake rather than to avoid pain, blame, or self-condemnation." He claims that it is through attempts to organize social experiences that the child comes to develop moral structures.

A child is at first quick to note when he is being treated unfairly. If a child in a group of children finds that an adult who is distributing candy gives him less than the others, he immediately complains. Somewhere in his development he goes beyond egocentric outlook to a construct of fairness that includes other people's points of view. The construct at that point is a moral value: *All* individuals *ought* to be treated fairly. Exactly what will be interpreted by an individual as constituting fairness in a specific situation will depend upon other values and beliefs of his that are relevant to the situation and to his own personal needs. Moral values do not stand alone, isolated from and uncontaminated by the many other beliefs and needs that enter into a human being's complex and intricate network of cognitions. Therefore, a person's actions cannot be related in a one-to-one fashion to any one moral value that is held by him. Yet we should not underestimate the importance of a moral value concept.

Values are abstract and general constructs. They need to be applied to concrete and specific situations. In the process of the application of our values to concrete and specific situations our values often guide and determine our actions and attitudes. On the other hand, our actions and attitudes in a given situation are often generated by our self-interests and might determine the manner in which we interpret our values. In a situation in which one's self-interests are involved it is very likely that they will direct one's interpretation of what is just within that situation. There is also the possibility that our situational attitudes will interact with our values in such a way that both will be partially transformed for the occasion. Also, two or more values may come into conflict when both are applicable to a particular situation.

Maccoby (1968) states that moral values are beliefs about what is good or right and that some moral imperatives are nearly universally found in all social groups while others vary from one cultural setting to another. As I have already said, a central moral value of the philosophy of nonviolence is the sacredness of human life. It may well be that, far from being unique to nonviolence, it is a nearly universal value. What might be less prevalent is the application of this and other values to means rather than to ends only.

White (1966, pp. 53–55) points out that the Communists of North Vietnam seem to believe that they have been upholding such values as peacefulness, independence, social justice, and even democracy—much the same values that the American government seems to believe that it has been upholding by its actions in Southeast Asia. Obviously, certain events and situations are being interpreted differently when incorporated into the opposing subjective realities. There need be no disagreement over that aspect of the situation that was capable of being directly perceived. For example, both the Communists and the American government would agree that American soldiers have been in South Vietnam. But when this perceptual fact is incorporated into one belief system, it is interpreted as aggression; when incorporated into the other—as defense. Yet these opposing belief systems, which are causing perceptual facts to be interpreted in two such discrepant ways, contain some similar values.

Are the values really similar? Does peacefulness, social justice, or democracy mean the same thing to both sides? Obviously, there are some discrepancies. However, I would contend that there is also some semantic overlap. White (1966, p. 55, footnote) claims that his research into the matter shows that the differences are not as great as many might think.

In this slight commonality of values we have another basis for agreement between two parties to a conflict. Yet, a strange and dangerous thing about conflict is that each of the opposing parties often believes that it is striving toward some ultimate common good.

Hitler, as indicated in *Mein Kampf* (1939), had a fanatical preoccupation with German nationalism, constantly glorifying the German "fatherland." Throughout his book he spoke of fighting for the "freedom and independence" of his nation (e.g., pp. 263, 288, 289, 375), albeit at the expense of the freedom and independence of the other peoples of the world (e.g., pp. 405–406, 580, 599). (He seemed to think he was offering them security instead [see pp. 405–406 and p. 406, footnote].) However, a careful reading of *Mein Kampf* reveals that Hitler believed he was fighting for no less a common good than the preservation of mankind (pp. 52, 65, 84, 175, 581, 593). German nationalism, for him, was related to this goal; it was a means to it.

He said of the Social Democratic Party that "mankind must rid the world of her as soon as possible, or otherwise the world might easily be rid of mankind" (p. 52). He talked similarly of the Jews (p. 84). He linked domination by Germany with the preservation of mankind and justified it in these cryptic terms:

> We all sense that in the distant future problems could approach man for the conquest of which only a highest race, as the master nation, based upon the means and the possibilities of an entire globe, will be called upon. (p. 581)

Hitler most likely believed himself to be a righteous man. He was against the "egoism and hatred" of the Social Democratic Party. And he had these words to say about the rulers of Russia (whom he thought to be Jews):

> We must never forget that the regents of present-day Russia are common bloodstained criminals; that here is the scum of humanity, which, favored by conditions in a tragic hour, overran a great State, butchered and rooted out millions of its leading intellects with savage bloodthirstiness, and for nearly ten years has exercised the most frightful régime of tyranny of all time. Nor must we forget that these rulers belong to a nation which combines a rare mixture of bestial horror with an inconceivable gift of lying, and today more than ever before believes itself called upon to impose its bloody oppression on the whole world. (p. 959)

How strange it is that Hitler could pass such judgment on others without perhaps ever seriously considering that similar terms could be used to describe his own deeds. In his mind, his murders were probably not crimes against humanity but necessary acts in his glorious and noble march toward the preservation of mankind.

The question of whether Hitler really *believed* what he wrote in *Mein Kampf* inevitably arises in the minds of some readers. But this question might arise primarily because *we* do not believe in what he wrote. What could he have been covering up? Certainly not his passionate hatreds that are revealed throughout the book. Beliefs are needed to support and sustain hatred. For example, his hatred toward the Jews, even if not caused by his beliefs about Jews, was certainly buoyed up by such beliefs. White (1966, p. 10) states:

> It is now fairly well established that in Hitler's mind the diabolical character of the enemy, especially the Jewish enemy, was extreme and unmitigated. Post-war studies have confirmed the proposition that his anti-Jewish delusions of persecution were no mere propaganda technique; he seems to have actually believed them.

And to ascribe his hatred to early childhood experiences psychoanalytically interpreted (if the reader be so inclined) is not to deny that beliefs sustained, if not caused, his adult hatred. Moreover, the repression-displacement (scapegoat) hypothesis of prejudice does not explain how the target of the prejudice comes to be set up. The setting up of the target requires getting an individual to *believe* certain things about that target. Only then does the scapegoat hypothesis have a chance of coming into play.

Finally, to say that Hitler's belief that he was fighting for the preservation of mankind was a rationalization, as some might, is not to deny that he *believed* it.

Once we allow ends to justify means in our thinking there is seemingly no limit to what our own self-righteousness will permit us to endorse. Each side has justified the death and destruction of the Vietnam War by interpreting it as in the service of its values. *In a conflict, when we look at our adversary we tend to focus on his means and condemn him for his inhumanity, but when we look at ourselves we focus on our ends and revel in our righteousness.* We often allow ourselves to find psychological consistency between means and ends by conceptualizing our means as in the service of those ends. The nonviolent activist rejects this particular subjective principle of consistency; he does not permit his mind its easy luxury.[6]

COGNITIVE CONSISTENCY

Man often strives toward consistency in his cognitions. Although this does not mean that this tendency will not at times be overridden by other tendencies and conditions, this proposition has been maintained by many social psychologists. Perhaps its best known formulation is Festinger's (1957) cognitive dissonance theory. Festinger maintains that when two cognitions stand in a dissonant (inconsistent) relation to one another a tension is set up toward dissonance reduction (cognitive consistency). Cognitive dissonance motivates the individual toward dissonance reduction, toward the attainment of cognitive consonance. A cognition can be defined as any knowledge, opinion, or belief about the environment, oneself, or one's behavior. Cognitive consistency, as already implied in the above, is a subjective thing. Two cognitions are dissonant if, in the mind of the individual, the opposite of one follows from the other. It seems apparent that dissonance exists and can be motivating only if the individual experiences it. If, to the individual, one cognition does seem to follow from the other, then cognitive consistency, or consonance, exists. When one cognition subjectively implies nothing at all about the other—that is, when one cognition is experienced as neither following from another cognition nor from its opposite—the two cognitions are said to be irrelevant to one another.

As an example of cognitive dissonance, my belief that a certain person is selfish might be inconsistent with my cognition that he just went far out of his way to do me a favor. As another example, my belief that the American people are humane might be dissonant with my belief that U.S. troops committed a massacre at Mylai. There are many ways that one might go about reducing dissonance, and they often do not involve the outright rejection of one or the other cognition in favor of its opposite. "Cognitive work" initiated in order to reduce dissonance can take interesting forms, some of which will be discussed below. The cognitive dissonance theory has been supported by numerous experiments in which attitude change was seemingly achieved by inducing dissonance, although some doubts have been raised from time to time about the theory and the supporting evidence.

Cognitive dissonance theory maintains not only that the individual strives to reduce dissonance but that he seeks to avoid information that might increase dissonance. As we shall see in Chapter 5, the latter conjecture is in doubt, for there is evidence to suggest that individuals sometimes seek out dissonance-producing information.

How does one go about incorporating new knowledge into one's belief system? While there might not be a tendency, within limits, to avoid potentially discrepant information, there are ways in which such information can be incorporated into a belief system without disruption (although often not without some change or accommodation on the part of the system). It can be incorporated in such a manner, in fact, that it is rendered through the organizing process as no longer really discrepant. For example, if a person I believe to be selfish has gone out of his way to do me a favor, I might interpret his act as due to an ulterior motive ("he wants something from me"). As another example, an individual who favored American involvement in the Vietnam War (and believed both himself and the American foreign policy to be humane) could interpret the Mylai massacre as an isolated incident, an "exceptional case." (See Krech, Crutchfield, and Ballachey [1962, pp. 44–45] for a discussion of "exceptions.") He could also interpret it in a nondissonant manner by claiming that such things cannot be avoided in war or by assigning guilt to a few supposedly unrepresentative soldiers who will be brought to trial for their "abnormal" actions.

Parenthetically, the importance of the distinction between perceptual facts and interpretations should again be noted. One might consider the killing of unarmed men, women, and children at Mylai as potentially drastically dissonant information for American "hawks." Indeed, when the information first became public, many people refused to believe it or claimed that it was not as yet clear that the event actually took place. But as verification flowed in to the public, even "hawks" no longer denied the event (although some might still not wish to call it a "massacre" because of the special connotations of that word). It was accepted as a perceptual fact. This fact then had to be contended with by the "hawks" in certain ways, some of which have already been discussed. They could, as shown, *interpret* the fact in a way that would not drastically disrupt the prior belief system. But often, even when a belief system assimilates information in a subjectively consistent manner, some accommodation or slight change is necessary on the part of the system. The importance of perceptual facts in bringing about this accommodative change will be discussed further here and more extensively in Chapter 4.

An event can also be incorporated into one's belief system by emphasizing, in interpretation, those aspects of an event most easily made consonant with one's prior beliefs and that are supportive of them, and deemphasizing (or putting out of awareness) other aspects of that event. For example, the above individual can take the event of the 1967 election in South Vietnam as proof that we are supporting a democratic government. An individual against the war will prefer to emphasize in his thinking the evidence supporting the notion that the election was unfairly conducted. The first individual can interpret this latter evidence—and note here that if presented with enough perceptual facts from what he considers to be reliable sources he might very well accept the evidence—as a minor fault to be expected in a country taking its first steps toward democracy.

In fact, any given event often has enough aspects to it to lend itself to consistent incorporation into a variety of different systems of beliefs.

Belief systems are, however, capable of changing. Although new information can often be interpreted in such a way that will allow it to be consistent with prior beliefs, the assimilation of the new information also often involves, as I have said, a slight change or accommodation on the part of the belief system. The individual who interpreted the Mylai massacre as an unavoidable incident in conducting war might have come to have some doubts about American involvement in that war. If new information does not adequately lend itself to being incorporated directly into the belief system in a consistent manner, it might be rendered quasi-consistent by treating it as an "exceptional case," thereby allowing prior beliefs to survive. For example, as already mentioned, the Mylai massacre can be treated as an "exception." If too many exceptional cases pile up for a given belief system, a major reorganization might take place, for the old system would no longer be adequately serving the purpose of meaningfully interrelating aspects of the individual's world, of rendering it understandable and predictable.

This kind of major disruptive change is rare. Many little "exceptions" more often add up to only one big "exception," allowing the remainder of the cognitive system to remain relatively intact after all. For example, a person might finally reject our involvement in the Vietnam War as a "tragic mistake." His mind has been significantly changed. However, he might continue to hold beliefs that allow him to regard the overall U.S. foreign policy as generally good.

There are certain cognitions that are more central than others. Some of the most deeply embedded beliefs we might call basic assumptions or premises about the world. For example, some people hold a basic premise about the world the flavor of which is as follows: "The world is a fearful place to live in; people are out to get you, to take advantage of you. People are not to be trusted." Such a view might lead one to be highly competitive (I'd better get them before they get me) and suspicious of others and might be highly influential in the determination of other beliefs. For example, such a view is consistent with and supportive of the beliefs that we had better get the Communists before they get us, that hippies are out to subvert the government and might even be controlled by outside forces, that we should not admit Communist China to the United Nations, that we should bomb North Vietnam, and that we should not fluoridate our water because fluoridation might be a Communist plot. I am not arguing that everyone who holds one of these beliefs holds the others or that in order to hold these beliefs one must have this basic premise or even that everyone who holds this premise holds one or more of the above beliefs. What I do wish to point out is that each of these beliefs can be easily generated from the premise. A cognitive system containing this premise and these beliefs would have an internal consistency to it, even though on the surface there is no apparent consistency. Being against fluoridation does not particularly seem to be related to being suspicious of hippies. Yet how strange it is that we are often able to predict the attitudes of a person on widely different issues by knowing his attitude on just one issue. The consistency is not horizontal (i.e., between beliefs) but vertical (i.e., between each belief and the underlying premise).[7] Note, too, that this cluster of beliefs becomes more understandable to us as outsiders once we know the underlying premise.

There are some people, on the other hand, who hold an opposite basic premise that goes something like this: "The world is a friendly place to live in. People are well-meaning and out to help you, and can be trusted." Similarly, as above, there are a number of beliefs that can easily follow from or be generated about concrete issues from this premise.

The complexity of the human mind is certainly not summed up here. There are many combinations of basic premises (certainly there are more than one to an individual and these interact to jointly generate beliefs), values, beliefs, and attitudes that make for the uniqueness of individuals.

Which of the two premises outlined above is valid? Is the world a fearful place to live in? Of course it is. Is the world a friendly place to live in? Of course it is. Each basic assumption reflects an aspect of the subjective reality of human beings. If anything, they are both valid. Each premise has been confirmed for the individual who holds it a thousand times over. If there were nothing in his experience that lent itself to being interpreted as support for the assumption, he would not have been able to form or hold to the assumption. As it is, however, there is no lack of subjective confirmation that can be wrested from the world or constructed out of the interaction between the human mind and the sensory input that the world affords us for such premises and many others. Then, too, each premise has its self-fulfilling prophecy aspects; so that each person, by acting in accordance with his premises, often receives the reactions from others that he had expected to receive, thus finding confirmation for his original premises.

The same can be said for entire belief systems, which are, however, sometimes more susceptible to change than the premises mentioned above. A belief system, like a scientific theory, is a construction based on perceptual facts and designed to fit the facts and to predict facts, but it is not the facts themselves. When it is able to incorporate many perceptual facts in a consistent manner, it stands strong. When it starts to lose the ease with which it can incorporate new perceptual facts consistently, the interpretations that it gives to these facts become more circuitous and elaborate for the sake of maintaining internal consistency, just as happens to scientific theories when faced with potentially discrepant new data. Under this strain, new concepts are added, old ones are stretched, and adjustments and change tend to take place within the system. But these kinds of changes are significant and are the ones that we should look for and hope to achieve in our persuasion attempts. Eventually, the system might be abandoned and replaced with a new one altogether, although such a complete overhaul is rare for the individual.

Belief systems are serviceable to the individual. They are his construction of the world; they are his world; they are what the world means to him. They incorporate aspects of perceptual reality, but they are not reality except for the person. They are not even perceptual reality, but systems of interpretations of that reality.

Rokeach (1968, pp. 167–168) has suggested that there are three methods that can be used in order to induce a state of inconsistency between cognitions, thereby setting the cognitive stage for change.

The proposition that if an individual is induced to behave in a manner that is inconsistent with his attitude, his attitude might change, will be explored in Chapter 3. It can be said that the nonviolent activist attempts to utilize this first method through noncooperation—a type of power that will be discussed in Chapter 6. Just how noncooperation might bring about attitude change through behavior change will be discussed in Chapter 7.

Another possible way in which to induce inconsistency that might eventuate in change is to expose the individual to information that is discrepant with the information he already has. When cognitive change is brought about through exposure to information intrinsically related to the issue at hand, I will call the result persuasion; this method will be discussed in Chapter 4. I have already indicated how change might come about through this technique. We have seen that it is both possible and tedious. Individuals are very likely to "work over" the new information, or to incorporate or process it in such a way that they experience it as indeed somewhat consistent with their prior information. They may also departmentalize the new information (cognitively isolate it) in such a way that they do not experience any relation at all (neither consistent nor inconsistent) between the new and old information. That is, they might simply never compare the two in their mind.

The third method is somewhat related to this last-mentioned difficulty. Rokeach has proposed that we expose the individual "to information about states of inconsistency already existing within his own value-attitude system." In other words, we can try to bring to the awareness of the individual inconsistencies in his own cognitive system with the hope of getting him to experience inconsistency of which he was previously unaware. This method, of course, can be very difficult and frustrating. The individual can often not be brought to "see" the relations you are trying so hard to reveal to him. However, Rokeach (1968, pp. 173–178) has obtained some interesting results using this method, and I will refer to them in Chapter 5. This method constitutes an appeal designed to activate a searching of conscience; I will construe it as a moral appeal. I will identify it with the "appeal to conscience" sometimes spoken of in the literature of nonviolence. In Chapter 5, using the civil rights movement as an example, I will argue that nonviolent protest can sometimes bring about cognitive change through this method.

Success with such an "appeal to conscience," while possible, is not easily achieved. One can hardly entertain the thought that it would have had much effect on Hitler, for example. But, while it is fortunate that the resources of nonviolence do not end but only begin here, there are numerous conflicts in which some success with an appeal to values is not implausible. Furthermore, I will argue that such appeals are most effectively directed at third parties (serving to mobilize the support of bystanders) rather than at the adversary himself.

Great patience and persistence are necessary at the very least. Individuals tend to believe that their actions and attitudes are quite consistent with the dictates of their consciences, and they have a great knack for bringing any momentarily experienced inconsistencies into line by instituting relatively minor changes in their cognitions, thereby avoiding more extensive "cognitive work" and avoiding any major upheavals in their belief systems.

Whether an individual first acts in accordance with his personal desires and self-interests and then tries to convince himself and others that these actions are indeed in some way consistent with his moral values, or whether his acts ensue from the prior careful and consistent reasoning from his values, individuals do often demonstrate a striving toward consistency. The first type of process we might call rationalization, and the second—rationalism. While it is often unclear which type of process is occurring in a particular instance, both types are prevalent in human thinking.

Such processes not only serve the purposes, spoken of before, of all cognitive organization—that is, of stabilizing one's world and making it meaningful, understandable, and predictable—but also of making one's self meaningful, understandable, and predictable to oneself.

I believe that one of the keys to the understanding of conflict between individuals, groups, or nations lies here in our understanding of the dynamics of cognitive systems. Without an understanding, we will not know well how to educate nor how to persuade nor how to resolve conflict; and so, when conflict arises, we will rather hastily complain and conclude that despite our efforts to resolve the conflict and despite the fact that our modest goals are merely fair and just, the obstinacy and evilness of the other side prevents us from resolution. We are therefore left with no alternative than to suppress rather than to resolve conflict, no recourse other than violence. It is for these reasons that the discussions of this chapter are so relevant to the study of nonviolence.

While engaged in conflict, I can momentarily step back from it, using my reflective consciousness to view myself as someone else engaged in conflict, even as I view the adversary. And with enough knowledge about my adversary, I can empathize with him; I can momentarily appropriate his belief system, appreciate the rationality of it, and see myself as he does. I might then gain the fuller understanding of the conflict that will facilitate conflict resolution. At the same time, however, I realize that I am not above the conflict, but an active participant in the arena of social interaction, motivated to engage the conflict and to act firmly on what I believe.

To understand is not to condone. The nonviolent activist *believes* what he believes. He does not waver and vascillate because of his awareness of the subjectivity and relativity of his knowledge, but he stands firmly against what he interprets to be social injustice because he believes in his interpretation until convinced otherwise.

What limitations does the nonviolent activist's conception of conflict and belief systems impose upon him? It directs him to understand that two parties can disagree about the nature of a situation even if they hold certain values in common, to understand that the adversary might feel just as self-righteous about his beliefs as does the nonviolent activist about his own. (The nonviolent activist is directed not to hastily attribute evil *intentions* to the adversary nor to presume that he is deceitful when he talks about his values. He is much more likely to be deceitful in the presumed *service* of his values. For example, the Army might have tried to cover up the Mylai massacre, but most likely for the purpose of not letting public outcries damage the war effort which, as the Army viewed it, was bringing "peace and freedom" to South Vietnam.) It directs him away from the tendency to justify means through ends. His understanding of the adversary leads him to sympathize with him, to see him as human as himself, and to be not *against* the adversary as a person.

However, to understand the adversary is not to condone his acts. The nonviolent activist is against those acts of the adversary that he considers unjust. He is not against the person himself, although it is this person with whom he will have to deal and attempt to change.

While this discussion leads us to consider that the adversary in conflict is often as sincere and as nobly motivated as we are, seeking to further moral values highly esteemed by even ourselves (and thus presents a possible basis for love and compassion rather than hatred for him), it also alerts us to the fact that man in social conflict is an extremely dangerous being. So long as he applies his moral values to ends and not to means, it can even be said that his danger partially stems from his very ability to generate such values. Contemplation of the massive destruction of human life wrought by human beings in pursuit of noble ends should alert us to the danger involved when we neglect to apply our moral values to our means themselves. In order to protect himself and others from both the adversary's and his own capacity for evil, the nonviolent activist must devise means that are not only humane but powerful enough to be used effectively in a conflict in which the adversary stands ready to use violence. It should be noted here that although the nonviolent activist always persists in trying to induce cognitive change (I have already discussed some of the great difficulties involved) the means that he employs will not exclusively be directed at bringing about cognitive change in the adversary.

With this analysis of subjective belief systems and conflict, we are led to seek (and should be in a better position to find) that kind of power that is both humane and potentially capable of achieving change and conflict resolution.

NOTES

[1]The nature of the physical object is inferred from other percepts. For example, the percepts involved in holding a ruler adjacent to the lines in Fig. 2-1 (percepts of continuous coincidence between the lines and ruler) are not consistent with the percept of curvature. One percept is checked against other percepts and is concluded to be misleading as to the nature of the physical object.

[2]For a description and listing of depth cues, see any textbook on perception, for example, Weintraub and Walker (1966).

[3]Although the organization of the perceptual world arises through nonconscious processes, it is possible for the perceiver to "work" with sensory material and to consciously construct those percepts that the sensory material is capable of supporting. Thus, within certain limits, he can actively switch from one perceptual organization of the sensory material to another.

[4]It should be noted that the way in which the term perception is used here is much narrower than the way it has been used in two works that discuss topics similar to the ones to be discussed in this chapter.

In his monograph, White (1966) states that he uses the broader sense of the term, in which perception "becomes synonymous with all forms of cognition, including even the individual's most basic assumptions about the nature of the world and of man" (p. 2, footnote).

In his book, de Rivera (1968) also uses a much broader sense of the term perception than I. While I separate perception from interpretation, de Rivera includes the latter within the former. Of course, there is no hard and fast line that can be drawn in that some instances can be found in which I would be hard put to say just where perception leaves off and interpretation begins. Nonetheless, we are left with a large area in which the distinction is not too difficult to make.

It might be said that the issue I raise here is a minor matter of semantics. Certainly, I do not wish to accuse anyone of "wrong" usage. However, the distinction I am making is important to some of my later discussions.

[5]According to my usage of the term belief system, one person can hold many belief systems pertaining to different objects. This is different from the way in which Rokeach (1968) employs the concept, for by it he means the total universe of a person's beliefs.

[6]Soon after I wrote this paragraph the White House issued a statement concerning the kidnap murder of a U.S. adviser in Uruguay by terrorists which included these words: "This callous murder emphasizes the essential inhumanity of the terrorists." One wonders whether there is anyone in the White House who ever considers some of his government's acts in the same light, or considers that the terrorists might feel just as righteous about their murders as the U.S. government does about its.

[7]Bem (1970) has also pointed this out in his book.

CHAPTER 3

Power and Nonviolence

The power that we seek in nonviolence is a humane and constructive power. The ideal that we strive for is power that can resolve and not suppress conflict, that can transform and not destroy, and out of whose use can emerge reconciliation rather than polarization. The power of nonviolence must be action based on the refusal to do harm, even knowing all the while that, as Gandhi noted, the perfect practice of nonviolence is difficult of attainment for man.

Nonviolence is not passive. It is not appeasement. It involves more than turning the other cheek. The nonviolent activist will endure suffering rather than inflict it, but he will not submit to what he considers to be injustice. There is power in nonviolence, not the destructive and repressive power of violence but the constructive power of a philosophy respectful of human needs in the immediate present as well as in the distant future.

Power is not amoral. The type of power used to gain certain ends, however humane those ends may be, can itself be inhumane. Cameron (1970, p. 24) has said:

> Violence . . . is centrally tied to the notion of human harm and commonly stands in need of justification, since it would seem absurd to advocate the harming of human beings.

Violence stands in need of "justification through the end it pursues" (Arendt, 1969, p. 51) perhaps because it is often regarded as intrinsically inhumane—and not merely because it is (often) instrumental in nature, as Arendt argues.

Nonviolence does not permit of means that are in themselves inhumane and that therefore stand in need of justification through ends. Although

55

the philosophy of nonviolence rejects violence solely on moral grounds (viz., on the premise that the violent act is intrinsically inhumane), it may well be that, as indicated before, power is not indifferent to the ends for which it is used.

Arendt (1969, p. 80) has said that "the danger of violence . . . will always be that the means overwhelm the end." Advocates of nonviolence have often maintained the belief that "the end is pre-existent in the means" (King, 1967, p. 71). Indeed, the power of nonviolence is, ideally, power that already demonstrates what it is designed to achieve, that already begins to build and set the example for what is to be. What it promises to achieve is not extrinsic to what it is. As Shridharani (1939, p. 316) said: "The means should be the end in process and the ideal in the making." The nonviolent activist believes that he cannot claim to seek a world of peace and yet not practice peace, or speak of a future social justice while perpetrating the injustice of violence in the present. Perhaps, if our goal is a world in which conflicts are resolved through reason, we must initiate rational discussion; if our goal is peace, we must behave peacefully; if our goal is justice, we must behave justly; and if our goal is human freedom tempered by social responsibility, we must behave as free and responsible individuals. Nonviolence is active love; it is humane power, power that does not do injustice or multiply evil. This is the ideal that the nonviolent activist, as imperfect as he is, strives to approximate. In succeeding chapters we shall see to what extent the above prescriptions for action are reflected in the various forms of nonviolent power. Let us first look more carefully at the concept of social power and at the various forms that power can take in general.

FORMS OF SOCIAL POWER

Social scientists have made many and varied attempts to define and analyze the concept of social power. Here I will follow Raven (1965) and Collins and Raven (1969) in defining power as potential social influence, where social influence is defined as change in an individual's cognition, attitude, behavior, or emotion that has its origin in another person or group. If an individual or group performs an act that results in such change, or in some way is the origin of such change, then influence has been exerted by that individual or group. Power is the capability of bringing about change of some psychological state of another person.

Six broad types of power have been identified and discussed by Raven (1965), French and Raven (1968), Collins and Raven (1969), and Raven and Kruglanski (1970). Following these authors, I shall refer to the influencing agent as O and to the influencee as P.

Coercive power involves the ability to use punishment and threats of punishment as a means of influence. *Reward* power stems from the ability to use rewards and promises of rewards as a means of influence. *Referent* power stems from one person's (P) identification with, or desire to identify with or be like or similar to, another person (O), in terms of cognition, attitudes, emotion, and/or behavior. It is thought that referent power can stem from P's attraction to, or liking for, another person. *Legitimate* power stems from P's belief that O has a legitimate right to influence him, and that he has an obligation to accept this influence. The individual believes that he is obliged to, or "ought to," comply. *Expert* power stems from P's belief that O has superior knowledge or ability in the particular area in which the influence is attempted. Finally, *informational* power involves the communication of information intrinsically relevant to the issue in respect to which O wishes to exert influence. The term persuasion is often reserved for a change in attitude brought about through this latter process. It is acknowledged that in any particular situation more than one type of power may be involved and that two parties may be trying simultaneously to influence each other.

Coercive power is often likely to produce behavior change without transforming the psychological forces of P, such as his inner attitudes and wants, which incline him toward the original behavior and which are therefore contrary to the changed behavior. We sometimes say that we have the feeling of behaving in a certain way against our will. We are behaving in a manner contrary to our original inclinations. In such cases, the maintenance of the changed behavior is dependent upon O's continued exertion of the coercive force. This was demonstrated in an experiment by French, Morrison, and Levinger (1960). Individuals subjected to coercive threats (of the loss of money) showed greater behavioral compliance (measured by speed on a card-sorting task) than individuals not threatened, but not after the coercive threat was terminated.

Thus, the direct effect of coercive power is to induce behavioral compliance that is not necessarily supported by the already existing psychological forces within the individual. A number of social psychologists (Festinger, 1953; Kelman, 1958; French and Raven, 1968) have stressed the importance of this distinction between public compliance and private acceptance. Where the outer condition is not a true reflection of the inner condition (to borrow Gregg's [1966, p. 62] terms), O must constantly stand over P with his coercive apparatus, for once he turns his back or removes his coercive system, *P* might revert to the behavior that stems from the opposing forces. In other words, if the psychological forces supporting the original behavior have not been changed, then once *O* lets up on the pressure and discontinues his surveillance, the original forces (which have been acting as opposing forces to the changed behavior) are likely to spur a reversion to the original behavior. It should be noted here that nonviolence aims ultimately at inducing private acceptance.

However, we shall see later in this chapter that under certain limited conditions coercion has some probability of initiating processes that will eventually result in attitude change. *P*, under certain circumstances, might be moved to rethink his original position or the coercive power might force him into a new interactional structure in which he may acquire new information that is inconsistent with his old attitudes. Attitude change could come about through these potential indirect effects of coercive power. This possibility is relevant to nonviolence because, although the nonviolent activist strives to induce private acceptance, the power of nonviolence is sometimes coercive in nature.

Coercive power must not only contend with and overcome opposing forces that it more often suppresses than changes, but it also must contend with the resistance that it itself generates. That is, in addition to the forces that support the old behavior, the very act of exerting coercive pressure can generate resentment, anger, and hostility. French and Raven (1968) have made such a distinction between opposition (i.e., opposing forces that do not have their source in the influence attempt of the agent) and resistance (i.e., the resisting force, in the opposite direction to the influence attempt, which is generated by the very act of influence). Even in a situation where there are no forces within the individual that incline him toward one behavior or another, resistance to the behavior desired by the influencing agent might be aroused directly through the induction of a coercive force. I shall refer to such resistance as resentment, hostility, and anger as reflexive or psychological resistance. It can be impulsive in origin and is emotional or strongly affective in nature. It might serve, as we shall see, to inhibit attitude change. But I wish to distinguish it from the thoughtfully planned strategies of action executed by individuals or organized groups in order to overcome the power of *O*. Such reflective or social resistance, if you will, can of course be stimulated and sustained in action by reflexive resistance.

An influence attempt might generate what Brehm (1966) has called psychological reactance, which might be included under the first type of resistance noted above. He has proposed that if an individual's freedom of action is reduced or threatened with reduction, a motivational state of psychological reactance will be aroused, which will incline the individual toward resisting any further loss of freedom and toward reestablishing the freedom or free behavior that had been lost or threatened. Brehm (1966) has reported a number of experiments that generally support this theory.

The resistance generated by coercive pressure often remains even after the pressure is terminated. We resent those who have coerced us in the past. Coercive pressure, once used, must sometimes be steadily increased over time in order to overcome the accumulating resistance. Coercion, once initiated, might necessitate greater coercion in order to maintain compliance.

There is no power that is likely to generate stronger psychological resistance than *violent* coercive power. Where there is a large differential in such power between O and P, it is also most likely to gain immediate compliance. Violence and threats of violence threaten health and life itself. According to Brehm (1966, p. 4), the magnitude of psychological reactance is a direct function of the importance and the proportion of free behaviors eliminated or threatened and of the magnitude of the threat. Violence threatens to eliminate *all* of the behavior of an individual. Threats of violence should generate the highest degree of psychological reactance. Then, too, two acts of coercive power might eliminate or threaten the same number of identical free behaviors, and yet one might generate more resistance because of the greater magnitude of the threatened punishment itself (or actual punishment) that it entails.

Although violent coercion is of course rejected on moral grounds, I have said that nonviolence does have its coercive aspects. It is undeniable that nonviolent action sometimes goes beyond informational and directly persuasive techniques (see, e.g., Bondurant, 1965, pp. 9–11). I will contend in Chapter 6 that nonviolent coercion (or *noncooperation*, as I will refer to it) is a decidedly unique form of coercion, which itself stems from moral grounds. Briefly, noncooperation involves the withdrawal of one's cooperation or compliance. It can have a coercive influence on others to the extent that they depend upon and have come to expect that support for their own actions. However, in the sense that noncooperation is a refusal to comply even in the face of coercive attempts of others to get one to do so, it is a form of resistance. When it is consciously planned and executed, with some intent of influencing others, it is a form of active, reflective resistance.

As Sampson (1971, p. 337) has said: "If power allows for resistance, the other side is also true: resistance confers power. That is, P's resistance provides a basis for power over O." He also recognized that "to the extent to which P can refuse to comply, he has power to influence O." In the face of coercive attempts of others to control my behavior, such resistance is possible to the extent to which I can exert self-control and am willing and able to bear the suffering that would be involved. And to that extent my resistance has a coercive influence on others at the same time that it frees me from the manipulative attempts of others to control my behavior. Thus, noncooperation has coercive aspects that inhere in active resistance to others' use of power. To be sure, it will be found to have some of the same deleterious aspects of coercive power in general, such as the generation of resisting forces that tend to inhibit attitude change, and I do not wish to belittle this fact. This unique form of coercive power will be discussed more fully in Chapter 6.

Since punishment may sometimes take the form of withholding from P something that he values (an illustration of coercive power used by Raven [1965, p. 373]), wants, desperately needs, or has come to expect, it is sometimes difficult to distinguish coercive power from *reward* power. So, for example, a manager might withhold from—or give to—a worker the salary raise that he may desperately need. Giving an individual, contingent upon certain behavior, something that he needs can often be viewed as a lack of punishment rather than as a reward. What is most important is the manner in which P interprets the situation. A worker who has to cope with economic inflation and who is barely maintaining what he considers to be a decent standard of living may view a small yearly raise in salary as a lack of punishment—a punishment he avoided by having performed his job adequately.

The concept of relative deprivation is relevant to understanding P's outlook. Relative deprivation involves the violation of expectations. An executive who is already receiving a far higher salary than his workers might feel very resentful if he does not receive a small raise, especially if some of his fellow executives have. Upon reflection, he might even feel that he does not need the raise, yet he is resentful because he expected it. His expectations and resentment stem from the fact that he compares himself with his fellow executives, whose situations comprise his frame of reference, and not with the workers.

The doubtfulness sometimes involved in trying to distinguish reward power from coercive power is further illustrated by the following examples. If, in a mental hospital in which a "token economy" has been instituted, a patient must earn tokens in order to eat lunch, and can earn the necessary amount by dressing himself "properly" in the morning, what kind of power is being used here by the therapists? Many therapists today like to avoid using such terms as "coercion" and "punishment" and prefer to talk about "positive reinforcement." In one therapeutic institution where patients are rewarded for "socially acceptable behavior," one reward is to allow the patient to stay up as late as he wants at night (Stanford, 1972). Since adults ordinarily expect to be able to go to bed when they please, such "therapy" can potentially generate much resistance.

Thus, if an individual harbors strong psychological forces against engaging in the compliant behavior, but feels he must only because he desperately wants or needs the reward and it will not be given otherwise, resentment might be generated. Since he might experience the reward power as reducing or threatening his freedom of action, psychological reactance might be generated.

From one perspective, noncooperation can be viewed as a form of reward power, that is, as the withholding of rewards. But my cooperation, which can be regarded as *mine* to give or withhold as a free individual, has often come to be taken for granted by others. In certain contexts, my noncooperation violates expectations, breaks a relationship that has come to be viewed by others as obligatory, frustrates others' self-interests, and generates hostility. Moreover, those to whom I give my support or compliance often believe that they desperately need it and that their freedom of action has been threatened by its withdrawal. For all of these reasons, noncooperation can quite properly be regarded as coercive.

There are certain conditions under which P might interpret a reward as a bribe. He might not desperately need the reward, but might comply because he *wants* it, even if the behavior itself is particularly obnoxious to him. When one interprets a reward as a bribe, for whatever reason, one sometimes becomes resentful even if it is accepted. I will return to this point later in this chapter. As with the use of coercive power, not only might there be opposing forces to the new behavior (i.e., those psychological forces that are supportive of the old behavior) but the influence attempt itself might generate resisting forces. On the other hand, there are situations in which the offer of a reward can generate attraction or positive feelings of liking toward O as might happen, for example, when an adult gives a child a promised toy for doing well in school. Also, if a reward inclines P to attribute generosity to O positive feelings toward O might develop.

It is reasonable to expect that the *immediate* effect of reward power is to induce behavioral compliance without simultaneous private acceptance, especially since only the outward compliance is necessary for the obtainment of the reward. One complies *in order to* receive a reward, just as with coercive power one complies *in order to* avoid punishment. Continued surveillance on the part of O is often needed to maintain the compliance in both cases. This compliance without acceptance is likely to occur even when reward power generates attraction. However, when reward power generates attraction toward O, it might stimulate the development of referent power.

Referent power, involving emulation of O without requiring his intent to influence, might lead to both behavioral compliance and attitude change. If one is eager to adopt the behavior of another, one might also be eager to adopt his attitudes and beliefs behind the behavior. While the process in this case would go beyond mere compliance to private acceptance, Kelman (1961) has distinguished between *identification* and *internalization*, which both involve private acceptance. Attitudes adopted through the process of identification are not integrated with the individual's basic beliefs or, according to Kelman, his value system. Rather, they tend to be isolated from his values. They are probably less stable than they would be if they did not lack the benefit of such integration, and they are dependent upon such variables as social support and the salience of the individual's relationship with O in a given situation. However, O's surveillance is not required for the maintenance of such attitudes. Internalization refers to a process through which attitudes are adopted by being integrated with the individual's value system, as when an attitude is formed on rational grounds or upon an intrinsic relation between new information and one's prior beliefs. Presumably, referent power often generates identification-based attitudes.

The referent power of an individual is not likely to be operating on his adversary in a conflict situation, but he may become a model for his own group and certain bystanders. It has been demonstrated that one determinant of attraction is similarity of beliefs (e.g., Rokeach, Smith, and Evans, 1960), and it might be that P is often drawn to emulate O through some initial similarity between some of his important beliefs and those of O. However, it must have been something beyond this that attracted millions of people to Gandhi. What might be involved in what is referred to as charisma (said to be possessed by an occasional adored leader) is not yet understood.

Whatever the attraction may have been based upon, it can well be argued that of those followers of Gandhi who were influenced specifically by his philosophy at all many adopted merely identification-based non-violent attitudes that never became internalized. Although this was probably the case here, the possibility of attitudes adopted through identification eventually becoming internalized should not be ruled out. When one accepts attitudes through identification, one might also come to accept the reasoning behind those attitudes and interpret one's values and prior beliefs within their context.

An individual might hold the belief that O has the right to ask his compliance, and that he has the obligation to obey, even if his attitude concerning the issue involved is not consistent with the behavior requested. Such is the nature of *legitimate* power. For example, a young man who is drafted into his government's army may have a negative attitude toward the military but yet feel obligated to go. Of course, in this situation, the government also utilizes coercive power, but the threat hanging over the individual might not generate a resisting force because he might even believe that the government has a right to threaten him. In the context of a work task, Raven and French (1958) demonstrated that attributed legitimacy increases one's attraction toward the agent of power, even when coercive power is employed.

Social life is often so structured—as is necessary for a group or society to function smoothly—that cooperation in the form of obedience to authority is often the "path of least resistance," the path for which the least amount of cognitive reflection is necessary, even if no tangible punishment has been threatened. It is disobedience that more often demands our contemplation before acting. It might not be too farfetched to state that our cooperation often takes the form of an unthinking blind habit of obedience. As de Jouvenel (1962, pp. 19–20) said:

> Someone says, "Come," and come we do. Someone says, "Go," and go we do. We give obedience to the tax-gatherer, to the policeman, and to the sergeant-major. As it is certain that it is not before them that we bow down, it must be before men above them, even though, as often happens, we despise their characters and suspect their designs.
>
> What, then, is the nature of their authority over us? Is it because they have at their disposal the means of physical coercion and are stronger than ourselves that we yield to them? It is true that we go in fear of the compulsion which they can apply to us. . . .
>
> It is, however, far from being the case that Power has always had at its disposal a vast apparatus of coercion. Rome, for instance, as it was for many centuries, had no permanent officials; no standing army set foot inside its walls, and its magistrates had but a few lictors to do their will. . . .

He concludes that: "The essential reason for obedience is that it has become a habit of the species" (p. 22). Whether or not one wishes to call it a habit, obedience can be aided and enhanced by a feeling of "oughtness," or a belief in one's obligation to comply.

As indicated above, there may be instances in which legitimate power is divorced from coercion. Such examples are difficult to find where governmental authority is involved, but such authority is not necessary for legitimate power. A particular Jewish individual may feel that he should not eat pork, and yet not fear any reprisals for doing so. What might be considered to be a form of legitimate power, albeit a unique one, is the process of influence involving the norm of reciprocity. According to Gouldner (1960), this norm obliges those who have internalized it to help those who have helped them and to refrain from harming those who have helped them. Thus, although such a norm might not often operate successfully between two parties to a severe conflict, we can frequently expect that a favor we do for someone will evoke a feeling of obligation on his part to return it. Such a feeling of "oughtness" characterizes legitimate power.

The studies of destructive obedience discussed in Chapter 1 most likely involved the dynamics of legitimate power. However, although Milgram did not employ any explicit coercive threat, the subtle threat of embarrassment, or of being placed in the lonely and taxing position of having to defend one's actions to those in one's immediate vicinity, is often present when one violates what one views to be the expectations of others that have arisen in a particular social context. Yet even in such situations one often focuses not so much on one's fears as on one's supposed obligations. The feeling of "oughtness" is present.

It is obvious, as I said before, that obedience can serve good as well as evil. What it often primarily serves is the smooth and effective functioning of a group. It should be noted, in fact, that Gandhi insisted on rather strict discipline among the ranks of his Satyagrahis. He recognized that much time and energy would be lost if every minor instruction were to be questioned and debated. He could not wage conflict on a massive level without some measure of unquestioning obedience. And it should not be supposed that fears of embarrassment, ridicule, and ostracism were not operating as coercive pressures within Gandhi's movements—as they do when any group arises with the attendant formation of group norms and expectations, whether the leaders intend it or not. Also expert power, to be discussed below, or the expertise that people often attribute to their leaders, probably aids in gaining the obedience that followers give to their leaders.

The nonviolent activist sometimes calls into question legitimate power and legitimate coercive power with acts of civil disobedience, but only in those situations in which he believes that a severe and otherwise unrectifiable injustice exists. Understanding very well the necessity of obedience for the functioning of society, he is ordinarily a law-abiding citizen.[1] But he believes that he must sometimes choose between the dictates of his conscience and those of governmental authority.

He may also have occasion to challenge *expert* power. Because of the tremendous complexity of our world, one person cannot have proficient knowledge of everything. We come to rely on people whom we regard as experts in certain areas. When a dentist informs his patient that one of his teeth must be extracted, the patient ordinarily defers to the dentist and does not go to the library to read up on dentistry. But before the nonviolent activist engages in action, even if the action be no more than persuasive attempts, he takes it upon himself to become an expert on the issue of concern, so that his conclusions and attitudes be his own, formulated on the basis of reasoning from the perceptual facts he has accumulated through careful study of the situation and not handed down by experts.

Of course, we often cannot avoid relying on the reports of others for our knowledge of perceptual facts. But we often rely on experts for their interpretations of facts without being given by them a knowledge of the facts themselves. We sometimes allow ourselves to be intimidated by expert power. For example, some American citizens have accepted their government's interpretations in regard to the Vietnam conflict without ascertaining the facts themselves. I would venture to say that in those cases in which an attitude is adopted without knowledge of many of the beliefs (including perceptual facts) from which it has developed (in the minds of the experts) and which could aid in integrating the attitude within the person's prior network of beliefs, attitudes, and values, acceptance is likely to be similar to that which occurs through identification. On the other hand, when we rely on experts merely as credible and reliable sources of perceptual facts, then, when we gain those facts, the attitudes that we form based upon them are likely to be internalized. Our attitudes are then more assuredly based upon understanding.

What the patient accepts from the dentist is his interpretation of facts unknown to the former. But it can be argued in regard to the example pertaining to Vietnam that it is the duty of a citizen to ascertain the facts. He may not be a dentist, but whatever else he might be, he is a citizen; it can be said he has the obligation to become an expert in his "field." That is, he does not have the responsibility of pulling teeth, but perhaps he does have responsibility for the actions of his government and for his action toward that government. Similar information can support different conclusions for different people. The nonviolent activist (as we shall see in Chapter 4) does not accept experts' interpretations of facts, but studies the facts himself and comes to his own conclusions on those particular issues about which preliminary information has caused him to contemplate action.

The direct effect of *informational* power, if successful, is to change cognitions. The basis of this power is the communication of information intrinsically relevant to the issue at hand. This is an important power base of the nonviolent activist, who seeks always to change attitudes, with the conviction that true conflict resolution entails more than mere behavioral compliance. He might at times reluctantly resort to noncooperation, but even then (and always) he attempts to communicate information and to persuade. The maintenance of a particular behavior change, if any, that stems from a particular attitude change is not dependent upon any relation to the influencing agent. In such a case, the outer condition reflects the inner condition. It is through the power of information that the process of influence that Kelman (1961) refers to as internalization would be most likely to occur directly. For when *O* communicates information that is intrinsically relevant to the issue in respect to which he wishes to exert influence, *P* might integrate that information into his belief system, that belief system might become modified to some extent, and attitudes dependent upon that belief system might undergo change.

According to Cartwright and Zander (1968, p. 221):

> It is commonly argued that the method of persuasion is an especially appropriate means of influence in "democratic" or "rational" social systems. This argument cites two features of persuasion. First, when a person *O* attempts to influence *P* solely by means of persuasion, he applies no extraneous inducements (rewards and punishments) for accepting his message. *P* is constrained only by his own evaluation of the merits of the message, even though this evaluation may be colored by his feelings toward *O*. Second, when *O* employs persuasion to control *P*'s overt behavior, he still permits *P* to behave "voluntarily" or "freely." A successful act of persuasion affects *P*'s behavior only indirectly by influencing the beliefs, attitudes, and values that guide his behavior, and *P* feels that his behavior is under his own control. Persuasion, then, respects the integrity of the individual.

Commenting on this statement with reference to nonviolence, I would say, first, that the nonviolent activist attempts to use the method of persuasion and to initiate rational discussion in whatever social system he happens to find himself. Second, I hope that it will become apparent in Chapter 6 that not only persuasion but also nonviolent noncooperation, although coercive, also respects the integrity of the individual. Furthermore, the feeling of freedom must be distinguished from the actual possibility of self-control. The latter will be discussed in Chapter 6.

At the time that the persuasive attempt is made, there are, of course, opposing forces to that attempt (unless the agent is trying to form an attitude in P rather than to change one). If the attempt is successful, at least some of these forces would have been changed or modified as a result of the assimilation of the communicated information. It is also possible that a persuasion attempt will generate resisting forces, depending upon the context and manner in which the information is conveyed (see Chapter 4), yet we would expect such resistance to be minimal as compared to that generated by coercive power.

ATTITUDES

I have not yet formally defined the concept of attitude. An attitude will be defined here as a relatively enduring organization of beliefs and feeling that is evaluatively oriented toward some object of experience. Thus, there are two components, cognitive and affective, and these components generally compose an interrelated system in that changes in one often produce changes in the other.

The cognitive component of an attitude consists of beliefs about the object. A belief is a cognition that concerns a relationship between two concepts. It often can be verbalized as an assertion having a subject and predicate. (A perceptual fact is one type of belief.) The affective component of an attitude refers to the pattern of feeling aroused by the object. (Emotion is only one acutely disturbed type of affective process [see Young, 1961, p. 352].)

An attitude entails an evaluative orientation, which is contributed to by both the cognitive and affective components. Although the two components often produce a consistent and unified evaluative orientation because changes in one component often effect changes in the other, it is sometimes possible to distinguish between the cognitive evaluation and affective evaluation.[2]

It is conceivable that if our cognitions about a particular object are changed, our feelings will subsequently change. We can, through a process of reasoning from our values and making use of the information we have assimilated about a social object, come to cognitively evaluate that object in a negative manner, and an affective evaluation of varying intensity might be generated. A person whose cognitions have led him to negatively evaluate American participation in the Vietnam War might have a fairly intense negative feeling about it and at times might be emotionally aroused. On the other hand, the affective evaluation of a social object might precipitate the use of our reasoning processes to bring our cognitions into consistency with our feelings. The latter process can be called rationalization. (See note 2.)

I shall conceive of attitudes as having one, and often both, of two very broadly defined motivational bases or determinants. Attitudes can predominantly be based upon, and developed from, self-interest. That is, they can be, to a greater or lesser extent, *self-interest-oriented.* Such self-interests might include the enhancement of self-esteem and ego-defensive needs (see Adorno, *et al.*, 1950; Smith, Bruner, and White, 1956; Katz and Stotland, 1959) and whatever an individual wants for himself. I also include under self-interest-oriented attitudes those in which the cognitive component develops out of the affective component. An individual who has a negative affective orientation toward Negroes might have developed justification for his feelings by developing beliefs that Negroes are inferior, etc. Attitudes can serve feelings. A person might also have the need to be accepted by certain groups and through that purpose not only adopt their attitudes but also the beliefs supportive of those attitudes.

In all of these cases, the attitude can stem from self-interests and often will direct the individual to search for supportive information. Self-interest can determine how one interprets new information. In any situation in which one's self-interests are involved, in fact, it is difficult for them not to partially determine one's interpretation of the relation of his moral values to that situation.

Attitudes can predominantly serve a cognitive organizational function. That is, they can be, to a greater or lesser extent, *meaning-oriented.* As indicated in the previous chapter, man is a construct maker whose constructs allow him to understand and deal with his world. He strives to comprehend his world, which necessarily means that he organizes it. Among the constructs he forms are attitudes. An American, for example, neither Protestant nor Catholic, might have heard of the continuing conflict between Catholics and Protestants in Northern Ireland. He might, out of curiosity, attempt to gain information about the conflict, without feeling that his self-interests are involved in any way. In what context, then, will he interpret his new information? He inevitably *will* interpret the information and moreover make an evaluation, forming an attitudinal construct. His evaluative interpretation might be guided by such values of his as justice, freedom, or equality, by other prior beliefs (perhaps pertaining to poor people or to "underdogs," etc.), and by his basic assumptions about the world. An affective component may develop out of the beliefs he has formed based on the information he has obtained, and out of the relations he has developed between these beliefs and his values and prior beliefs.

The two broad motivational bases are not mutually exclusive, and often both contribute to the same attitude. An attitude that develops from self-interest itself serves the function of meaningfully organizing one's world, but also can guide further meaning-oriented development of the attitude. On the other hand, our American in the above example may at some point in his information gathering interpret some of it in a manner that indicates to him that his self-interest is indeed involved.

The affective component of an attitude can vary in sign and intensity. The cognitive component can vary in differentiation (i.e., the number of different beliefs related to the attitude) and in the degree of integration of those beliefs. Attitudes can be supported by elaborately differentiated and integrated belief systems. The cognitive evaluation can vary in sign and extremity. An attitude based on intense affect or strong need (which might generate intense affect) as well as one based on an elaborate belief system (which also might generate intense affect) will be very resistant to change.

I have described an attitude as relatively enduring. But attitudes can vary widely in their stability—i.e., in their resistance to change. I would hypothesize that an attitude can be increased in its stability either through increased differentiation and integration of its cognitive component or through intensification of its affective component. The two components are interactive, so that the increased differentiation and integration of the cognitive component might increase the intensity of the affective component, and increased intensity of the affective component might lead to increased incorporation of information being rendered as supportive of the attitude, thereby increasing the differentiation and integration of the cognitive component. Strong self-interest can also generate a stable attitude, intense affect, and the inclination to seek supportive information that will increase the differentiation and integration of the cognitive component. Also, some beliefs are more important to the individual than others and will have a greater stabilizing effect than less important beliefs.

An increased amount of new information potentially supportive of a new or changed attitude can increase the stability of that attitude by relating it to certain values, to other beliefs, and to self-interests. Stability is increased if a subjective link to other belief systems can be established, thereby enlisting these other beliefs as additional cognitive support.

The stability of an attitude can be tested in at least two ways, but prior to or in the process of this assessment we should try to ascertain whether we are actually dealing with a true attitude. There are characteristics of an experimental situation that might elicit compliant behavior (e.g., an individual's markings on a questionnaire might indicate mere outward compliance) and this behavior might not be an indicant of the private attitude. We cannot always correctly infer that an individual's responses are an indicant of his private attitude. Orne (1962) has defined what he calls the "demand characteristics of the experimental situation" as "the totality of cues which convey an experimental hypothesis to the subject." He proposes that the subject tries to ascertain the true purpose of the experiment and the cues he picks up become significant determinants of his behavior. He might want to respond in a manner that will support the hypothesis that he thinks is being tested. Orne (1962) states that

> if a test is given twice with some intervening treatment, even the dullest college student is aware that some change is expected, particularly if the test is in some obvious way related to the treatment.

Rokeach (1968, p. 155) has argued that the experimental literature on what has been called attitude change

> is a literature concerning changes which, in the main, seem to be localized in the region of the lips and do not seem to affect the mind and heart, nor the hands and feet.

According to Rokeach, one way to increase our confidence that the private attitude is being tapped is to attempt to assess it in at least two different situations or contexts.

One way to assess the stability of an attitude is by testing it on a number of occasions over time. Another way to test the stability of an attitude is to directly try to change it. With this latter method we can study whether a particular persuasive technique produces relatively stable or unstable attitude change by subjecting the changed attitude to a persuasive communication that argues in a direction opposite to the changed attitude. In other words, how relatively effective was the original persuasive communication as an inoculation against subsequent countercommunications, or how resistant to change is the changed attitude? In situations in which one persuasive communication is tested against another, this latter technique for assessing stability can yield results that will increase our confidence that true attitude change has been measured, for the demand characteristics conveyed by the second communication are likely to be opposite to those conveyed by the first. The reader should be cautious about his acceptance of any experimental evidence in regard to attitude change (some of which will be presented in this chapter and the next), because many studies have been devoid of checks that would increase our confidence that private attitudes have indeed been assessed and that would indicate that relatively enduring changed attitudes, rather than only momentary modifications, have been produced.

ATTITUDES AND BEHAVIOR

It is, of course, commonly assumed that an attitude predisposes an individual to behavior consistent with that attitude—that attitudes have behavioral consequences. Therefore, if an attitude is changed, certain changes in behavior should result. Although some investigators have raised evidence to suggest that measured attitudes are often poor predictors of behavior (see Wicker, 1969, 1971), others (e.g., Green, 1972) have found evidence for such consistency.

Despite the paucity of supportive experimental evidence, I would be willing to say that there is obviously widespread attitude-behavior consistency in everyday life. We would not have expected to find a person who favored American involvement in the Vietnam War actively participating in an anti-war demonstration. A person who favors a certain candidate for political office is not likely to vote for his opponent. There are, however, many circumstances that could be expected to lessen the probability that an attitude will eventuate in a particular behavior that is consistent with it. In addition, even when such a correspondence between attitude and behavior exists, we might fail to observe it if the responses (e.g., on a questionnaire) we elicited in order to detect a private attitude were a function of the demand characteristics of the testing situation, noted above, rather than a valid indicant of the attitude.

However, even if we have correctly ascertained the attitude, we should not expect behavior consistent with it to be exhibited at some later time if the attitude did not persist over that period of time. In other words, an attitude must at least be stable if we would expect a behavioral consequence to be manifested at some future time (Ehrlich, 1969).

Then, too, we must consider that a behavior is determined by many attitudes, not just one. Rokeach (1968) has distinguished between attitude-toward-object and attitude-toward-situation and has demonstrated (Rokeach and Kliejunas, 1972) that the interaction of such attitudes must be considered in order to increase accuracy in predicting behavior. Out of two individuals holding the identical negative attitude toward American involvement in the Vietnam War, one might have engaged in such behavior as joining in marches and demonstrations and distributing anti-war literature, while the other might not have. The second individual may have held, in addition to his anti-war attitude, the conviction that such activities are ineffective, that marching in the streets is undignified, etc. He might have believed also that he was too busy with other matters and did not have the time. Our first individual might have gone on to participate in tax and draft resistance. Again, the second individual might have refrained, perhaps for the same reasons as before, but perhaps also because of certain situational pressures that mitigate against the expression of an attitude in certain forms of behavior. He might have feared imprisonment and other possible reprisals, such as ostracism by his friends. In other words, coercive/reward power might induce a person not to manifest his attitude in certain behaviors. He might also have a certain belief in legitimate authority that makes the breaking of any laws unthinkable for him. Thus, a particular behavior is determined by the interaction of a number of attitudes and situational pressures.

Just as a particular behavior is a function of several attitudes, a particular attitude might predispose one to any of a number of different behaviors. Our reluctant "dove" might have finally engaged in at least one behavior that was consistent with his Vietnam attitude by voting for an anti-war candidate, although, of course, even here he might have refrained because he might not have, for example, liked the candidate's views on local issues.

If we want to get a person to take a particular action, we must be concerned not only with changing his attitude but also with the degree of positiveness or negativeness of the change and the intensity of the changed attitude. Surely, the more strongly anti-war a person is, and the more concerned he is about the war, the more likely he is to perform certain actions and the more weight as a behavioral determinant will this attitude have relative to his consideration of his other attitudes about the behavior and of the situational pressures counter to his anti-war attitude. But, as indicated, even a person with a strong attitude can have many reasons for refraining from action. To get a changed attitude to eventuate in behavior, we must also deal with (and change, if necessary) the individual's attitude toward the particular activity, such as marching, and we must also minimize the situational pressures. Insofar as the situational pressures are not within our control, we must seek to reduce his fear of coercive power or awe of legitimate authority. In other words, once we have succeeded in changing an individual's attitude on a particular issue, we must then proceed to reduce all blocks to the actualization of that attitude in behavior.

While the situational pressures of coercive/reward power can prevent the expression of an attitude in behavior, and can sometimes elicit behavior contrary to that attitude, it can be asked whether such power can ever eventuate in attitude change. I have been discussing the circumstances that limit the probability that an attitude will eventuate in behavior, but I will now consider the conditions that might enhance the possibility that behavior change will subsequently eventuate in attitude change consistent with that behavior. Under what conditions, if any, does behavior have attitudinal consequences? Because, as previously mentioned, nonviolent action has its coercive aspects and yet is aimed partially at changing attitudes, this issue is of considerable relevance to it.

An interesting derivation from Festinger's (1957) cognitive dissonance theory is that when a person is induced to perform an act that is contrary to his attitude, the less the pressures (such as coercion or reward) applied to elicit the behavior, the greater the attitude change that will occur. This hypothesis is related to the various ways in which the theory postulates that cognitive dissonance—in this case between one's attitude and one's cognition of one's act—might be reduced. One way is through the addition of new consonant cognitions. An individual's cognition that he has behaved in a manner contrary to his attitude is not, supposedly, cognitively inconsistent with the knowledge that he was greatly pressured to do so. Such pressure will reduce the dissonance generated by the performance of the act by offering sufficient justification for the discrepancy between the act and the private attitude. Presumably, when such pressure has been the minimal amount needed to elicit the act, there is less justification for performing the act, and therefore greater dissonance, which must be alleviated through greater attitude change toward consistency with the act (since it would be difficult to deny to oneself that one has indeed performed the act).

Put in another way, it might be said that a person has good reason to perform an attitude-discrepant act if threatened with severe punishment or offered a large reward. But if he succumbed to a mild threat or was lured by a small reward, insufficient justification for the act leaves lingering dissonance that can be reduced through attitude change. It is as if he must come to grips with doubts as to whether the scant pressures were sufficient reason for him to have acted contrary to his attitude in the first place.

This hypothesis has received support from a number of experiments. For example, Aronson and Carlsmith (1963) had children rank the attractiveness of a number of toys, one of which they were then forbidden to play with. Children in one condition were mildly threatened in regard to playing with it, while children in another condition were more severely threatened. Each child was then left alone in the room for ten minutes and was observed through a one-way mirror. None of the children actually played with the forbidden toy. The experimenter then returned and the child again rated the toys for attractiveness. It was found that only in the mild threat condition was there a decrease in preference for the forbidden toy. Presumably, while a child's knowledge of severe threat was consonant with the knowledge that he did not play with a toy that he liked, mild threat was less reason for not having played with an attractive toy. In this case, a child could reduce dissonance by derogating the toy—a "sour grapes" approach.

One of the most frequently discussed experiments in social psychology is that of Festinger and Carlsmith (1959). In this experiment, subjects (college students) engaged in an exceedingly dull task and were then induced to tell another person that the task was very enjoyable. In one condition, subjects were told that they would be paid 20 dollars for describing the task as enjoyable to the person, while in another condition subjects were told that they would be paid one dollar. In another context, after the subjects had done this, they were asked how enjoyable they thought the initial task was. The subjects in the 20-dollar condition rated the task as less enjoyable than those in the one-dollar condition. This finding, although other explanations have been offered, is consistent with the hypothesis under discussion. Presumably, a person's cognition that a task he had just performed was very dull is discrepant with his cognition that he just told someone that it was enjoyable. But if he had been paid much money for saying this, then he had good reason for acting in a manner (telling someone the task was enjoyable) discrepant with his attitude. The small reward would have less sufficiently justified the attitude-discrepant act. In order to satisfactorily reduce cognitive dissonance in this case, the subject could decide that the task was fairly enjoyable after all, thus bringing his attitude more into line with his act.

In this type of experiment, it is often not clear whether the individual suddenly expressed a different attitude, as if through some self-regulation of forces set off by the stress of cognitive dissonance, or whether he convinced himself out of his initial attitude by developing reasons as to why he should have acted the way he did. I doubt whether a stable, cognitively complex attitude could be changed without such self-persuasion, or counter-attitudinal advocacy, or whether a stable attitude can be formed solely through a simple counter-attitudinal act. For if an individual changed his expressed evaluation of an object without dealing with the intrinsic supports of his original attitude, he would thereby have created dissonance at least as great as that which he had reduced. In order to reduce this new dissonance without self-persuasion, he would have to change back to the original attitude, leaving him where he started with a discrepancy between his act and attitude. In order to maintain a new attitude—that is, in order to develop a stable changed attitude, regardless of whether his initial attitude was stable or not—an individual might have to engage in counter-attitudinal advocacy.

Rosenberg (1965, 1966) has made such a distinction between a simple counter-attitudinal act and counter-attitudinal advocacy. Perhaps the dissonance aroused through a simple counter-attitudinal act itself could directly bring about a change in attitude. However, it seems to me that even if such an automatic readjustment or thermostatic-like regulation were possible with regard to simple affective evaluations (such as a child's attraction to certain toys or an adult's reaction to a dull, montonous task), it would not be possible with a cognitively complex attitude (such as one *might* have toward socialism) without running into the difficulties mentioned above. If the prior attitude was cognitively complex, or if it was stable, and especially if the new attitude is to be stable, the individual will have to come to grips with the cognitive supports for his old attitude and will have to create ones for his new attitude. That is, sooner or later, he will have to engage in some degree of counter-attitudinal advocacy.

Thus, an individual might be induced, perhaps through the act itself, to conjure up and dwell upon information that he has that is potentially inconsistent with his attitude. That is, he might be induced to interpret information he already has in a manner that is inconsistent with his old attitude, and to develop and elaborate arguments counter to it. The dissonance thus aroused secondarily to the act might be more crucial for producing stable attitude change than the mere fact of an experienced discrepancy between act and attitude. It would seem reasonable to assume that when behavior change induces attitude change, it often does so indirectly through stimulating counter-attitudinal advocacy.

A number of experiments have been performed in which a subject is paid a certain amount of money to write an essay defending a position opposite to his own attitude. Cohen (in Brehm and Cohen, 1962, pp. 73–78) found an inverse relationship between amount of incentive for writing a counter-attitudinal essay and attitude change. Thus, he found the same relationship between reward and attitude change as that obtained in the Festinger and Carlsmith experiment. However, when Rosenberg (1965) had subjects (students at Ohio State University) write a counter-attitudinal essay (supporting a ban on Rose Bowl participation by the university's football team) for either 50 cents, one dollar, or five dollars, he found that the *more* the subjects were paid, the *greater* was the degree of attitude change toward the position advocated in the essay. Rosenberg had predicted this relationship on the grounds that larger monetary incentives should incline the subjects toward writing more persuasive essays and toward more readily internalizing the counter-attitudinal arguments.[3] Parenthetically, it should be noted that neither of these experiments tested the stability of the changed attitudes, and I have suggested that counter-attitudinal advocacy is most important for the development of a *stable* changed attitude.

Other experiments that have dealt with counter-attitudinal essay writing for various amounts of monetary reward have found both direct and inverse relationships between amount of reward and attitude change, depending upon subtle variations in the manner and context in which the rewards were offered, and of the tasks involved (e.g., Janis and Gilmore, 1965; Carlsmith, Collins, and Helmreich, 1966; Linder, Cooper, and Jones, 1967).

These experiments present a confusing picture. However, what might be an important difference between Cohen's and Rosenberg's experiments is that in the former the subject was offered the money before he actually committed himself to writing the essay, while in the latter the subject had already committed himself before he was offered the money. The possible significance of this fact will become clear shortly.

As indicated before, coercive power generates resentment or resistance. Although this resistance is related to the coercive pressure itself and not to the original attitude, it might foster a reluctance to engage in counter-attitudinal advocacy. It was also indicated before that reward power is sometimes difficult to distinguish from coercive power and that when a person feels a desperate need for the reward it might generate resistance when its offer is made contingent upon certain behavior. More importantly for the immediate discussion, I also mentioned previously that resistance might be generated if a reward is interpreted as a bribe, but that there are situations in which a reward can generate attraction.

In a situation in which it is possible to interpret a reward as a bribe (such as in Cohen's experiment where the reward was offered *before* commitment) it is possible that it can more readily be interpreted as such the larger it is. Indeed, in investigating the paradigm employed in such experiments, Kauffmann (1971) has found that a large monetary reward offered before commitment is likely to be interpreted as a bribe, and that the same size reward offered after commitment is more likely to be interpreted as a bonus. There was no clear tendency to interpret smaller rewards one way or the other. His evidence also suggests that more resentment might be generated when the money is offered before commitment. Thus, we could expect to find an inverse relationship between the amount of reward and attitude change, as in fact was found in Cohen's experiment.[4]

On the other hand, in a situation in which a reward is not interpreted as a bribe and therefore does not generate resistance, we might expect that the individual might engage more enthusiastically in counter-attitudinal advocacy the larger the reward that is offered. A direct relationship between amount of reward and attitude change might then result, as was the case in Rosenberg's experiment, in which the reward was offered *after* commitment. Indeed, in this experiment the reward could have been interpreted as unnecessary and generous—the larger the more so— and therefore attraction might have been generated that would have facilitated counter-attitudinal advocacy.[5]

Of course, in the experiments referred to here that involved reward, the specific nature of the task itself was that of counter-attitudinal advocacy. That is, the advocacy was not spontaneous but was itself the counter-attitudinal act. However, I have argued that the individual, in the context of an action that he has been induced to take, might be stimulated to reexamine his attitudinal position on his own. As Kelman (1962) states,

this *action may provide the occasion for the person to re-examine his attitudes toward the object.* That is, the situational demands on the person to take or consider taking a particular action may be such as to bring into play an active process of re-evaluation of his position.

In this process, he might reorganize or reinterpret his old information.

This process of re-examination may provide attitudinal support for the induced action and lead to attitude change. The resulting attitude change would, then, be occasioned by the induction of overt action, but it would actually be produced by the internal processes that precede and accompany the action. (Kelman, 1962)

Due to external pressure, the individual will have to make a decision about whether or not he will comply, and perhaps whether or not he should have complied, and the necessity of that decision might induce him to rethink the attitudes supporting his old behavior.

> The situational requirement to take or consider taking the action has served to force the issue, and has provided the occasion for the person to re-examine his attitudes. (Kelman, 1962)

Kelman recognized that one important variable to be considered in predicting when the induction of action would lead to attitude change is the degree of pressure applied.

In speaking of pressure, the factor of sufficient justification must not be overlooked. To the extent that I *feel* forced into a particular act, there will be no inducement to engage in counter-attitudinal advocacy. I am least likely to engage in it if someone holds a gun to my head. Thus, when coercive power is employed, resentment and the factor of sufficient justification are likely to be working together and in the same direction, that is, the greater the coercion, the less the attitude change. When a desperately needed reward is made contingent on one's behavior, resentment might be generated, and sufficient justification will be experienced. Thus, again, attitude change would not be expected. However, when a person is offered a reward that he does not believe he desperately needs, he cannot have the same feeling of being "forced," no matter how large it is. He might perform the act simply because he wants to obtain what is offered, and, although he might not have any doubts about what he is doing, he might still be inclined to rationalize his act, perhaps in order to maintain his self-esteem. However, when such a reward is interpreted as a bribe, resentment might inhibit the rationalizing process. But when viewed as a "bonus," neither resentment nor a feeling of being "forced" is created, and the rationalizing will proceed uninhibited. Thus, the businessman who had been earning fat profits from the Vietnam War through transactions with his government might have been inclined to develop a pro-war attitude complete with such supportive beliefs as that the "domino theory" is correct and that the North Vietnamese are aggressors. Or a business executive who has found a "rewarding" position with an automobile company might happen to develop the attitude that cars are built safely and that the focus of public attention, for safety's sake, should be on driver education rather than the automobile industry. In other words, self-interest-oriented attitudes may develop.

The foregoing discussion leads to the conclusion that the possibility of attitude change, as a consequence of behavior change, is enhanced the less resistance, the greater the attraction, and the less the feeling of being "forced" is generated. The practical implication for nonviolent action is that when one seeks attitude change as a consequence of behavior change through coercive power, one should apply the *minimal* pressure necessary to obtain the behavior change.

It should be noted that while the minimal coercive power needed to obtain the behavior change desired is most likely to induce attitude change, very great coercive power is not always ineffective in this regard. If *O* views the coercive power as legitimate, or in some way justifies its use on the part of the agent, less resistance will result. Sometimes even the victims of violence can justify the violence committed against them, thereby reducing their own resentment, so flexible is the human mind.

The counter-attitudinal advocacy discussed thus far involves conjuring up potentially discrepant information that one already has and interpreting it in a manner that is inconsistent with the original attitude. There is another way in which behavior change can indirectly lead to attitude change. The changed behavior of the individual might take the form of immersion into a new social interaction through which he is exposed to new information that he did not have before. For example, enforced contact, or integration, between whites and blacks might initiate an interaction between them that exposes each to new information about the other that is potentially discrepant with their prior prejudices. As Kelman (1962) put it, the induction of action may lead to attitude change because

the *action may provide the occasion for the occurrence of new experiences in relation to the object.* Once the person has taken a particular action, he may have certain new experiences that were unanticipated, in the sense that the expectation of these experiences did not form the basis of his taking the action in the first instance. These new experiences and the information they provide may, in turn, be of such a nature as to produce a reorganization of attitudes.

One of the best known findings of the reduction of prejudice through intergroup contact is that of Deutsch and Collins (1951). They found a greater reduction of prejudice in integrated housing projects in which black and white families were assigned to apartments on a nonsegregated basis than in those in which they were assigned to apartments on a more segregated basis (to different buildings or areas of the project). There was evidence of more frequent and intimate interracial contact in the more integrated projects. The weight of the evidence seemed to indicate that the housing patterns, presumably through this factor of contact, were responsible for the results.

Contact between ethnic groups does not always, however, lead to favorable attitude change. Amir (1969) has reviewed the studies in this area and has summarized the conditions that tend to increase or decrease its likelihood. Involuntary contact is one condition that might serve to increase rather than decrease prejudice, but it would seem that, again, the desired results are more likely to be obtained when the minimal pressure necessary to produce behavior change (in this case, interethnic contact) is used, thereby generating the least resistance. If the individuals viewed the power as legitimate or justified, they would likely be less resentful than otherwise.

Amir (1969) lists the following conditions of intergroup contact as ones which tend to reduce prejudice:

> (a) when there is equal status contact between the members of the various ethnic groups, (b) when the contact is between members of a majority group and *higher* status members of a minority group, (c) when an "authority" and/or the social climate are in favor of and promote the intergroup contact, (d) when the contact is of an intimate rather than a casual nature, (e) when the ethnic intergroup contact is pleasant or rewarding, (f) when the members of *both* groups in the particular contact situation interact in functionally important activities or develop common goals or superordinate goals that are higher ranking in importance than the individual goals of each of the groups.

Perhaps when the new information that an individual receives through the intergroup contact is of such a nature as to be readily interpretable by him as support for his negative attitudes, the likelihood of reduction of prejudice is decreased. But when the information is of such a nature as to evade easy interpretation in the context of such attitudes, attitude change is more likely to occur. This issue of intergroup contact will be revisited in Chapter 7.

In summary, under certain conditions behavioral change can induce attitude change through at least two channels: by inducing the individual to reorganize and reinterpret his old information and by exposing him to new information.

Nonviolent action is ultimately concerned with resolving conflict through attitude change. Mere behavioral compliance can only be maintained through the external maintenance of pressures. Yet, at times, in an attempt to combat injustice, coercive aspects of nonviolence come to the fore in the form of noncooperation. The question of the possibility of inducing attitude change indirectly through behavior change will again arise in Chapter 7.

NOTES

[1]When one obeys laws through internalized reasons for doing so, or from understanding, it can be argued that legitimate power as defined here is not involved.

[2]It is possible for the cognitive and affective components in relation to an object to be so minimally integrated so as to make for quite discrepant evaluative orientations toward that same object. For example, an individual might have a negative affective orientation toward blacks and yet intellectually be inclined to react favorably toward them. Both components might have important behavioral implications. For instance, his affective response might prevent him from moving into an integrated housing development, and yet his cognitive orientation might lead him to contribute money to a black civil rights organization or to not refrain from voting for a black political candidate.

Rokeach (1968, pp. 121–122) indicates that a positive or negative preference toward an attitude object can either be due to the fact that the object is affectively liked or disliked or that it is cognitively evaluated as good or bad. He points out that the two dimensions of *like-dislike* and *goodness-badness* need not necessarily go together. "It is possible to like something bad, and to dislike something good." An example he uses is that of an individual who believes cigarette-smoking is bad, but enjoys it. Another one is that of a person who thinks that a particular medicine is good, but does not like to take it.

Often, however, the two components are better integrated and incline the individual toward a consistent evaluation of a social object and a consistent set of behaviors toward that object. This consistency between the two components comes about because a change in one component often induces a consistent change in the other. Rosenberg (1960) hypnotized his subjects and induced in them, through post-hypnotic suggestion, a feeling opposite to their original attitude. For instance, those who were against blacks moving into white neighborhoods were told under hypnosis that they were going to feel very positively about the idea. It was found that after hypnosis subjects changed their cognitions toward consistency with their new feelings.

The example above concerning a simultaneous negative affective orientation toward blacks and a positive intellectual orientation is based on an individual I once met who said something to the following effect: "Intellectually, I have nothing against Negroes. I know it is wrong, but emotionally I react negatively to them and so, for example, I can't bring myself to move into an integrated neighborhood." He seemed deeply concerned and disturbed about this situation, and I believe that it is very possible that such a person could eventually experience his feelings being transformed by his beliefs, but only because this person was not allowing his emotions to dictate to his intellect, in a way that would lead him to interpret perceptual facts in a manner consistent with his feelings.

[3]He did indeed find that the high-incentive essays were generally more persuasive than the low-incentive essays, as determined by impartial judgment. However, when the groups were matched on essay-persuasiveness by discarding from the analysis low-incentive subjects who wrote particularly unpersuasive essays, the original relationship between amount of incentive and degree of attitude change still stood. Rosenberg interprets this as meaning that high incentive induced a greater degree of internalization of arguments in addition to better quality of essays. It is also possible that the persuasiveness of the essay was not a crucial factor. But another possible interpretation is that the correlation between incentive and persuasiveness of the essay is merely a rough indicant of the relationship between attitude change and counter-attitudinal advocacy, and not all arguments thought up are eventually

written down in the essay. Moreover, it is possible that a subject could have been refuting, in his own mind, each counter-argument as he was writing it down. This might have been less likely to occur in the high-reward condition.

[4]Events outside of the laboratory can be found that seem to support the contention that if a reward is interpreted as a bribe it will generate resistance. For example, a few years ago I read that the Polaroid Corporation had given a twenty thousand dollar contribution to a black community organization in Boston. A group of present and former employees, the Polaroid Revolutionary Workers Movement (which has been fighting against Polaroid's business dealings with South Africa on the grounds that the government is racist), denounced the gift as an attempt to buy off the black community. The community organization voted to divert the money to groups working for the liberation of South African blacks. It would seem, then, that those who interpreted the financial contribution as a bribe had more contempt for the corporation than ever. Perhaps a smaller reward, say, one hundred dollars, could not have been interpreted as a bribe, and would not have increased resentment (although it might not have lowered it either).

[5]In the Cohen experiment, attraction might have been operating in the low-reward condition. It has been found that when an individual performs a favor for someone, he tends to increase his liking for the recipient of the favor (Jecker and Landy, 1969). When a subject commits himself after a low or nominal reward has been offered, he might really feel that he is committing himself to do a favor, and his attraction might thereby increase. In Rosenberg's experiment, where the subject already committed himself, high reward would have increased attraction more than low reward. In other words, if you already have committed yourself to do someone a favor and he then offers you much money for it, you might feel even more attracted to him.

CHAPTER 4

The Power of Information

Nonviolent action begins with—and, I might add, never abandons—persuasion through reason (Bondurant, 1965, p. 11). Nonviolent persuasion involves reasoning, or the stimulation of reasoning, based on perceptual facts, from moral values and human needs. An essential preliminary step is the accumulation of factual knowledge of the particular issue of concern and a thorough analysis of the situation. As Horsburgh (1968, p. 71) has written:

> Gandhi held that one must appeal to people's concern for justice and one another's welfare rather than to fear, greed, or hatred. A great deal of his propaganda was purely factual, being intended to make both Indians and their British opponents aware of existing conditions. In this he was greatly assisted by the strong local roots of his movement which helped him both to gather information and to spread it.

Both the theory and past practice of nonviolence suggest that the nonviolent activist gathers as many facts as is possible, gains firsthand knowledge of the views of all parties involved in the issue, and, before making any public commitment, consults his conscience and evaluates his facts in the context of moral values and human needs. He thoroughly convinces himself of his case before he begins to attempt to persuade others, and even then stands always ready to be persuaded through reason from his position.

This approach was exemplified by Gandhi in his Champaran campaign.[1] Gandhi had been called to Champaran in northern India in 1917 to help the peasants on the indigo plantations there who, it was claimed, were being grossly exploited by the planters. These planters were allegedly extorting money from the peasants through a variety of coercive means. Upon hearing one person's account of the peasants' plight, Gandhi (1954a, pp. 494–495) stated: "I can give no opinion without seeing the condition with my own eyes."

Gandhi said that his object in Champaran was to inquire into the condition and grievances of the peasants. First, he called upon the planters and the government in order to ascertain their side of the story. Later he and his coworkers interviewed thousands of peasants who came to him to give statements of grievances. Gandhi (1954a, p. 511) states:

> Those who took down the statements had to observe certain rules. Each peasant had to be closely cross-examined, and whoever failed to satisfy the test was rejected. This entailed a lot of extra time but most of the statements were thus rendered incontrovertible.

He then took it upon himself to meet the planters against whom serious allegations had been made.

The inquiry led to the establishment of a government committee to which Gandhi was appointed as a member. Nanda (1958, p. 160) states:

> With the evidence of 8,000 tenants in his hands, there was no aspect of the agrarian problem with which Gandhi was not thoroughly acquainted. Knowledgeable, persuasive and firm he was able to make out an irresistible case for the tenants.

The committee submitted a unanimous report that favored the peasants, and a bill was passed a few months later that redressed the peasants' grievances to some extent.

There is some indication that Gandhi's success might have been at least partly due to the pressure that the Government of India—for its own reasons in wanting to avoid a full-scale local Satyagraha struggle (Gandhi's actions in Champaran had greatly aroused the peasants)—applied to the local governor, who, in turn, may have brought more than persuasion to bear on the members of the committee in guiding the bill to passage (see Gandhi, 1954a, p. 519; Nanda, 1958, p. 160). But, as will be discussed later in this chapter, the power of information is not limited to persuasion.

Thus, the nonviolent activist first engages in thorough fact-finding in regard to the issue of concern. He must be convinced in his own mind that a definite injustice exists before he will take further action. Perhaps his first impression about the issue, based on few or no facts and bolstered only by the belief that there are others who claim that a particular injustice exists, or based on social support but not on factual support intrinsic to the issue of concern, is not, in the end, the construction that most satisfactorily encompasses and relates the facts and his moral values. Gandhi, influenced to go to Champaran by a peasant from the area, would not have persisted in his campaign if his fact-finding did not, to his mind, reveal injustice unequivocally.

Thoroughly convinced of an injustice and committed to eradicating it, the activist then continues to try to understand the viewpoints of those he will attempt to persuade. He will have to *listen* to them and attempt to put himself in their shoes in an effort to understand their subjective reality as well as he does his own.

Barring a change of mind even at this stage, the nonviolent activist—firmly convinced of his own position—is now ready to persuade. However, as noted above, he will continue to stand ready to be persuaded himself. While he is not prepared to yield any position that he believes in, and will attempt to convert others to it, he *will* yield a position that he has been persuaded from, and he openly invites persuasive attempts (Bondurant, 1965, pp. 196–197). There is an important difference, not always acknowledged, between being firm and committed to a point of view and being dogmatic.

It should be noted that the nonviolent activist attempts to influence a number of different groupings of people, often simultaneously. He strives to influence the general public (or bystanders), many of whom might not have formed an attitude in regard to the issue. He also tries to strengthen the attitude of those bystanders and supporters who are already inclined toward his view. Finally, he wishes to influence the adversary, if one can be identified in the situation, who might hold an attitude contrary to his own. The adversary's attitude might be especially difficult to affect, sometimes being grounded in intense self-interest and supported by many beliefs. But no matter whom a particular persuasive attempt is directed at, it need not vary in regard to stressing information and reason.

Perhaps it should also be noted at this point that when I speak of attitude change I will use this one term as a matter of convenience to refer not only to a change in the sign of an attitude (i.e., from "pro" to "con" or vice versa) but also to a change in extremity of an attitude and even to attitude formation. What is referred to as the research literature on attitude change often contains conclusions based upon the last two categories of attitude activity.

In this chapter, I will examine the processes through which information might affect attitudes. It is not my purpose here to present a guide or activist's manual on how to change attitudes nor to review the social psychological research literature on persuasion, which deals largely with the question of how best to present information or with *techniques* of persuasion. Many of these techniques would not be inimical to nonviolence, although some would. The emphasis in nonviolent persuasion might be said to be on the fullest dissemination of information as possible concerning the issue in question, even including facts that might more easily be construed to support our opponent's viewpoint than our own. The object is not only to persuade but to arrive at a mutual adjustment of attitudes consistent with the facts that might result in partial or full agreement.

All techniques of persuasion involve the communication of information. When one party goes to the trouble of discovering and disclosing relevant information to the fullest extent possible, it can be wondered to what extent the techniques are important relative to the information itself. That is, I suspect that techniques of persuasion often involve, or at least thrive upon, a manipulated and incomplete exposure of information. They are effective to the extent that information is held back, or that the knowledge possessed by those who are to be persuaded is meager. When techniques of persuasion are tested in the laboratory, it is often under conditions in which only certain facts are made available to the subject and others are purposely withheld. Of course, such manipulation of attitudes is often attempted on a massive scale in everyday life—as implied, for example, when we talk about the "packaging" of a political candidate. Perhaps one effect of exposing an issue through the dissemination of information, such as the nonviolent activist would do, is that of bursting such one-sided bubbles as are the attitudes formed on the basis of controlled doses of spoon-fed information. One might refer to the activist's work as that of muckraking, or investigative reporting, which has a fine tradition in American history. Although not usually referred to as such, I would propose that it is an important aspect of nonviolent action. At any rate, Ralph Nader did not need to learn elaborate techniques of persuasion in order to expose the automobile safety issue. He patiently compiled facts and presented them to the American public, together with rational argumentation from those facts.

In whatever form the nonviolent activist might decide to present his information, it can be said that an essential ingredient of nonviolent persuasion is the honest and straightforward dissemination of information. It is also clear that the withholding of information, the making of unsubstantiated charges, the cynicism involved in the "packaging" of an issue, and appeals to greed, prejudice, and hatred cannot under any circumstances be reconciled with the philosophy of nonviolence.

When I refer to certain techniques of persuasion in this chapter, I will do so only through an interest in elucidating the process of attitude change. I will not be recommending the specific techniques themselves, although there are, as I have said, certain techniques of persuasion that would not be incompatible with nonviolence.

PERSUASION

It was pointed out in Chapter 2 that the interpretation of perceptual facts is not as restricted by those facts as perceptual organization is restricted by stimulation. Perceptual facts can support multiple interpretations. However, an increasing number of facts can sometimes restrict the number and kind of interpretations that can be made of them as a set, or at least elicit the modification or qualification of certain of those interpretations. The facts are partially, but not wholly, determinative of the resulting cognitive organization.

The more perceptual facts presented, the more limited might be the number of alternative interpretations that can be made of them as a whole. However, facts occur not only in the context of other facts but also in the context of the needs, goals, values, and prior beliefs of the individual, and their meaning arises through their subjective relations in both contexts.

Even when a particular set of facts itself is highly determinative of the resulting subjective cognitive organization, that organization is itself potentially supportive of multiple more inclusive interpretations in the context of needs, goals, values, and prior beliefs, through which the evaluative aspects of cognitive organizations arise.

For example, a "hawk" might have accepted the fact of the Mylai massacre and might have regarded it as an "exceptional case." If he could have been presented with other facts of possibly many other similar events in Vietnam, the "hawk" might have had to regard this set of facts as indicative of a pervasive aspect of warfare in Vietnam. However, this fact-necessitated interpretation need not have been subjectively inconsistent for the "hawk" with his beliefs about the necessity of the war for ultimately furthering such things as national self-interest, justice, freedom, or self-determination for the South Vietnamese people.

The presentation of facts, then, might not be enough for successful persuasion. Through rational argumentation, developed by either O (influencer) or P (influencee) himself, those facts must be linked to the needs and values of P, and help to link the needs and values to the attitudinal object in a manner that is discrepant with his original attitudinal position.

It has been demonstrated that the cognitive structure of an attitude consists of beliefs that the attitudinal object facilitates or blocks the attainment of important valued states or goals, and that the sign and extremity of an attitude is a function of those beliefs. Rosenberg (1956) assessed the attitudes of his subjects toward "allowing members of the Communist Party to address the public." Three to five weeks later, he assessed the importance attributed by each of his subjects to certain valued states (such as everyone should have equal rights, American prestige abroad, and education) and also each subject's estimate as to whether and to what extent each of these goals would tend to be facilitated or blocked through the "policy of allowing members of the Communist Party to address the public." Rosenberg found that the sign and extremity of the attitude was related to the sum of the products of the estimated instrumentality of the attitudinal object for achieving a particular goal and the attributed importance of that goal. In a similar vein, Woodruff and DiVesta (1948) found that attitude change will accompany changes in believed instrumentality of the attitudinal object for the attainment of certain valued states.

Carlson (1956) tried to raise arguments that "allowing Negroes to move into white neighborhoods" would facilitate the attainment of four goals: American prestige in other countries, protection of property values, equal opportunity for personal development, and being experienced, broadminded, and worldly-wise. Tests administered three weeks later revealed increased agreement with the four propositions, and a corresponding significant attitude change on the housing segregation issue.

THE STIMULATION OF ARGUMENTATION

Before an individual is influenced by facts and arguments, he has to accept and understand them and perhaps relate them to his own beliefs and values. He has to *think* about them. "People enjoy and affirm the changes they make for themselves; they resist changes imposed on them by others" (Watson, 1966, p. 550). While this profound hypothesis was formulated in regard to social change and innovation, I wish to point out that, when broadly interpreted, it can refer to attitude change as well as behavior change. People enjoy and affirm what they *think* for themselves.

When one really attempts to comprehend a communication, one thinks about it, reconstructs it, and casts the ideas stimulated by the communication in one's own language. We sometimes say that a person really understands something when he can put it into his own words. We then know that he has comprehended the thought behind the words. That which is merely rote learned is insulated from one's cognitive system because it is not dealt with in a thinking manner. Facts and arguments must engage one's cognitive system and be interpreted in its context in order to be understood. The meaning and comprehension of the communication arises out of the active constructive process through which it is incorporated into the cognitive system in whose context it is interpreted. The thought or idea that emerges will therefore be personal to some degree; it might differ somewhat from what the communicator had in mind. But the greatest comprehension might occur when an individual formulates his *own* arguments.

A communication must necessarily be limited in scope and time, while P has relatively unlimited time to explore the issue in his own mind. The arguments that he himself spontaneously produces might be more important for attitude change in the long run than those presented to him in the communication itself, not only because there might be more of them but also because, as we shall see, he tends to accept them more.

In the previous chapter it was noted that behavior change can sometimes beget attitude change, but that the process of inducing a behavior that is contrary to one's original attitude can generate resistance. Even when the resistance does not prevent capitulation in the form of changing one's behavior, it can prevent attitude change by discouraging counter-attitudinal advocacy. The greater the resistance generated, the less the likelihood of attitude change.

As we shall see later, resistance can also be generated by certain persuasive attempts or during the process of attempting to persuade. We would expect that, in general, the greatest resistance is generated by pressures to directly induce behavior change and the least by persuasive attempts. Informational power allows for a greater feeling of subjective freedom. But anything that occurs during the persuasive attempt that restricts P's feeling that he is changing his own mind or that he is free to do what he wants with the information provided to him might engender resistance. Regardless of this particular possibility, resistance in the form of anger or resentment can be generated by O during or prior to his persuasive attempt, perhaps by certain comments or arguments he makes, and may prevent counter-attitudinal advocacy. Overwhelmingly good arguments can sometimes overcome this resistance and obtain attitude change anyway, just as considerable coercion can obtain behavior change despite the resistance it generates. Yet there is something special to *P* about the arguments he himself produces.

I will propose that, in general, effective persuasion attempts will be ones that do not induce any resistances to the potential self-generation of arguments or even the reconstruction of arguments in the communication and that, on the contrary, they stimulate *P* to look at the other side, or both sides, of the issue, to actively think about it on his own, and to engage in counter-attitudinal advocacy. For he might be more likely to accept, internalize, and be convinced by the arguments he himself produces. A communication that contains much and diverse information might itself tend to stimulate thought about an issue.

A number of recent lines of research lend support, though as yet weakly, to the notion that the arguments that *P* himself has generated may be more effective in attitude change than those communicated to him.

Many of the experiments on role-playing or active participation indicate that, if an individual is asked to argue against his own position, his attitude will change more than if he is passively exposed to arguments against his original position. Janis and King (1954) found that subjects who were asked to defend a particular attitudinal position by giving an informal talk based on an outline that summarized the main arguments to be presented changed more in the direction of that position than those subjects who merely read the prepared outline and listened to the talk. Although there are a few exceptions, most of the studies in this area have demonstrated that improvised role-playing, either orally or written, yields greater attitude change than hearing or reading persuasive communications (King and Janis, 1956; Culbertson, 1957; Janis and Mann, 1965; Watts, 1967; Greenwald and Albert, 1968). In Greenwald and Albert's (1968) experiment each subject was asked to improvise, in response to five neutrally worded questions, five arguments advocating either specialized or general undergraduate education. They were randomly assigned to these positions. They also studied arguments supporting the other side that had been written by another subject in the experiment, so that each subject's arguments served also as a communication for another subject who had written arguments on the opposing side. The subjects were found to be more swayed by their own arguments, tending to favor the position that they had been asked to advocate. They also tended to recall more of their own arguments than those they had studied, and tended to rate their own arguments as more original than the others.

The relative stability of attitude change induced by improvisation of arguments was studied by Watts (1967). In his improvisation condition, subjects were given an attitudinal statement (such as "The Secretary of State should be elected by the people, not appointed by the President" and "Courts should deal more leniently with juvenile delinquents") and were asked to write a strong convincing argument supporting the side of the issue indicated. It was found that subjects who improvised persuasive arguments maintained greater attitude change over a six-week period than did those subjects who had read a persuasive communication, even though this communication had been specially constructed so as to induce immediate attitude change equivalent to that produced by improvisation. Those who had written persuasive arguments were more likely to have subsequently discussed and read about the topic than those who had read the prepared communication, and, regardless of treatment condition, those who had claimed to have discussed the topic showed greater persistence of attitude change.

The findings of these experiments, while open to more than one interpretation, are consistent with the notion that counter-attitudinal advocacy is an important factor in the persuasion process.[2]

Studies reported by Greenwald (1968) support the notion that self-generated thoughts are important in the process of persuasion, and raise the possibility that the effects of persuasive communications are mediated by counter-attitudinal or communication-consistent advocacy. When subjects were asked to list their thoughts in regard to the attitudinal object after the receipt of a communication, it was found that they listed more self-generated thoughts than they did ones conveyed by the communication itself. While the nature of the thought-listing request itself might have partially determined this difference, what is of most interest is the differential effects of communications on the nature of self-generated thoughts and attitude change. A two-sided communication—one that acknowledges some opposing arguments and refutes them where possible—was not only found to more effectively produce attitude change than one-sided communications, but was also found to have induced the most favorable set of self-generated thoughts supportive of the position advocated in the communication, relative to unfavorable or nonsupportive self-generated thoughts, while inducing the least supportive cognitive pattern of those thoughts conveyed by the communication itself. These findings indicate that self-generated thoughts may be more determinative of attitude change than the communication-originated ones. Although a cause-effect relationship between the nature of the self-generated thoughts stimulated by a communication and attitude change has not been conclusively demonstrated, the correlational evidence presented by Greenwald (1968) strongly implicates their role.

Attitude change is an active process. It is possible that in order for a communication to be effective, P must first work on it, cognitively react to it, reconstruct it, and be stimulated through the communication itself to think about the issue.

But there is no guarantee that, if the communication stimulates thought relevant to the issue, this thought will consist of arguments in the same direction as the position advocated in the communication. Indeed, it can sometimes stimulate the generation of arguments supportive of P's original attitudinal position. In order to obtain attitude change, the communication must stimulate counter-attitudinal advocacy; a two-sided communication, one that at least refers to some arguments for the other side, seems to be effective in this regard.

Other lines of research implicate the role of the self-generation of arguments as an important one in inducing resistance (or opposition) to persuasive attempts. In one type of experiment, subjects listen to a communication while being distracted by having to attend to another task, such as monitoring flashing lights on an instrument panel. Other subjects are not distracted. It has been found that attitude change *increases* with distraction and that distraction reduces the number of counter-arguments generated by the subjects. Thus, the generation of arguments counter to the communication might help to reduce the impact of persuasive attempts (Osterhouse and Brock, 1970; Keating and Brock, 1971).

Although such evidence again points to the importance of self-generated arguments, the distraction technique perhaps cannot be recommended to anyone who wishes to create changed attitudes that are stable rather than ones that change momentarily and do not last. McGuire and Papageorgis (1961) have suggested that techniques most effective in producing immediate attitude change are sometimes least effective in immunizing the attitude against future attack. Sometimes such techniques do not really produce attitude change at all, but merely what appears to be change due to the demand characteristics of the experiment, as discussed before. Similar situational demands are influential in our everyday lives. If I try to persuade someone on an issue, he might pretend to agree with me because he does not want to be discourteous or start an argument, or because if he expresses disagreement he might be dragged into a long conversation that he might want to avoid. However, as is possible in regard to the distraction technique, he might sincerely agree at the moment, but change his mind again after he has had an opportunity to really think about the issue and weigh the arguments by himself. Until that time, he might be inclined toward the side being taken by anyone communicating to him at the moment. Specifically in regard to the distraction technique, there is nothing to prevent P from generating counter-arguments at his leisure sometime after the distraction has ended. The same communication that stimulated counter-argumentation in nondistracted subjects immediately, quite likely stimulated it in the other subjects sometime after the distraction.

In asking what *does* produce *stable* attitudes, the possible importance of the self-generation of arguments supportive of the desired attitude once again arises, and has already been seen in the experiment by Watts (1967) reported above. In that experiment subjects were *asked* to improvise arguments supportive of a particular position. Stability has also been found to be imparted to attitudes by the inoculation techniques of McGuire (1964). Central to his theory is the idea that certain kinds of communications can in themselves stimulate counter-argument to subsequent persuasive attack. He has explored a number of ways in which the immunity of certain beliefs to persuasive attack can be increased. Employing a biological inoculation analogy, he has reasoned that preexposing an individual to weak forms of arguments against a particular belief that he holds can stimulate defenses of that belief, making it less vulnerable to strong persuasive attack, just as preexposure to a mild dosage of a virus can make a person resistant to a later viral attack. But the dosage must be "not so strong that this preexposure will itself cause the disease" (McGuire, 1964, p. 200).

The inoculation analogy inclined McGuire to work with beliefs that had been maintained in a "germ-free" environment or, in other words, beliefs that the person is not likely ever to have heard attacked and that, because they probably have been held without much cognitive support, are likely to be quite vulnerable to persuasive attack. "Cultural truisms" are this type of belief, and McGuire (1964) chose examples such as the following with which to work: "It's a good idea to brush your teeth after every meal if at all possible"; "Mental illness is not contagious"; "The effects of penicillin have been, almost without exception, of great benefit to mankind"; "Everyone should get a yearly chest X-ray to detect any signs of TB at an early stage."

In the first experiment stemming from the inoculation analogy, McGuire and Papageorgis (1961) compared the effectiveness of supportive and refutational defenses in inducing immunity to subsequent attacks on the "truisms." A supportive defense consisted of four arguments in support of the "truism." The subject was presented with a statement of the "truism," which was followed by the mention of several arguments in support of it. Then followed four paragraphs, each elaborating one of these arguments. In the refutational defense, the statement of the "truism" was followed by the mention of four arguments against the belief and then four paragraphs, each refuting one of the arguments. Immediately after the defensive treatments, opinion questionnaires were filled out.

Two days later came the attacks. An attack consisted of the elaboration of arguments against a belief—in this case the same four arguments that were mentioned, but not elaborated, in the refutational defense. Opinion questionnaires were again administered.

Immediately after the defensive treatments, the refutational defense was found to be no more effective in strengthening the belief than the supportive defense. However, the second measure indicated that the refutational defense was more effective in sustaining the belief against subsequent attack than the supportive defense and, of course, than no defense at all. In this latter condition (attack without any prior defense treatment) the belief held up very poorly as compared with another condition in which the belief was neither attacked nor defended. The differential effects of the defenses were as predicted, for it was reasoned that the supportive defense, while providing belief-bolstering material, does not provide a threat to the belief and thus does not stimulate the individual to assimilate belief-bolstering material, as does a refutational defense.[3]

A refutational defense might increase the immunity of a belief to subsequent attack by refuting the same arguments that are to be used in the attack. In the McGuire and Papageorgis (1961) experiment, the arguments mentioned and refuted in the refutational defense were in fact the same ones elaborated in the subsequent attack.

But McGuire has argued that the immunity produced by the refutational defense derives not only from the presentation of refuting arguments but also from the mention of opposing arguments, which presumably motivates the individual to "accumulate belief-bolstering material," which, of course, will take time if such material is not directly presented to him (McGuire, 1964).

In line with this reasoning, Papageorgis and McGuire (1961) predicted that the refutational defense should be as effective against an attack consisting of arguments neither mentioned nor refuted in the defensive treatment as against an attack consisting of arguments dealt with in the refutational defense. With the attack coming seven days after the defense, the defense was found to be about as effective for the novel attack as for the other, and both conditions were superior to an attack-only condition.

Presumably, a period of time between defense and attack in the last experiment allowed for the assimilation of belief-bolstering material, stimulated by the threatening component (the mention of belief-opposed arguments) of the refutational defense. An attempt to directly measure this assumed mediating process was made by asking the subjects at the end of the experiment to list supporting arguments. Unsupportive of the theory, no significant difference was found between the number of arguments listed by subjects in the defense conditions and those in the attack-only condition. Another measure, however, revealed that the attack was regarded as less credible and of lower quality when preceded by a defense. Rogers and Thistlethwaite (1969) have also found that when a defense was effective it did not increase the number of arguments that could be listed, but did increase the tendency to discount the attack. Tannenbaum (1967; pp. 303–304) also reports that the refutational defense was found to weaken the judged fairness and believability of the attack.

However, McGuire (1964, pp. 213–215) has found that the mere mention of belief-opposing arguments, without refutation, is a significant factor in producing immunity to attack, as well as is the actual refutation of mentioned opposing arguments. It is difficult to see how the mere mention of opposing arguments without refutation can decrease the apparent credibility of a subsequent attack without in some way stimulating refutational and belief-supporting arguments, even if they be vague and inarticulate ones.

McGuire's work on immunity to persuasion seems on the whole to at least sustain the possibility that part of the reason why refutational defenses are better in conferring opposition to subsequent attack than supportive defenses is because the refutational defenses stimulate or motivate the individual to assimilate material that will support his original attitude. They stimulate him to prepare his own defenses or arguments, thereby making his original attitude less vulnerable to attack. But if the individual is merely stimulated to prepare defenses and is not given the material with which to formulate his arguments or the time in which to do so, his motivation might be to no avail. So that, in addition to stimulating the individual, some guidance might also need to be supplied. This idea is further supported by the results obtained when comparing active and passive defenses. An active defense consisted of instructing subjects to write an essay containing arguments supporting the belief (active supportive defense) or to write refutations of possible arguments against the belief (active refutational defense). In the McGuire and Papageorgis (1961) experiment referred to above the passive defenses proved to be superior to the active defenses, especially in regard to the refutational defenses. Presumably, the active refutational defense and supportive defense were threatening and thus provided motivation, but the individual did not have the material with which to argue. The passive refutational defense, on the other hand, provided both the threatening component and the material for counter-arguments. The more time given between defense and attack, however, the more effective are the active defenses. Active defenses were found to be more effective against an attack that came one week after than one that came immediately after (McGuire, 1964, pp. 225–226).

Other experiments on active participation, or role-playing, some of which were cited earlier, also seem to indicate that when subjects meet with difficulty in improvising arguments (perhaps because of the unfamiliarity or complexity of the issue), lack of sufficient guidance will leave the attempted improvisation ineffective. *Information* is needed with which to generate arguments.

The communication that would supply the most information along with the motivating component would be one in which the supportive and refutational defenses are combined. In an experiment in which there was no delay between the defensive treatment and attack, McGuire (1961) found that such a combinational defense was more effective than either one alone.

Since McGuire's findings are all based on work with "cultural truisms," we must be cautious about generalizing to other types of issues. However, the combinational defense discussed above is similar to what has been called a two-sided communication, which has been found to offer better immunity to subsequent attack than a supportive defense (or one-sided communication) alone (Lumsdaine and Janis, 1953; Insko, 1962).

The strategy of presenting "both sides" was originally tested by Hovland, Lumsdaine, and Sheffield (1949). In 1945, they presented American soldiers with communications arguing that defeating Japan would be difficult and would take a long time after the defeat of Germany. One group of soldiers heard a 15-minute communication that presented only arguments indicating that the war against Japan would be long (at least two years after VE Day). Another group heard a 19-minute communication that presented the same arguments but also included *some* consideration of opposing arguments that stressed U.S. advantages and Japanese weaknesses. In this two-sided communication, however, attempts were rarely made to refute the opposing arguments made; rather, attempts were made to offset each opposing argument by immediately presenting supporting arguments.

Overall, both communications proved to be quite effective, and about equally so, as assessed by a questionnaire administered immediately after the communication. However, for those soldiers who initially opposed the view expressed in the communication (i.e., those who initially estimated that the war in the Pacific would last for less than two years after VE Day), the communication that presented "both sides" was found to be more influential than the one-sided communication. For those men who initially favored the stand taken in the communications, the one-sided communication was found to be more effective. Furthermore, when the data from those men who had graduated high school were compared with the data from those who had not, it was found that the communication that presented "both sides" was more effective among the better educated, while the one-sided communication was more effective among the less educated.

In the above study, change was measured immediately after the communication. Lumsdaine and Janis (1953) tested the stability of the effects produced by one-sided as compared with two-sided communications. The experiment was conducted with high school students a few months before the Soviet Union had exploded an atomic bomb for the first time. The communications took the form of a recorded radio program, and in both versions the commentator advocated that it would be at least five years before the Russians would be able to produce a large number of atomic bombs. Several weeks after the administration of an initial questionnaire, one group of subjects was presented with the one-sided and the other with the two-sided communication. In the two-sided communication: "The opposing arguments were interwoven into the relevant sections of the communication and in some instances no attempt was made to refute them." One week later, half of each group was exposed to a one-sided counter-communication in which a strand opposite to that taken in the first communication was advocated. The final questionnaire was then immediately administered to all subjects. For those who had not been exposed to the counter-communication, there was no significant difference in effectiveness between the one-sided and two-sided communications. For those who had been, the two-sided communication was much more effective.

Thus, the two-sided communication was more effective in producing immunity to subsequent counter-influence. The earlier cited Greenwald (1968) finding indicates that a two-sided communication tends to be superior to a one-sided communication in facilitating counter-attitudinal, or communication-consistent, self-generated thoughts. Whether counter-attitudinal advocacy is the mediating process whereby two-sided communications generate immunity to subsequent counter-communications or produce stable attitude change is not yet clear. It is possible, as Lumsdaine and Janis (1953) indicate, that when a communication persuades while at the same time taking into account opposing arguments, one is given an advance basis for discounting an opposing communication. Some of the findings reported above point to this discounting effect.

Yet there is also at least some support in the research presented in this chapter for the notion that self-generated arguments are an important mediator in the effects of communications on the attitude change process. The stimulation of issue-relevant thought and, more specifically, counter-attitudinal or communication-consistent advocacy might be an important goal for the influencing agent. But it is also necessary for the agent to supply the information or material for such advocacy, or make sure that such material is available to P. Once P is stimulated, the counter-attitudinal advocacy might not occur all at once, but it might be performed leisurely over a long period of time. A "sleeper" effect has sometimes been found in attitude change studies, whereby there is a delayed effect of the original communication (Hovland, Lumsdaine, and Sheffield, 1949; Hovland and Weiss, 1951; Stotland, Katz, and Patchen, 1959).

One sometimes accepts facts without being able to immediately incorporate them in a consistent manner into the belief system relevant to a particular issue. They "lie around" in one's mind as it were, until such time as they are incorporated or related to the relevant belief system through an insightful reorganization. For example, solely by way of his negativity toward the American government's role in the Vietnam War, an individual might have developed a positive attitude toward the Viet Cong. A negative attitude toward the Viet Cong might have appeared inconsistent with his attitude toward American involvement, even though he accepted the fact of Viet Cong atrocities. He might therefore have previously made an attempt to rationalize this fact, but perhaps without complete subjective satisfaction of consistency. He might have at some later time achieved an insight that it is not necessary to have a positive attitude toward either of two opposing party's involvement in a conflict, that it is possible that both sides are behaving immorally, and that the two negative attitudes are not inconsistent. He might have achieved a transcending subjective consistency that incorporates the previously troublesome fact. Another example is that of an American who loves his country and has accepted certain negative evidence about its foreign policy. His positive attitude toward his country might have prevented the formation of a negative attitude toward its foreign policy until it occurs to him that one can still love one's country while being critical of some aspect of it.

In a discussion with an individual, I seldom find that he immediately admits that I have convinced him about the issue under discussion, or confesses that he now suddenly sees the light and I have changed his attitude. What I do find is that he begins to make more qualifications on his own arguments than he did before, and begins to concede certain points he would not concede before, but nonetheless he maintains that these concessions are not inconsistent with his original viewpoint. In this manner cognitive modification might have come about which he does not admit to. Such results might be frustrating to the influencing agent, who often does not detect this modification, and who would prefer to have P come out and admit that he was "wrong," which is a rare event in persuasion. The persuasion attempt might have been successful if only it planted the seeds of inconsistency, or implanted excess "data" that might not be incorporated into the attitude system until a much later time, after P has had much time to think about it, has gathered additional inconsistent material, and finally, has found a new way to interpret all of his relevant data in a manner that makes most of his thoughts on the issue consistent with each other. Attitudinal reorganization has a chance of occurring only when a new organization is found that renders some aspect of the individual's world just as or more comprehensible to him than his former organization, and that is experienced as more supportive of his needs and values.

Also, as Stotland, Katz, and Patchen (1959) point out, immediate resistance might be aroused by the initial influence attempt, and this resistance might dissipate over time, thereby paving the way for a delayed, or sleeper, effect. I have already proposed in the last chapter that counter-attitudinal advocacy will be hindered by resistance and facilitated by attraction. The manner of the influence attempt is important; a communication that is rammed down someone's senses, so to speak, has a minimal chance of stimulating counter-attitudinal advocacy. But the process is more complicated here. While resistance might foster a reluctance to engage in counter-attitudinal advocacy, the communication itself, or that part of it containing information intrinsically relevant to the issue, might simultaneously be tending to stimulate it.

It has been found that, under certain conditions, the effectiveness of a persuasive communication is reduced through the inclusion of an explicit attempt to tell P what to believe, such as in telling him that he "must inevitably draw the same conclusion" as the one drawn in the communication, or that he "must by all means agree" (Brehm, 1966, pp. 108–116; Worchel and Brehm, 1970). However, if resistance was thus created, we do not know from the findings whether perhaps such resistance was only momentary, allowing the substance of the communication to have a delayed effect over a period of time.

Individuals who were directly insulted by a communicator who was attempting to persuade them were less likely to agree with the communicator's statements and were even inclined to increase the extremity of their initial attitudinal position (a boomerang effect). However, the investigators indicated that such effects due to insulting remarks were not easily detectable three weeks later (Abelson and Miller, 1967).

Experiments have indicated that attitude change can be facilitated when the agent is attractive to, or liked by, P (e.g., Tannenbaum, 1956). Also, O might be in a better position to persuade if he is regarded by P as being similar to himself in certain ways. Weiss (1957) found that when a communicator established that his attitude was congruent with that of P on a particular issue of importance to P (academic freedom), the effectiveness of a subsequent communication from the same agent on a different issue (opposing the fluoridation of drinking water) was enhanced. In these experiments, however, effects on attitude stability were not assessed.

Some recent experiments have purported to demonstrate that if an individual believes that a communicator has the *intention* of persuading him, attitude change will be inhibited. It would seem that the mere intent to persuade might be construed as a threat to one's attitudinal freedom and might arouse resistance. But such resistance might wash out over time, giving rise to a sleeper effect (a possibility not yet tested, for in these experiments attitude change was measured only immediately after the communication). Moreover, Mills (1966) found that when a communicator was presented as liking P and having a concern for him, his stated intent to persuade did not lessen attitude change.

Whether the effects of resistance and attraction would decrease over time relative to the effects of the communication itself is not known.

Abelson and Miller's (1967) results, cited above, suggest that this might be the case for resistance. However, if the resistance generated were to persist over a period of time, it might continue to prevent counter-attitudinal advocacy. Attraction, on the other hand, might help to stimulate counter-attitudinal advocacy, even at the time of the communication, which may contribute to stability. Resistance might play a role in determining whether P is going to receive the communication in the first place. For example, in a study involving the distribution of political leaflets in a shopping center, it was found that shoppers were more likely to accept and keep a leaflet when approached by a conventionally dressed student than when approached by a student who had the appearance of a "hippie," with long hair and a beard (Cooper, 1971).

CREDIBILITY

In any event, in order for the substance of a communication to have an impact, it must at least be believed. We do not, of course, believe everything we hear or read (although there often does seem to be a strong tendency to do so). Psychologists have been interested in the differential effects of the credibility and lack of credibility of the source of a communication on attitude change (e.g., Hovland and Weiss, 1951; Kelman and Hovland, 1953). We might not accept the validity of statements made in a gossip magazine in regard to some government official as much as we would statements appearing in *The New York Times*.

However, barring sources that we have good reason to believe are unreliable, credibility can be established by the communication itself. A well-reasoned communication incorporating many facts is likely to be viewed as a credible one. Ralph Nader did not have to establish his credibility before his book, *Unsafe at any Speed*, was to be influential; the book, revealing much research and containing many detailed examples, generated its own credibility.

Statements of fact are perhaps more readily accepted than their interpretations. We sometimes accept the facts reported by *The New York Times* without accepting its interpretation of those facts or the conclusions it draws from them. I might accuse a magazine of being biased in that I believe that it only presents certain facts and ignores many other important ones. But I might still believe the facts it presents, some of which might be new to me and might influence my attitudes.

ATTITUDINAL VACUITY

On the other hand, for some of the people who did not read Ralph Nader's book, merely the belief that someone had found enough information to write a book critical of the automobile industry in regard to safety, or had merely made claims, might have been enough to convince them. This would be the case especially if this new belief was not contrary to other beliefs they hold, and perhaps consistent with their beliefs about big business in general.

The belief "Other people (peers, expert X, people I like, people whose views are generally similar to mine, etc.), who probably have more information than I, hold to position Y" is itself supportive of a particular attitude. Such an attitude would become more stable if, in addition to this belief, the individual would assimilate *intrinsic* information related to the issue that is supportive of the attitude. Attitudes that do not have such support are more vulnerable to attack, as indicated by the inoculation research reviewed above.

It might be that the more factual and rational a communication is, the more likely it will be to overcome extraneous factors, such as the attributed characteristics of the source of the communication (e.g., whether I like him or not, whether I regard him as prestigious or not, etc.) or the number of people who subscribe to it. When intrinsic information is given, sooner or later the individual might come to evaluate it on its own merits. In other words, once he has the information and time to evaluate it, he might be less likely to depend upon the mere stated positions of others. If I have not received any communications containing facts and arguments intrinsically relevant to an issue, I might form an attitude based merely upon my exposure to the stated positions of certain others. In regard to certain local elections in which I had not, for one reason or another, gotten to learn much about the candidates, I had formed attitudes toward them on the basis of the stated choices of other people whose political views I knew to be similar to my own. (It is difficult to prevent oneself from forming "pro" or "con" evaluations, even if one's information be extrinsic and skimpy.)

The oldest trick in controlling attitudes is to withhold information. An individual, to the degree that he is not given or cannot or does not gather information intrinsic to the issue at hand and does not *assimilate* it, is inclined to rely on extrinsic factors such as the number and prestige of the other persons who hold a particular attitude. To the extent that one has intrinsically relevant information on an issue, one is in a position to form an attitude on the basis of one's evaluation of this information itself, and one need rely less on extrinsic factors. However, it is quite natural that an individual would adopt the attitude of others, especially if he attributes expertise to these others or has trust in their judgment, if he does not have the opportunity to evaluate the intrinsic information on its own merits.

One who is trusted often takes advantage of this trust by attempting to influence people on the basis of it, without divulging information that would allow the trusters to make independent evaluations. This is quite natural, for to divulge the information would be to take the chance that P would form a divergent attitude—a chance that one who is trusted need not take. Government officials often take advantage of this. Recall that a primary task of the nonviolent activist, as I have construed it, is to expose an issue by accumulating and disseminating as much intrinsically relevant information as he can. (Note that in this discussion I do not mean to imply that, in regard to any given issue, there exists a finite amount of intrinsically relevant potential information, or that, even if this were the case, it is possible for any one person to assimilate it all.)

The strangely rapid fluctuations reflected in public opinion poll data—Rosenberg (1968) speaks of the "easy malleability that is revealed in week-to-week shifts of public opinion"—might indicate that people in general do not have well-formed cognitively supported attitudes in regard to the issues probed. One perceptual fact, such as George Romney's famous "brain-washing" charge after his return from a visit to Vietnam, is enough to drastically shift public opinion about him, perhaps because many people did not have attitudes rich in cognitive support toward Romney in the first place. In short, when an attitude is not supported by much cognitive information, one new fact relative to the little information one has already is heavily determinative of the attitude, and that attitude is likely to shift again when only one or two more new facts are acquired. For a person who already had many beliefs and much information about Romney, one new fact would make relatively less difference to the overall attitude. (However, there are times when an individual might regard the one new fact as more important than all of the many facts he might already have.) Rosenberg (1968) has written about what he calls "attitudinal vacuity," and he reports evidence that consistent cognitive supports lend stability to attitudes.[4]

As I have said, the knowledge that "many other people who are similar to me believe X" is often a sufficient basis for attitude formation in the absence of intrinsically relevant information. Often propagandists try to create the illusion that many similar people believe X and, if successful, the reality springs from it. In such a case a vacuous attitude is created in millions of people overnight. It is possible that informational exposure can break this reality. An attitude that has been formed on the basis of extrinsic information should be less stable and yield more easily to intrinsic information than one that has been formed originally on the basis of intrinsic information. Rosenberg (1968, pp. 82–89) has demonstrated that an evaluative orientation that is not supported by a context of consistent cognitions will be relatively unstable and relatively more changeable by communications, even ones that convey merely extrinsic information.

Walker and Heyns (1967, p. 94) concluded from their experiments on conformity that:

> The larger the amount and the better the quality of the information possessed by a person about an object of attitude or behavior, the more intimate and personal the association, the less effective will be social pressure toward conformity. In short, the better the education, the more independent and self-determined the behavior, the less the conformity under social pressure.

In the experiments cited above involving the inoculation approach it had been shown that imbuing "cultural truisms" with cognitive support makes them more stable or less vulnerable to persuasive attack. In regard to the dearth of cognitive support with which "cultural truisms" are assumed to be held, they are probably similar to many other attitudes that people commonly hold. If this is the case, then McGuire's findings with "truisms" are perhaps more generalizable than he has been willing to grant.

Although more research on these issues would be useful, it seems that because attitudes are often of a vacuous nature (based more on extrinsic factors than on intrinsically relevant information), they often can be changed through communication of information. Attitudes that appear to be strong and extreme on the surface are often quite changeable because they are nonetheless based on little or no intrinsically relevant information. Appreciable progress toward a more rational society can be greatly assisted by those who are willing to patiently gather and disseminate information. Such informational power does not require great numbers of people or unique status. In a society that maintains freedom of speech even only one man can exercise great power of this sort. Ralph Nader is an excellent example. Even in a society that maintains censorship, only the personal risks are greater—the curiosity of people is difficult to squelch and the dissemination of information is hard to prevent.

Informational power, then, should not be underestimated; it is the foremost weapon of the nonviolent activist. We can successfully appeal to the rational side of people. It often appears that people are not rational only because they of course need information with which to make rational decisions; without such information, they necessarily base their attitudes on extrinsic factors not intrinsically relevant to the issue at hand. Their behavior is thus as rational as it could be under those circumstances.

RATIONALIZATION

An attitude that has been centrally determined by a particular self-interest and contains such self-interest as its most weighty or important and therefore most stabilizing belief might be embellished with rationalizations. Rationalizations are not necessarily worthy of our scorn, and many of our attitudes have obvious self-interests at their base. Whatever the motives that result in their formulation, rationalizations can be quite rational. They may in themselves be arguments that might convince us to adopt an attitude with the same evaluative orientation as that of the self-interested party, although perhaps not containing the same self-interest belief.

Rationalizing is thinking, and the rationalization of a self-interest-oriented attitude can mean the development of a reasonable justification of a particular position beyond self-interest. A young man of a few years ago who had just turned 18 and had received an unfortunate number in the draft lottery might have been led to reflect upon the morality of the war and might have found support for his self-interest-oriented attitude against it.

Rationalizations serve the function of not only convincing others but also of further stabilizing the attitude of the self-interested party. A person who is acting solely in self-interest, especially if it is contrary to others' interests, sometimes has to protect *himself* from this fact, for such action might be in conflict with his own image of himself as moral and just. One might find that efforts at rational argumentation directed at stripping away these rationalizations are not a waste of time from the point of view of persuasion. Although such rationalizations are not the core of the attitude of the self-interested party, they might protect the individual from guilt or shame—i.e., from having to confront something about himself that he does not want to face. Because of this important function of rationalizations, they might be extremely difficult to strip away. But if this is successfully done, we might find that the individual will change his attitude rather than have to think less of himself.

A particular businessman might have developed a self-interest-oriented attitude toward the Vietnam War because of his financial gains from it. This attitudinal determinant could be responsible for the elaboration of a complex system of beliefs, dealing with self-determination for the South Vietnamese, that is supportive of the attitude. It could be argued that persuasion attempts directed at these beliefs would be useless in that they would in no way alter the central determinant of the attitude. Indeed, the immediate self-interest—financial profit—might be an undeniable fact, not itself subject to persuasive attack. Moreover, the surrounding beliefs, because of their self-interest-oriented determinant and protective function, might be extremely resistant to change.

I would contend, however, that as difficult as the attempt might be, a persuasive attack on the surrounding beliefs is worthwhile, precisely because rationalizations often do serve an important attitude-protective function. The stripping away of rationalizations, if it can be accomplished by the communicator, might leave our businessman squarely facing a subjective inconsistency between his position and his moral values. Cognitive conflict (in this case in the form of guilt) might shake him deeply and precipitate attitude change. It is because an individual often strives to maintain a lofty moral self-image that rationalizations are necessary.

There are of course those situations in which one of the parties that the nonviolent activist wishes to persuade has a very stable attitude based upon a great deal of information. Let us suppose that the nonviolent activist has seen to it that all of the information that he possesses has been brought to the awareness of the other party. He has made certain that the other party's attitude is not merely vacuous. Yet the other party's interpretation of the information conflicts with that of the activist, who still strongly believes that an injustice exists. Any argument that the activist raises in an attempt to influence might have already been considered and thought through by the other party. Of course, the adversary in a conflict situation is likely to be such a party, and the persuasive attempts of the activist are more often likely to directly influence third parties, bystanders, or the general public, than the adversary himself. How the adversary might be indirectly affected by such influence will be briefly touched upon in the remainder of this chapter. Later stages of nonviolent action will of course partially depend upon such influence of third parties for mobilization of support. However, the *direct* effects of the power of information beyond that of persuasion have not often been acknowledged, and will also be briefly discussed below.

Persuasive attacks on rationalizations have functions other than changing the attitude of the individual who has generated them. There are times when an individual can live perfectly well with his self-interest-oriented attitude, even without rationalization. However, he may form rationalizations for public consumption, to protect himself from others. Since they are still serving a function, attacks on those rationalizations will also serve a function, even though it will not be the direct persuasion of the self-interested party. For one thing, such an attack might change the attitudes of the public toward the individual, thereby causing him embarrassment. He might still wish to pursue his course of action, but he might refrain from it not because his original attitude has changed but because he is afraid that others will think poorly of him. If he is heading a business, he might fear that pursuing his course of action in the face of adverse public opinion might eventually hurt him economically. Because of diffusion of responsibility, corporations or large bureaucratic organizations are probably less susceptible to embarrassment of any sort than the individual. But the potential economic effects of adverse public opinion can be a potent force for change.

When an issue is exposed to the public (such as the danger of automobiles), a change in the policy or behavior of a company might occur without attitude change. Ralph Nader's book, *Unsafe at any Speed*, focused public attention on the neglect of safety factors on the part of car manufacturers. Such publicity is damaging to the "image" of a car company, and corrective steps might be taken. A company can be influenced indirectly through a change in the public's attitude toward it.

Such informational exposure often succeeds by way of resulting economic effects on the company, legislative actions, and law suits rather than by pure social embarrassment. Embarrassment works best on an individual level. An individual might rationalize his actions to his satisfaction and yet be upset if his actions have been exposed to others who view them in an unfavorable light.

At any rate, informational exposure is an important and effective strategy for the nonviolent activist. The approach employed by Ralph Nader in his consumer campaigns can be regarded as an important nonviolent strategy.

Informational power can also bring about what I will call a "releasing" effect. There is often the possibility that directors of business corporations are locked in to certain policies that are at variance with their private attitudes. Even if certain car executives had wanted to concentrate on safety as opposed to style, they might not have felt in a position to do so due to their obligations to unseen stockholders who are presumably interested in maximal profit. Public opinion aroused through information could "release" the executive to do what he felt was right all along. Specifically, an informed public might begin to shop for safety features in cars, thereby making it more of a competitive factor among manufacturers than style, or stimulate the passage of safety legislation governing all car manufacturers. Either event would "release" the executive. A politician unduly concerned with his reelection to the detriment of his being a true leader might have been blocking civil rights legislation, not because he was privately against it but because he thought that the majority of his constituency was. Attitude change among his constituents (perhaps through the work of civil rights groups) could have "released" him even to lead the cause of civil rights legislation in the political arena.

NONPERSUASIVE FUNCTIONS OF INFORMATION

Exposure can be an important function of informational power, even without any persuasion of the public taking place. Segments of the public might already have a negative attitude toward some corporation engaging in practices detrimental to the public interest or toward some injustice existing within the society. Exposure through the gathering and communication of specific facts might confirm and increase the intensity (without necessarily shifting the extreme nature of the evaluative orientation) of these attitudes, bring them to the focus of attention, promote increased confidence in them, and stimulate the people who hold them to action. Such informational exposure can also point the way to just what specific action should be taken.

Thus, before Ralph Nader's exposure of the automobile industry on matters of safety, there were probably many people (including politicians) who, if pressed for it, would have revealed a belief that cars were unsafe, without being able to provide specifics. Nader's documentation could have worked to bring this previously undifferentiated attitude from the back of their minds into their focus of attention, to make them think more about it, and to push the politicians—now armed with facts and also with a knowledge of citizens' heightened awareness on the issue—to action. Such exposure helps to insure that the issue will not be ignored.

As discussed in the previous chapter, it is not enough to change an attitude toward a particular issue. We also want to make that attitude salient for its holder and also deepen his commitment to it, or deepen the intensity of his attitude, for only then can we rely on him to act upon this attitude. In addition, in order to elicit certain behavior that is consistent with the attitude, persuasive attempts are again needed, this time directed toward attitudes in regard to particular actions. For example, once we had persuaded an individual to be against the war, we might then have had to work on his attitudes toward voting, demonstrations, civil disobedience, etc.

The power of information goes beyond persuasion in at least one more very important way. It can make others' attitudes more cognitively complex, or differentiated, without necessarily changing the overall evaluative orientation of those attitudes. (The evaluative dimension has been the traditional focus of concern in attitude research.) By doing so, it can increase areas of overlap and agreement of individuals holding conflicting overall evaluative orientations.

Informational power, without changing the global evaluative aspect of an attitude, might promote greater cognitive differentiation of that attitude as in the following example. One who has an overall negative reaction to abortion might be made to think of special cases in which it would be a reasonable alternative. His overall reaction might not change in regard to abortion per se. An attitude that is made more cognitively complex might still retain its global evaluative response and yet permit exceptions in regard to certain situations related to the attitudinal object. In other words, for certain agreements to arise between two individuals who hold contrary general evaluative reactions toward a particular attitudinal object, it is not necessary that either individual change the other's overall reaction. If each individual's attitude is sufficiently cognitively complex, areas of overlap can be found without actual persuasion or change taking place. This would not be the case with attitudes that are vacuous or lacking in a differentiated cognitive underpinning, for there would not be much that could overlap in the cognitive area. We would have solely two conflicting evaluative responses.

Hence, an important goal of informational power is to promote greater cognitive differentiation of attitudes. This paves the way for, and is part of, the process of *negotiation*, for then two conflicting parties can settle their dispute through negotiation—seeking out areas of agreement— without any global attitude change necessarily taking place on either side. In regard to the Arab-Israeli conflict, one cannot expect a resolution to come about through attitude change on either side or, for that matter, through violence. However, through negotiations it might be possible to reach a settlement that encompasses the self-interests and wants of both parties: the obvious desire of the Israelis to maintain their state, the aspirations of Arabs for a Palestinian state, and peace—which would be mutually beneficial. What at first glance might appear to be mutually exclusive self-interests between two parties can reveal themselves to be compatible upon closer inspection and through mutual reflection. One problem is that the prior development of distrust often prevents meaningful negotiations from taking place (see Chapter 7).

Perhaps it can be said that the nonviolent activist seeks not only to persuade through his use of information, but also to insure that attitudes are based on facts and rational argumentation rather than upon factors that are extrinsic to the issue itself, such as reference group pressure or extrinsic reinforcement schedules. In using information, he is seeking not merely to persuade but to appeal to the rational side of man, always attempting to uplift human interaction to a rational plane. In fact, if his communications did not in the end succeed in persuading but merely stimulated rational thought on the part of others so that perhaps their original attitudes, though unchanged, have become more reflective and cognitive ones, grounded more in facts and reasons and moral considerations, they still would have served a purpose—that of promoting rational discussion and reflection.

I have said at the beginning of this chapter that the greater the number of perceptual facts, the more limited is the number of alternative interpretations that can incorporate those facts in a consistent manner. The nonviolent activist never shies away from the collection of those facts, for he believes that they will support his attitude; if they do not, he will not hesitate to admit that the position he was defending does not merit his defense after all. Those whose main motive is not the correction of injustice but perhaps the furtherance of only their *own* self-interest are the ones who might look upon the collection of facts with some apprehension.

The implicit and perhaps unintended assumption that is conveyed by the current attitude research literature is that we need only discover and develop effective techniques of attitude change and that these techniques can then be employed with equal effectiveness on any issue and on any side of an issue. But if we are talking about the changing and forming of cognitively complex attitudes and not unstable, vacuous orientations, then I would have to doubt that attitude change is merely dependent upon an abstract arsenal of techniques that will function effectively without regard for the substantive matter of the issue itself. Especially if the other side is to be heard, much certainly depends upon the bulk of the facts themselves. The facts might be more supportive of one interpretation than another and the mere, even clumsy, exposure of these facts might stimulate thought and be successfully pitted against the skilled ordering, arrangement, and wording of the arguments for the other side. I do *not* maintain that this is so with every issue, that the same perceptual facts—even many of them—cannot be interpreted in widely divergent ways (I pointed this out in regard to the Arab-Israeli conflict) or that the development of techniques of persuasion account for naught. I merely wish to dispel the commonly held notion that the manipulation of human attitudes is akin to the manipulation of machines and that we merely need to discover the appropriate techniques, without much regard for substance.

NOTES

[1] See Rajendraprasad, 1949; Gandhi, 1954a, pp. 494–519; Nanda, 1958, pp. 156–162; Sharp, 1960, pp. 10–37, for brief accounts of this campaign.

[2] The mere commitment to argue for a particular position, even without actually going through the process of generating arguments, might itself induce attitude change, as dissonance theory would predict, although it is not clear that a stable attitude can thus be formed (see Chapter 3), or that one can get subjects to anticipate a role-playing task without the commitment already stimulating them to start thinking up arguments. Moreover, it has been found that actual advocacy leads to more attitude change than merely committing oneself to role-play (even when this latter event already induces some thinking up of arguments), at least under conditions in which resistance is not generated (Janis and Gilmore, 1965). As was argued in the previous chapter, to the extent that the conditions that are set up to induce counter-attitudinal advocacy simultaneously generate resistance that will interfere with it, attitude change will be inhibited.

[3] As compared with the control condition in which the subject received an attack on a belief without any prior defense treatment, the supportive defense was not found to produce immunity against attack. Tannenbaum (1967, pp. 282–283; Tannenbaum, Macaulay, and Norris, 1966), however, using similar belief issues, has found supportive defenses to decrease vulnerability to attack (when the attack came one week after the defense), although not as much as refutational defenses (Tannenbaum, 1967, pp. 291–292).

[4] I am so taken with Rosenberg's term "attitudinal vacuity" that I have adopted it even though I use it slightly differently than Rosenberg had intended. He uses the concept to refer to a false attitudinal representation masking an indifference in regard to an issue that one has little (intrinsic) information about, whereas my use of the term is based on a distinction between extrinsic and intrinsic information. According to my conception, a person might truly have an orientation even though it be based on only extrinsic information. In this case, I would say that it is vacuous.

CHAPTER 5

Nonviolent Protest

The rectification of injustices, or the redress of grievances, sometimes requires that we go beyond persuasive attempts and negotiations. Words sometimes fall on deaf ears, an affliction that can be bred by complacency.

In this chapter I will comment on the tactics of the second phase of a nonviolent campaign. Such actions are sometimes referred to as agitation, and more often as protests. They include demonstrations, marches, public meetings, vigils, leafletting, renouncing honors, and other forms of dramatization of an issue (see Sharp, 1970, p. 32 and 1973).

It should be made clear at the outset that such actions are not automatically or inherently nonviolent. Nonviolence cannot be equated with the tactics employed.[1] The philosophy of nonviolence entails certain attitudes toward the adversary and toward conflict and its resolution, and a program of action of which a particular tactic is but one aspect. In this book I am attempting to describe the constructive and reconciliating approach of nonviolence that should permeate or manifest itself in any action that is intended to be consistent with the philosophy of nonviolence.

For example, the street protests in Chicago in connection with the 1968 Democratic Convention were not generally nonviolent. Provocation of the police through throwing things at them or taunting them by calling them "pigs" and directing other verbal insults at them is not consistent with the nonviolent philosophy, which entails treating the adversary with dignity and respect. Calling the police "pigs" is destructive behavior in that it increases polarization and mitigates against reconciliation.

Nonviolent action ideally strives to be constructive and reconciliatory. Not all protest demonstrations in which the demonstrators do not initiate or even react with violence are necessarily nonviolent.

The general class of actions that I am attempting to focus upon in this chapter, and that I will call protest, are to be distinguished from acts of noncooperation, which are directly and intentionally coercive and are generally more sustained actions than protests. Noncooperation is the concern of the next chapter, but, because there are certain features and effects that it has in common with nonviolent protest, reference to certain instances of noncooperation in the past (such as those that occurred during the civil rights movement) will be made in this chapter in order to enrich the present discussion.

FUNCTIONS OF PROTEST

A protest action is a complex social event; it is multidimensional, having many facets and potential implications. It would be difficult to conceive of it as serving only one function or having only one potential effect. Moreover, protest is often different things to different people.

Protest actions can serve the purpose of drawing public attention to a particular issue or to an alleged injustice. They can pave the way for subsequent persuasion by arousing curiosity and promoting a state of receptiveness to new information. Also, a protest action can draw sympathizers with the cause into active participation, thereby getting them to commit themselves in a behavioral and public manner. Cesar Chavez, the nonviolent organizer of migrant farm workers, once said that it is on the picket line that a worker makes an irrevocable commitment to the cause (Matthiessen, 1969, p. 84). The act of commitment can have a stabilizing effect upon one's position, perhaps by increasing the saliency of cognitions related to it, as indicated by the experimental findings of Kiesler (1971). Moreover, protest actions can embolden individual sympathizers by showing them that they have social support—that they are not alone. Increased confidence and determination can incline them toward further action. Thus, protest actions can serve the purpose of mobilizing people in preparation for other action, such as mass noncooperation.

There are a number of ways in which a protest action might have a coercive effect on others, even if unintentionally. It can sometimes be construed by the adversary as a threat that, if the alleged injustice is not rectified soon, action of a more direct nature will be taken. Demonstrations might indicate to the adversary that the numerical strength for mass noncooperation is available. They can warn him of potential economic and political consequences. A protest action might be more immediately coercive in that it might drive away business from the area in which it is taking place, or create fear and discomfort in the adversary. Then, too, it might be construed by the adversary as a portent of violence.

Protest actions can demonstrate to the adversary that there are many people who are not content with the situation as it stands, thereby perhaps shattering one of his rationalizations. Protest actions can possibly embarrass the adversary, or might have the "releasing" effect discussed in the previous chapter.

I mentioned that a protest action might pave the way for persuasion by drawing attention to the issue. There is also the possibility that a protest action might be persuasive in itself in that it might directly change other people's attitudes toward a particular issue. That is, it might constitute a persuasive communication in itself. However, following an attempt to apply theories of attitude change to an analysis of the possible persuasive effects of nonviolent actions, Perloe, Olton, and Yaffe (1968) concluded that such actions have very limited persuasive capability. I would argue that protest actions, such as demonstrations and marches, are generally not effective means of stable attitude change because they fail to convey much information intrinsically relevant to the issue at hand. Rather, a potentially more effective function of such actions might be to draw the attention of both the general public and the adversary to the alleged injustice. They can make the issue salient and heighten public awareness of it, and arouse curiosity and concern. This function of protest can be regarded as a form of power, but one that is not easily subsumed under any of the classifications described in Chapter 3.

DRAWING ATTENTION TO THE ISSUES

Perhaps, as Horsburgh (1968, p. 72) has suggested, "the more specifically nonviolent function of demonstrations is that of drawing attention to particular injustices." Frazier (1968), in analyzing some aspects of the civil rights sit-in movement (which went beyond protest), observed that to be successful the movement "must be attention-compelling and public."

This function often seems to be regarded by the participants themselves as a major purpose of a protest action. Solomon and Fishman (1964b) concluded from their interviews of participants in a student peace demonstration in Washington, D.C., in 1962 that "almost everyone hoped that the publicity given the demonstration would somehow result in increased public arousal and awareness of the issues." The presumed effect of marches most frequently mentioned by British and Danish marchers against nuclear weapons was to draw public attention to the issue and/or to convince, perhaps by having the general public confronted with the marchers' arguments through the press (Boserup and Iverson, 1966). Interestingly, the investigators noted:

> In this perspective, having a large number of participants in the demonstration is important only in so far as it adds to the publicity value; in this respect the march does not differ from hunger strikes and other individual demonstrations.

Indeed, the sheer numbers might help in drawing press coverage and in getting people to stop and think about an issue that so many apparently feel so deeply about. An individual might be curious as to what so many participants might know that he does not know, and he might be moved to an awareness of doubts about his own attitude or lack of it. But a creatively unique dramatization of an issue might call attention to it without the need for large numbers of participants.

If we look upon the major function of nonviolent protest (the second phase of a nonviolent campaign) as being that of drawing attention to the issue, one might ask why this phase should come after rational persuasion attempts have long since begun, rather than before. It would seem logical that the nonviolent activist first draws attention to the issue and, once he has received attention and aroused interest, he then attempts to persuade. However, some protest actions involve mobilizing large numbers of people, which always involves some risks. We lose some degree of control over our own actions and those of others when we move from persuasion attempts to protest actions. In addition, as I mentioned before, protest actions might be construed as coercive threats by the adversary. As such, they would produce a polarizing tendency, which the nonviolent activist would try to offset as much as possible if, indeed, running the risks of protest actions, becomes necessary. But he first strives to avoid having to go beyond persuasion and negotiation. Persuasion is a less drastic step than protest actions and it is based more on reason. To go beyond this step before it is felt that there will be no other way to deal with the alleged injustice would be equivalent to startling people in order to get their attention, before we have determined that we would have to go that far to get it. Besides, the persuasion attempts are at least partially directed toward the adversary. It is only after we have failed to persuade the adversary that we begin to concentrate more fully on the general public and attempt to arouse it.

Complex social events that are designed to be attention-getting are often bound to be alarming to the general public. Even protests that are peaceful in fact and noncoercive in intent are likely to be regarded by others as a threat to the status quo. That which is strange often evokes anxiety and feelings of insecurity. Potential disruptions of the status quo cannot immediately be expected to be favorably received by the general public. Protests are launched in the first place because for many people things seem fine and right the way they are. That which cannot be readily categorized into the security and regularity of the normal flow of events of an organized society has attention-getting value, but at the same time it has the potential to arouse fear. There is bound to be some resistance. The nonviolent protest, if it must be initiated, must be potent enough as an attention-getting and curiosity-arousing device so as to overcome the resistance that it is simultaneously creating. The potential for generating resistance must be held to the minimum that is possible without simultaneously necessitating the sacrifice of its curiosity-arousing value.

We can now ask what characteristics of a protest action might allow it to best fulfill the function I have been discussing. Relevant experimental research on the factors involved in attracting attention and arousing curiosity has been performed, but has not involved such molar events as protest actions. The value of such research for our concern here is that we can draw abstract principles from it that might be applicable to the understanding of a protest action. Since this research has largely employed geometrical and pictorial patterns, inferences drawn about protest actions are, of course, highly speculative.

Experimental findings indicate that more complex stimulus patterns attract visual exploration more than do less complex ones (Berlyne, 1958a, 1958b). They are also rated by subjects as being more interesting (Berlyne, 1963, 1970; Berlyne, Ogilvie and Parham, 1968). However, there is some indication that both exploration time (see Berlyne, 1966) and rated "interestingness" (Day and Berlyne, 1966) decline with extreme complexity. That is, it seems that very complex stimuli are less interesting than moderately complex ones, although there are likely to be wide individual differences in regard to the degree of complexity at which "interestingness" starts to decline.

Using randomly generated geometric figures, Munsinger and Kessen (1964) found that figures with an intermediate amount of variability (number of independent turns) were most preferred (liked better), but so also were the least complex figures. Day and Berlyne (1966), also using randomly generated geometric figures, showed that "interestingness" remains comparatively high with high levels of variability while "pleasingness" drops. Berlyne (1963) found that with some sets of stimulus patterns, the more complex patterns that are rated as less pleasing are also rated as more interesting. Apparently, a stimulus pattern does not necessarily have to be pleasing in order to stimulate curiosity.

Cognitive uncertainty has been described by Munsinger and Kessen (1964) as the interrelationship between stimulus variability (i.e., complexity) and cognitive structure (e.g., meaningfulness). Cognitive uncertainty can be reduced by decreasing the complexity of the stimulus pattern, but also by increasing its judged meaningfulness. There is some optimal level of cognitive uncertainty that is most preferred, and also one that elicits a judgment of most interesting; these two levels both fall in some intermediate range of cognitive uncertainty. However, the two functions of cognitive uncertainty ("pleasingness" and "interestingness") do not coincide, as can be seen from the results of the experiments cited above (Berlyne 1963; Day and Berlyne, 1966), although they are similar (i.e., both functions can be roughly described by inverted U-shaped curves).

A figure that possesses a large number of elements might form a shape that is meaningful to the perceiver, perhaps by allowing it to be recognized as a familiar object. The subjective meaning might render the pattern of stimulation less confusing and more likely to be preferred despite its high variability (see Munsinger and Kessen, 1964). It is possible that meaning might also increase the "interestingness" of very complex stimuli that would otherwise be judged as relatively uninteresting.

Protest actions are, of course, on a much higher level of complexity than are the stimulus patterns employed in the above research. But, because of their greater meaningfulness, they might not be much higher in cognitive uncertainty for the average perceiver. Being already very complex social events, they might benefit in terms of arousing curiosity by conveying some easily comprehended overall meaning that can serve to structure the perceived event for the public. A protest that resembles a confused mob scene is likely to be overly aversive, and attempts to convey complex meanings are not likely to offset the inevitable diversity of a protest action nor to arouse interest.

It has been found that novelty attracts attention and increases the duration of exploratory behavior (Berlyne, 1958a; Berlyne and Lawrence, 1964). That is, patterns that recur (are familiar) are less likely to attract attention and be explored than those that are new. Berlyne (1970) has found that in general both "interestingness" and "pleasingness" increase with novelty. However, he has also noted: "Instead of eliciting exploration—which means approach and sustained contact—novel, surprising, and strange objects 'may provoke terror and flight" (Berlyne, 1966). That which is inconsistent with our past experience is often found to be interesting. However, there is a limit to how drastic this novelty might be and still elicit approach-type responses. Hebb (1946) found that chimpanzees exhibit great fear and avoidance tendencies at the sight of a clay model of a human head. It could be that extreme novelty induces extreme negative affect, such as fright.

The findings gathered by Zajonc (1968) indicate an *inverse* relationship between novelty and rated preference. Thus, even within the limits noted above, the findings pertaining to whether novelty increases or decreases "pleasingness" appear to be contradictory. A tentative resolution of this problem has arisen from some further experimentation of Berlyne (1970). He has found evidence in support of his hypothesis that the hedonic value ("pleasingness") of complex stimulus patterns rises as they become less novel (i.e., as they are seen more often), while simple stimulus patterns become less preferred as they become less novel. Furthermore, he found that complex patterns reached a peak and then declined in hedonic value with increasing familiarization (decreasing novelty).

I would argue that the demonstrations against the Vietnam War continued to be mounted long after they had actually outlived their usefulness. At least with regard to this particular issue, they had ceased to be novel. They could be passed off without much interest as "just another demonstration." After many demonstrations had already been staged, more demonstrations delivering only the message "There are many of us who want our troops brought home immediately" and always in the same way did not have much effectiveness in drawing attention or stimulating thought. Such demonstrations lost the novelty they once had, at least for this particular issue. People became used to them, which means that they perhaps ceased for a time to elicit negative affect, but it also means that people began to take them in stride. The sheer number of people who participated could not really be a potent factor, especially in a democracy and especially in a country where opinion polls are frequently taken, because everyone knows that this cannot indicate what proportion of the total citizenry is for or against the view propagated by the demonstration. Novelty, both on a perceptual and higher cognitive level, was again introduced into anti-war demonstrations perhaps only when in April of 1971 Vietnam veterans demonstrated in Washington and threw their medals onto the steps of the Capitol. This action was dramatic and novel, and accordingly drew wide coverage by the news media. Nonetheless, it is my belief that a crucial flaw of the anti-war movement was not going beyond the protest phase to noncooperation at the point at which demonstrations began to be taken in stride by the American public.

Incidentally, anyone who has ever participated in a demonstration knows that the events of the day as reported in news media often fail to correspond with one's own account. Certain incidents seem to be blown up out of proportion to their significance, and sometimes seem to be erroneously reported. This has led to charges that the news media are biased and that the reporting reflects the prejudices of the reporters. While there is little doubt that a person's prior beliefs will play a role in determining his interpretation of present events, and that a pro-war reporter's account of a demonstration might differ considerably from that of an anti-war observer, it seems to me that a good case can be made for the notion that in a country with a free press one of the most important single determinants of what events will get reported at all is novelty, which, after all, is implicit in the word "news." Reporters, and even such people as newspaper owners, are not much different in their exploratory and information-seeking tendencies than the average citizen whose interest is also drawn by novelty.

As I mentioned before, a protest action is not likely to be pleasing to the general public. It is bound to generate some resistance. But we have seen that a stimulus can be comparatively interesting even if it is not comparatively pleasing. It does not have to be liked in order to stimulate curiosity. Also, we have found that complex stimuli become more pleasing as their novelty decreases. For the sake of novelty, which attracts interest and encourages exploration, pleasantness might automatically be sacrificed to some extent.

However, I mentioned before that the meaningfulness of a highly variable pattern can decrease its cognitive uncertainty and might increase its "interestingness." It is possible that the comprehensibility—i.e., the meaningfulness—of a very complex stimulus pattern increases up to a point with repeated encounters, so that up to a very limited number of repetitions "interestingness" might actually increase. That is, for very complex patterns, there might be a brief increase in "interestingness" with decreasing novelty before "interestingness" begins to decline. A protest action can be at first startling and perhaps incomprehensible to the general public, and it might benefit from a few repetitions in that its comprehensibility and consequently its "interestingness" might increase. But very much of the same is boring and easily ignored.

The generalizations and speculations presented here are certainly not overly convincing; they are dependent upon the generality of a set of functions across situations that are of vastly different orders and that differ in many ways. Experimental research employing protest actions themselves as stimuli would of course seem more appropriate for our purposes, but such research would be extremely difficult if not impossible to carry out.

A protest action must not only attract attention and induce exploration at the perceptual level but also certain aspects of the action must stimulate epistemic curiosity relevant to the issue once the perceptual attention has been attracted. Epistemic curiosity is that which motivates the quest for knowledge and is relieved when knowledge is procured (Berlyne, 1960, p. 274). While the process of attracting attention might generate some resistance, the nonviolent activist will seek to offset this resistance in ways that will be discussed later. This is important if he seeks to stimulate epistemic behavior and not the avoidance of thought and, moreover, if he does not want to insure that the only thought and information-seeking stimulated will be in a direction selectively contrary to the activist's views.

Berlyne has made a beginning to the study of the determinants of epistemic curiosity. He has claimed that conceptual conflict—"conflict between incompatible symbolic response patterns, that is, beliefs, attitudes, thoughts, ideas"—is the principal factor underlying epistemic curiosity (1965, p. 255). The concept of conceptual conflict is, of course, similar to that of cognitive dissonance. The induction of conceptual conflict can motivate the individual to seek information that will relieve the conflict. In order to stimulate information-seeking behavior, we wish, for example, to raise doubts in the individual's mind about certain beliefs that he holds.

Berlyne (1960, p. 289) has noted that a question can be a powerful inducer of epistemic, or knowledge-seeking, behavior. He (1954) found that he could increase curiosity about a particular topic merely by asking questions prior to presenting the information. He also found that questions involving more familiar concepts and those that related concepts that seemed incompatible aroused more curiosity than others.

It would seem that a stimulus relationship in which concepts with which the individual is familiar are related in a novel way would induce more conceptual conflict than a stimulus relationship in which more unfamiliar concepts are related in a novel way, which in turn would arouse more curiosity than a familiar relationship involving familiar concepts. This might be so because more familiar concepts would be more likely to arouse thought patterns that could potentially conflict, while a familiar relationship would not arouse conceptual conflict but would merely confirm what the individual already knows.

Certain situations might arouse an individual to formulate a question. Using children as subjects, Berlyne and Frommer (1966) found that stories and pictures that were more novel (in terms of concepts), surprising, and incongruous elicited more questions than others.

A protest action must shake beliefs, raise doubt, and promote discussion. It is often directed at a situation that is unjust but taken for granted by the public. At this stage the nonviolent activist is attempting to make it an issue of public concern. He is trying to bring the alleged injustice to the awareness of people who perhaps never before questioned the status quo and who might have taken their beliefs and attitudes in regard to the issue for granted, without perhaps much underlying cognitive support. He seeks to promote conceptual conflict.

The factors of cognitive uncertainty and novelty are probably important in regard to the higher cognitive aspects of a protest action, as well as in regard to its perceptual aspects. A protest action is limited in the duration of attention that it will generate. Highly complex information will not get through and will probably elicit avoidance. A protest action is a brief and limited event; the information that it does present is probably best kept concise and easily comprehensible. That which stimulates too much cognitive uncertainty does not stimulate interest. For example, a highly technical journal article in physics can be extremely interesting to the physicist but not at all interesting for a novice to the subject. The information presented in a protest action must be brief and clear. It should be novel in order to stimulate epistemic curiosity, and it should be designed to raise doubts in people's minds about where they stand on the issue—it should stimulate them to think and seek information about the issue, and to discuss it.

The doubts raised will be more salient to an individual if he is induced to believe that the issue is important to *him*. The chances of inducing this experience of importance might be increased if one or more of the concepts conveyed in the information and related to other concepts involves the individual's self-interests or important values.

One way in which SANE (A Citizens' Organization for a Sane World) has tried to stimulate doubts about American foreign policy, especially in regard to armament, has been to print leaflets that present a "pie" divided up so as to show what proportion of federal tax money goes for military expenditures (59%) as related to other expenditures, along with the question: "Do you know what war costs you?" The same organization also widely circulated a cartoon (see Fig. 5-1) with the caption: "From the people who brought you Vietnam: The anti ballistic missile system." (Humor, of course, also involves invoking familiar concepts and relating them in novel ways.)

Effective protest actions present novel information in novel ways and convey some easily comprehensible, overall meaning to the public. As I mentioned before in regard to the protest action as a whole, it might be beneficial to repeat the information in the same way a few times—but many repetitions would be futile. Creative new ways must be found to inform the public of the alleged injustice. Novelty is needed to draw the publicity of the news media as well as the attention of the public.

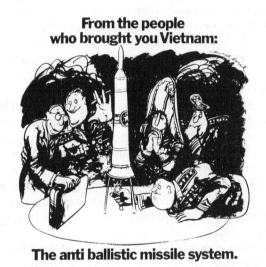

From the people who brought you Vietnam:

The anti ballistic missile system.

Fig. 5-1   (Cartoon by E. Sorel, used with permission from SANE.)

DETERMINANTS OF SELECTIVE EXPOSURE TO INFORMATION

One of the most serious drawbacks of Festinger's cognitive dissonance theory lies in its prediction that while an individual will tend to seek out information that will reduce dissonance, he will actively *avoid* information that is potentially inconsistent with his prior beliefs, attitudes, values, actions, and decisions; that is, he will avoid information that would potentially increase dissonance. If this were unequivocally the case, attitude change would be almost impossible except in those situations in which the individual's choice of information to attend to was in some manner constrained.

However, as I briefly noted in Chapter 2, there is some evidence to suggest that people do not always tend to avoid information that they believe to be potentially inconsistent with their prior beliefs (see Freedman and Sears [1965] for a review). Taken together, the studies on selective exposure to information have indicated that, while people do tend to seek out information that is likely to be consonant, they do not avoid potentially dissonant information and are sometimes equally desirous of both kinds of information.

The fact that individuals sometimes seek out dissonant-producing information might be considered as consistent with recent findings in experimental psychology concerning curiosity and exploratory behavior, some of which were cited above. These studies have shown that, within limits, the individual seeks out varied stimulation. There seems to be a need to seek out and explore the novel, complex, and unusual—a need to receive varied and changing stimulation—and the same might be true for information on a higher cognitive level than perception.

The act of exploration is intrinsically satisfying. That which is inconsistent with our past experience is often found to be interesting. Dissonant information is often novel information and may have attention-getting qualities. However, there is a limit as to how drastic this novelty might be and still elicit approach-type responses. It will be remembered that Hebb's (1946) chimpanzees exhibited fear and avoidance reactions to a clay model of a human head. Hebb (1955) states: "It appears that, up to a certain point, threat and puzzle have positive motivating value, beyond that point negative value."

Man has a need for variation in information and stimulation. Perhaps it can be said that he seeks out potentially consonant information, not to tell him what he already knows or believes (because no variation would be obtained then) but to increase variation within the context of the prior belief system. So, for example, a socialist reads socialist magazines not because they tell him what he already believes, which he might find boring, but because they expand upon what he already believes in a manner consistent with his prior beliefs, thereby allowing him to incorporate change or novel information while at the same time allowing the structure of his belief system to remain intact.

Like a scientist with a theory (belief system), the individual looks for new evidence that simultaneously supports his belief system and expands the area of new information that the belief system can cover or incorporate. He will be led to examining even potentially discrepant information but might avoid information potentially so discrepant as to endanger the belief system by precipitating the replacement or reorganization of that belief system.

In other words, potentially consonant information is often not sought out for dissonance reduction but for variation in information and stimulation that will not be so dissonant as to induce reorganization. Change is welcome; reorganization is not. Potentially dissonant information, however, will be preferred to unchanging, unnovel, potentially consonant information, which might be considered boring. But, when the danger is too great—i.e., at a point where the new information is potentially so dissonant as to portend an inability to assimilate it without drastic disruption—it will be avoided. We look for new, novel, more complex, and even seemingly incongruous information and stimulation and seek to interpret it in a manner consistent with our prior beliefs.[2]

It has been found that individuals tend to prefer to expose themselves to dissonant arguments if they anticipate that they will be easy to refute, but tend to avoid dissonant material that they anticipate will be difficult to refute (Lowin, 1967, 1969). During the 1964 presidential campaign, Lowin (1967) mailed letters out to people whose political views were ascertained earlier. The letters contained samples of brochures that could be obtained free by returning the enclosed postcard. The samples contained a series of arguments that were either easy or difficult to refute (as rated by independent judges) and either consonant or dissonant with the person's own view. The letter was made to appear to have come from a partisan organization that was interested in convincing the person to vote for a particular candidate (either Johnson or Goldwater). Each person received one of four letters, which differed only in whether the sample arguments favored Johnson or Goldwater and whether they were very easy or very difficult to refute. Preferences (selective interest) for strong or weak consonant or dissonant information were determined by comparing the percentages of postcards returned in the four categories. It was found that strong consonant communications were preferred to strong dissonant ones, but that weak dissonant communications were preferred over weak consonant ones. In a second experiment that employed a different procedure, weak dissonant messages were not found to be preferred to weak consonant ones, but the original finding was replicated in a more recent study (Lowin, 1969).

Selective interest in communications in favor of or against the draft-resistance movement among men who had varying positions in regard to an anti-draft pledge was investigated in a field study by Janis and Rausch (1970). The study was carried out in 1968, after a "We-Won't-Go" pledge had been circulating at Yale University for some time. Yale undergraduates with known stands in regard to the pledge were each shown brief summaries and titles of eight magazine articles, half of which were clearly supportive of the pledge and half of which were clearly against it. The students were asked to rate each of them in terms of how interested they would be in actually reading the article. It was found that undergraduates who were opposed to the pledge were less interested in reading anti-pledge articles than those who were in favor of signing. For the pro-pledge articles, there was no difference in interest ratings between those who were opposed to and those who were in favor of signing the pledge. While those who favored the pledge were equally interested in both types of articles, those who were opposed appeared more interested in reading the pro-pledge than the anti-pledge articles. In regard to the low interest ratings that the men who opposed the pledge gave to articles that supported their position, Janis and Rausch (1970) speculated that these men may have been uninterested in articles supporting their position because they were already overly familiar with such arguments.

In a study by Sears (1965), subjects were given brief synopses of criminal trials to read. Each synopsis strongly suggested that the defendant was either guilty or innocent, and was found to have the intended persuasive effect. After reading a synopsis, the subject's preference for type of additional reading material (either the defense attorney's summation, the prosecution attorney's summation, or the judge's charge to the jury) was assessed. Some subjects were told that the additional material would contain new information, and others that it would be substantially the same as that covered in the synopsis, although more detailed. It was found that, overall, subjects preferred nonsupportive information. That is, most of the subjects who had read the "innocent" synopsis preferred the prosecution summation, while most of the subjects who had read the "guilty" synopsis preferred the defense summation. Furthermore, the subjects who expected the additional material to contain new information did not prefer nonsupportive information as much as did those who expected it to cover essentially the same matters. That is , if the information to be presented on both sides of the issue was not expected to be new, subjects tended to prefer to expose themselves to the potentially dissonant side, but this preference was less marked when new information was anticipated on both sides.

One possible interpretation of Sears' (1965) findings is that the preference for familiar information is increased when that information is organized in a novel way. (In this case, it is dissonant organization that produces novelty.) But the increased preference for new information conferred by novel organization is not as marked.

This evidence is fairly consistent with the view I expounded above. Although there are other important variables that I have not discussed (e.g., the subjective importance of the information), the novelty of information is a major determinant of selective exposure. The processing of potentially consonant novel information fulfills both the need for variety and consistency. The processing of potentially dissonant novel information can also fulfill both needs, but not if the potentially dissonant information is too dissonant, whereupon it might be avoided. Potentially dissonant information might be preferred to unnovel potentially consonant information. However, in the Sears (1965) study, despite the relative differences found between the old and the new information conditions, the preference was for nonsupporting information in *both* conditions.

Novelty of information is a variable worthy of further investigation in selective exposure research. As suggested here, novelty of information may often override the potential consonance or dissonance of the information as a determinant of selective exposure, although potentially consonant information is more likely to be preferred to potentially dissonant information when the information is unfamiliar than when it is not. When the information is familiar, the fact that it is being used to support an unfamiliar side of the issue itself produces novelty. Too much novel dissonance, however, is aversive.

Certainly the individual will try to incorporate novel information in a manner that will make it consistent with prior beliefs, but, as pointed out in Chapter 2, the incorporation of new information is also likely to involve some modification of the belief system.[3]

Gaining attention and stimulating epistemic curiosity can pave the way for persuasion but it is not persuasion itself. The communication process by which persuasion takes place was discussed in the previous chapter. It was pointed out there that the stimulation of issue-relevant thought is only one aspect of persuasion. This thinking process might need to be guided and fed by the presentation of relevant information that will hopefully (from the point of view of the communicator) steer the thinking into counter-attitudinal advocacy.

In other words, once we have stimulated information-seeking behavior, we might have to provide the information. Protest actions are short-lived and not the place for the presentation of extensive information and argumentation. They can incorporate a statement of position, or brief statements of potentially doubt-arousing facts or arguments, but not elaborate informational discourse. The complexity of information involved in such a function is actually incompatible with the attention-getting and curiosity-arousing function. Therefore, protest actions might serve as priming devices to be followed up by extensive information and persuasion campaigns (which, ideally, also would have preceded the protest actions).

THE CONSEQUENCES OF PROTEST IN THE CIVIL RIGHTS MOVEMENT

Opinion surveys show that in the early 1960s a large proportion of the American public disapproved of the tactics of the civil rights movement (Sheatsley, 1966). Yet these same surveys show that during this time more and more people were claiming attitudes favorable to racial integration. The proportion of whites that approved of school integration climbed from 30% in 1942 to 49% in 1956 (two years after the Supreme Court school desegregation decision and the year of the Montgomery bus boycott, which drew national and world attention to Martin Luther King, Jr. and the civil rights movement) and to 62% in 1963 (three years after the sit-in movement had been launched). The white South, taken alone, showed an upward trend. The proportion of whites nationwide approving of integration in public transportation rose from 44% in 1942 to 60% in 1956 to 78% at the end of 1963 (Sheatsley, 1966). Only 4% of Southern whites approved of integrated public transportation in 1942, but 27% did in 1956 and 51% did at the end of 1963 (Sheatsley, 1966). Similar trends were observed for attitudes toward housing integration (Sheatsley, 1966). Yet, in 1963, 59% of white people in the North and 78% of white people in the South generally disapproved of the tactics of the civil rights movement, and these percentages can be seen to overlap with the percentages pertaining to approval of integration.

If we were to assume that the protest aspects of the civil rights movement set the stage for attitude change toward integration by drawing attention to the issue, then these findings are consistent with the conclusions drawn earlier from basic research into attention and curiosity. That is, a stimulus does not have to be liked in order to be effective.

It should be noted that on this particular issue of race relations Sheatsley (1966) claims that there was a relatively small proportion of people expressing "No opinion," compared to the public's answers on most other national issues. He states:

There have been no masses of apathetic or undecided people, swayed this way and that by events, and drifting from segregationist to doubtful, from doubtful to integrationist, and perhaps back again. Rather, support for civil rights today comes from a younger generation that, during the last two decades, has come of age and has replaced an older, more segregationist generation in our population; and from former segregationists whose senses and consciences have been touched by the Negro protest, or who have simply changed their opinions as segregation appears increasingly to be a lost cause.

Sheatsley (1966) concludes:

Certainly there is no evidence that the majority of American whites eagerly look forward to integration. Most are more comfortable in a segregated society, and they would prefer that the demonstrators slow down or go away while things are worked out more gradually. But most of them know also that racial discrimination is morally wrong and recognize the legitimacy of the Negro protest. Our survey data persuasively argue that where there is little or no protest against segregation and discrimination, or where these have the sanction of law, racial attitudes conform to the existing situation. But when attention is kept focused on racial injustice and when acts of discrimination become contrary to the law of the land, racial attitudes change.

The increasingly favorable attitudes toward integration were probably not due, at least in the early 1960s, to increased contact between the races. In the 1963 survey the vast majority of those interviewed said they had not been affected at all by integration, and most claimed little (less than every day) or no contact with Negroes (Sheatsley, 1966).

To what extent could the increasing approval of integration be attributed, however indirectly, to the nonviolent civil rights protest movement? Hardly any survey data relevant to race relations had been collected prior to 1942. A positive trend has actually been visible since then, even on the survey questions asked after 1942 but prior to 1956. However, it can be argued from the data that the increase has been especially accelerated since 1956.

Yet although, as Sheatsley (1966) notes, the survey data are persuasive, it is difficult to conclusively determine the effects of such a movement. The best we can do is to observe the correlation of events with the attitude changes indicated by the surveys, but such correlations do not in themselves necessarily reflect cause-effect relations.

Here, of course, we are faced with the fact that it is very difficult to assess the effectiveness of mass social movements. Experiments cannot be performed on such a molar scale, and history omits control groups. The best that can be done is to perform experiments on a small scale involving what are thought to be crucial variables of some aspects of the larger phenomenon. With this procedure, cause-effect relations within the experiment can be pinpointed with some certainty, but inferences to the larger social context are speculative and hazardous. For the most part, this is the approach being taken in this book. On the other hand, one can observe the correlations of events in the larger social context. In this case, generalizations from a different level or context are avoided, but inferences as to the cause-effect nature of the occurrences are highly speculative.

Yet some inferences are more convincing than others. The most conservative statement that can be made is that the civil rights movement could not have greatly hindered the favorable trend in attitudes, because its increase was so dramatic during that time. But changes of any kind cannot be attributed to time alone. Something happening within that time must be responsible for the changes. The argument that the civil rights movement was one great event that contributed to the improvement of racial attitudes (not only in its more convincingly causal relation to the enactment of civil rights laws but also in more direct ways) is no more nor less than fairly persuasive.

Of course, doubts can be raised about the meaning of the survey data themselves. I have already noted Sheatsley's observation that on the issue of integration, unlike many other surveyed issues, the changes detected are stable. However, one can ask: *What* has changed? Perhaps because of the great furor over race relations in recent years people have come to believe that it is socially unacceptable to express attitudes of a racially discriminatory nature, especially to strangers such as interviewers, and they might respond in the way that they think is expected of them. If this is the only thing that has changed, it is at least obvious that there is a new social climate and a new social norm. If it is socially unacceptable to discriminate in word, it might also or soon will be socially unacceptable to discriminate in deed. Discrimination will have to be carried on more covertly than in the past, and this does not mean that discrimination simply goes "underground." It means that discrimination becomes more difficult to get away with, that it becomes taboo, frowned upon, and a new social norm gets passed on to new generations. The young people are likely to internalize it as the norm, directing them into increasing interracial contact.

However, Hyman and Sheatsley (1956, 1964) strongly believe that the people interviewed honestly expressed their true attitudes in regard to racial segregation. They note that the people were not at all reluctant to talk to the interviewers about the issue and showed great interest in it; that they freely expressed opposition to full integration and freely expressed criticism of Negroes; that emphatic comments accompanied the answers, and both were often given without hesitation but with confidence and certainty; and that there was a low percentage of people expressing "No opinion" or who were lukewarm about the matter.

For those who believe, as I do, that the anti-war movement made slower progress against the Vietnam War than the civil rights movement did against racial discrimination, it is interesting to note some differences between the two movements. The civil rights movement utilized noncooperation to a much greater extent than did the anti-war movement, which relied heavily on noncoercive protest demonstrations. But even at the protest level, I would speculate that the civil rights movement had an important advantage that accounted for its effectiveness—in order to induce attitude change, it was sufficient to call the Negro's plight to the attention of the general public. It was not imperative to present facts and figures in the context of a persuasion campaign because many people already realized that the Negro was not getting a fair shake in our country. Such beliefs merely had to be made more salient for many people; the people had to be induced to think about the issue; they had to be prevented from pushing their beliefs back into dim awareness. They had to be shaken out of blind adherence to an accepted custom, to a norm with which they had become comfortable but which really did not square with their moral and democratic values. In other words, in this case, nonviolent protest might have initiated the process of bringing to the individual's awareness states of inconsistency already existing in his value-attitude system, making him uncomfortable, and thereby bringing about attitude change.

I have already noted in Chapter 2 that such bringing to awareness of inconsistencies has been suggested as one method by which to accomplish attitude change in another individual. I have said that this method of inducing an individual to experience inconsistency can activate a searching of conscience and can be construed as a moral appeal or an "appeal to conscience."

After having assessed subjects' attitudes toward equal rights for black people, equal rights for other groups, and American policy in Vietnam, Rokeach (1968, pp. 173–178) presented his subjects with a list of values and asked them to rank-order the values in terms of importance. He found that if he then suggested to some of his subjects that it is inconsistent for a person to rank freedom high and equality low (unless he is only interested in his *own* freedom), there was a tendency for these subjects to raise their preferences for the values of equality and freedom. Attitudes toward the issues also changed. These changes in value preference (especially equality) and attitudes were found to persist over substantial periods of time.

Such changes were apparently most marked among subjects to whom an additional suggestion was made. It was proposed to these subjects that people who are against civil rights, and rank freedom high while ranking equality low, might really be demonstrating that they are concerned about their own freedom but are indifferent to other people's freedom. For these subjects, significant increases in their ranking of equality and freedom were found three to five months later. Furthermore, among those who had originally ranked equality high but were anti-civil rights, there was significant attitude change in a "pro" direction on this issue. Those who had· originally ranked equality low but were pro-civil rights generally increased their ranking of equality, became more favorable in attitude toward equal rights for other groups and, to a lesser extent, more dovish in their attitude toward American involvement in Vietnam. Sleeper effects were found in that attitude change that was not detectable after three weeks showed up after three months. In later experiments, Rokeach (1971) found attitude change in regard to civil rights to persist after 15 to 17 months. He also found that subjects who had been exposed to the experimental treatment (the suggestions) were more likely to respond to a letter from a civil rights organization soliciting money than those in a control group.

While this process of arousing inconsistency might have been operating in regard to nonviolent protest during the civil rights movement, the Vietnam War issue was different. The general public did not even have much information about the war and often felt that support of the war effort was quite consistent with their values. There was no subjective inconsistency to arouse, and so protest was not enough. Protest could dramatize and call attention to the issue, but attitude change could not take place without something more, such as extensive information campaigns. On college campuses, where perhaps the most attitude change took place, protest demonstrations had been followed up with "teach-ins." However, I have already expressed my belief that the anti-war movement should have put heavier emphasis on noncooperation than it did.

An improvement in attitudes toward race relations was not the only gain made in recent years. Black people just now are in the process of becoming better educated, of being trained for better jobs, and of taking advantage of their rights. Progress is necessarily slow. Education and training take time. Expectations rise faster than gains. And the necessity for continued nonviolent action has not yet passed. Black people must continue to push hard and fast, but the tangible gains inevitably come less quickly.

As Martin Luther King, Jr. (1958, p. 221) said:

> The nonviolent approach provides an answer to the long debated question of gradualism *versus* immediacy. On the one hand it prevents one from falling into the sort of patience which is an excuse for do-nothingism and escapism, ending up in standstillism. On the other hand it saves one from the irresponsible words which estrange without reconciling and the hasty judgment which is blind to the necessities of social process. It recognizes the need for moving toward the goal of justice with wise restraint and calm reasonableness. But it also recognizes the immorality of slowing up in the move toward justice and capitulating to the guardians of an unjust status quo. It recognizes that social change cannot come overnight. But it causes one to work as if it were a possibility the next morning.

And while, as I noted before, correlations do not necessarily reflect cause-effect relations, the close contiguity of events in time and place can convincingly indicate such relations. Such was the case more so with regard to specific behavioral social gains made following particular segments of the civil rights movement than with regard to the movement as a whole and overall attitude change. Many of these specific gains, however, were due to acts of noncooperation and not merely protest. As Martin Luther King, Jr. (1968, p. 67) noted:

> The 1960 sit-ins desegregated lunch counters in more than 150 cities within a year. The 1961 Freedom Rides put an end to segregation in interstate travel. The 1956 bus boycott in Montgomery, Alabama, ended segregation on the buses not only of that city but in practically every city of the South. The 1963 Birmingham movement and the climactic March on Washington won passage of the most powerful civil rights law in a century. The 1965 Selma movement brought enactment of the Voting Rights Law.

PSYCHOLOGICAL EFFECTS ON PARTICIPANTS

But many years of oppression must have taken their toll, not only on the society in general and not only in terms of the restrictions that have socially imprisoned black people but on the black people themselves.

Perhaps one of the most important gains to be made by a nonviolent movement is not the effects it might have on others but the psychological effects it can have on the participants themselves. According to Frazier (1968), the building up of self-respect is not only one of the most important goals of a nonviolent movement but also the one most likely to be achieved.

It has been found that those students at a Southern Negro college who were more inclined to participate in civil rights action in the first place were more likely to believe that they were in control of their own fate than those who were not (Gore and Rotter, 1963). But there is evidence based on interviews that participation in nonviolent action might itself *increase* self-confidence. Pierce and West (1966) reported that black children who participated in sit-ins in Oklahoma City manifested a "remarkable sense of latent power" six years later and expressed "an almost magical conviction that they can influence the course of events by their own behaviour." Comparisons made between active participants in sit-ins and nonparticipating individuals of similar background apparently supported this finding of increased self-confidence.

Speaking about the effects of the Montgomery bus boycott, Martin Luther King, Jr. (1958, p. 187) observed in regard to that city's black community:

> Although the intense solidarity of the protest year has inevitably attenuated, there is still a feeling of closeness among the various classes and ages and religious denominations that was never present before. The increased self-respect of even the least sophisticated Negroes in Montgomery is evident in the way they dress and walk, in new standards of cleanliness and of general deportment.

He also noted: "There has been a decline in heavy drinking. Statistics on crime and divorce indicate that both are on the wane" (1958, p.187). Evidence gathered in one study suggests a reduction in crime by blacks during periods of organized civil rights activity in certain cities, although the data do not indicate a sustainment of this reduction afterward (Solomon, *et al.*, 1965).

As Bem (1970, p. 67) points out, here is an instance in which behavior change begets attitude change—in this case nonviolent action begetting a change in attitudes toward the self. To the extent that the black people in general identified with the activists and took pride in and learned from their courage and determination, it is likely that they too began to reorient themselves and to experience an enhancement of self-esteem. No longer would they neither expect nor demand respect from others as human beings, and no longer would the old social norms and the strange security of accepted custom blind them from their awareness of their human rights. Undoubtedly, the civil rights movement contributed to a new pride and self-respect on the part of black people.

It is also likely that the civil rights movement helped to elicit a new respect for black people on the part of whites. Survey data indicate that in 1963 most white people at least knew that the Negroes wanted the right to vote, equal job opportunities, and equal access to public accommodations (Sheatsley, 1966). It is quite possible that this awareness had been heightened by the nonviolent protests of that time. As Solomon and Fishman (1964a) said:

> By protesting, the Negro students in the civil rights movement have exploded stereotypes, showing that they are neither childlike nor contented.

SELF-SUFFERING AND PROTEST

However, nonviolent protest can be expected to extract a price from its participants. It can be viewed as a threat to the status quo, and may elicit hostility on the part of some or the planned violence of government officials who may regard the situation as a problem to be dealt with through violent force. The nonviolent activist must at all times be willing and prepared to suffer.

Solomon and Fishman (1964a) have stated:

> The suffering experienced at the hands of abusive opponents is suffering in the name of dedication to the "cause." It enormously strengthens individual and group identity.

But what effect does self-suffering have on others? In his book on nonviolence, Gregg (1966, p. 53) has stated:

> The sight of a person voluntarily undergoing suffering for a belief or an ideal moves the assailant and beholders alike and tends to change their hearts and make them feel a kinship with the sufferer.

Gandhi (1954b, p. 17) said:

> Real suffering bravely borne melts even a heart of stone. Such is the potency of suffering or *tapas*. And there lies the key to Satyagraha.

However, contrary to the hypotheses that can be gleaned from the literature on nonviolence, recent experimental evidence suggests that the awareness of another person's suffering, far from "melting hearts," can in some instances elicit a negative reaction toward the victim. In others words, in some cases we tend to dislike those who suffer, because they suffer. Lerner (1970, pp. 212–213) found that people who are led to believe that they will see a person suffer (they expected to observe her receiving strong electric shocks) evaluate her less positively than those who do not expect her to suffer.

Observers' reactions to the suffering of an innocent victim (one whose behavior did not seem to merit the suffering) was more extensively studied in an experiment by Lerner and Simmons (1966). College students who thought that they were participating in an experiment on the judgment of emotional arousal were led to observe what they believed was another experiment, on human learning, in which another student was to participate. The student subjects (observers) were to watch the experiment on a television monitor although, unknown to them, what they actually saw was a previously made ten-minute video tape. The students were told that the subject they would observe in the learning task would receive electric shocks for incorrect responses made during the course of the task. The victim appeared to receive several painful shocks during the task, to which she was observed to react with expressions of pain and suffering. (Unknown to the observers, the victim was a confederate of the experimenter, and was not actually being shocked, but was acting.) After the tape was shown, the observers' reactions to the victim were assessed by means of a number of rating scales.

Students who were told that they were halfway through their observation, and who thus expected that the victim would continue to be shocked in a second session after the ratings, devalued the victim more than did students who were led to believe that the suffering was at an end and that the victim had been financially compensated.

In another condition, almost all observers given an opportunity to alter the victim's fate voted to place the victim in a situation in which the suffering would be ended and she would be compensated. Observers who were told of the positive outcome of the vote were found to reject the victim less than those who, without having a vote, had been led to believe that the second session would be similar to the first. However, observers who were not told of the outcome of the vote rejected the victim as much as did the observers who expected more of the same and had not been given a vote. Apparently, rejection occurred unless the observer was *assured* that the suffering was at an end or that the victim would be compensated. When observers were unable to end the suffering of an innocent victim and compensate her for it, they devalued her.

In what was called the martyr condition the observers had been led to believe, prior to seeing the video tape, that the victim was reluctant to take part in the experiment (they saw her protest and express fear of shock) and that she finally consented to it only so that the other students might receive their needed lab credits for participating in the experiment as observers. The impression was created that she had agreed to undergo suffering out of altruistic motives, solely to benefit the observers. It was found that the observers in this condition rejected the victim much more than did those in the condition in which the observers were merely led to believe (as were those in the martyr condition) that the learning experiment was over at the time of the rating, but had not been exposed to a martyr performance. Of all the conditions, the martyr condition produced the most rejection. The general findings of this experiment were confirmed in later studies (Lerner, 1970, 1971).

Lerner (1970) noted that it is possible that the martyr act in the above experiment produced the impression that the victim, rather than being altruistically motivated, was someone who was overly submissive to authority or overly concerned about gaining others' approval. This impression could have elicited the strong rejection and devaluation of the victim that was found. The results of further experimentation reduced the likelihood of this possibility (Lerner, 1970, 1971), although perhaps did not entirely eliminate the hypothesis that this impression, aided by the expectation of suffering, facilitated the devaluation.

Since the martyr in the Lerner and Simmons (1966) experiment had made it clear that she would participate in a task involving shock only for the sake of the observers (so that they could obtain credit), they might have felt indirectly responsible for her suffering. Lerner and Matthews (1967) found that when a person felt responsible for a victim's suffering, she tended to derogate her. This feeling of responsibility and perhaps guilt might account for the strong rejection in the martyr condition. However, in further experimentation (Lerner, 1970, 1971) other observers were called in who believed that the martyr was to suffer for the other students, but who were themselves not implicated in the suffering. These observers, who could not feel responsible for the suffering, rejected the victim as strongly as did the other observers.

The findings of these studies were explained by Lerner (1970) in the following way. He claims that people have a need to believe in a "just world" in which people get what they deserve and deserve what they get. "We want to believe that good things happen to good people and serious suffering comes only to bad people." Thus, a person who sees another suffering, or expects that the other will suffer, will be motivated to persuade himself that the victim in some way deserved his fate. Apparently, knowledge that the victim will be compensated for his suffering will alleviate the threat to his "just world" belief and reduce this motivation. He can also reinforce his belief in a "just world" by compensating the victim himself, and he will do so if the means are easy and readily available. But if he is unable to compensate the victim he can maintain his belief in a "just world" by persuading himself that the victim deserves to suffer. He can do this by convincing himself that the victim brought about his own suffering by behaving poorly. But if the victim is clearly innocent of any kind of behavior that might have caused his suffering, he can convince himself that the victim has undesirable personal traits and deserves his fate because of them.

The martyr's suffering is the most unjust of all because he is presumably acting from altruistic motives. His suffering is the most threatening to the belief in a "just world" and therefore elicits the greatest attempt to derogate the victim and convince oneself that he deserves his fate.

Lerner (1970) states:

> If the observer is unable to alter the fate of the victim he is likely to be compelled to find some undesirable attributes in the victim which makes his suffering appear to be a relatively acceptable, just fate. This personal rejection can become rather extreme if the victim appeared initially to be suffering out of altruistic motives. Most people do not want to believe that suffering can be visited upon decent, good people who did nothing to merit such a fate.

In a recent experiment subjects observed a slide in which a black man involved in "a peaceful demonstration to call attention to poor city maintenance in certain areas of the city" was being attacked by a white policeman with a dog. The subjects devalued the victim when they thought that the attack was *unjustified* (Lincoln and Levinger, 1972). This finding is consistent with Lerner's theory. However, this devaluation was slight as compared with the more drastic devaluation of the attacking agent himself. Moreover, when observers who thought that the attack was unjustified were led to believe that their evaluations might affect the fates of the people in the slide (they were told that the ratings would be made available to an investigating commission, and to the victim and policeman), they rated the victim more highly than did observers who saw a slide in which the black man did not seem to be attacked.

Devaluation of the victim of an unjustified attack is not what we would expect. Lerner (1970) himself notes that the findings in regard to his martyr condition apparently contradict common sense. He notes that we often love and revere martyrs, and react to them with compassion and admiration rather than with condemnation and rejection. One of the possible reasons that Lerner (1970) offers as to why, aside from his experimental findings, martyrs are often revered instead of rejected is as follows: "Our prior cognitions surrounding the martyrdom are likely to be stable and important to us, so we suffer along with the martyr and the injustice of his fate."

Berscheid and Walster (1969, p. 25) state:

> It may be easy enough to convince ourselves that a stranger deserved to be hurt; it is much more difficult to convince ourselves that the victim deserved to suffer if we know many good things about him which contradict our distortion.

Indeed, in such a case the suffering might increase our attraction toward the victim and elicit sympathy, although I am not aware of any experimental evidence that would support this conjecture.

The preceding experiments deal with the measurement of attitudes toward the victim that have been formed on the basis of a single experience. One's prior information about either the issue in regard to which the victim has undergone suffering or about the victim himself might determine how he will react to the suffering (although information that we might have expected to favorably incline the observer toward the victim was not entirely lacking in the Lincoln and Levinger [1972] study). Prior attitudes toward the issue or the victim might crucially determine how the cognition of suffering will be incorporated into one's belief system. Many Americans, although revulsed by the thought of the Japanese kamekaze pilots during World War II, admired American soldiers who sacrificed their own lives through daring acts for the sake of the war effort. Especially if one has a prior positive attitude toward the issue or victim that is rich in cognitive support, far from convincing oneself that the victim deserved to suffer, one might have a higher regard for him than ever before. The evaluative direction of a prior cognitively well-differentiated attitude might determine the direction in which the cognition of suffering will influence the attitude toward the victim.

Nonviolent actions will sometimes be met with insults and violence. Sometimes they will be met with force on the part of the police or the military. In such instances the nonviolent activist does not retaliate in any way, but endures the inflicted suffering. He suffers the violence and perhaps imprisonment. The background information presented to observers in the Lincoln and Levinger (1972) study was rather meager. Perhaps those of the general public whose attitudes toward the issues are consistent with those of the demonstrators or who had prior positive attitudes toward the demonstrators will be drawn to sympathize with them, while those of the general public who hold attitudes contrary to those of the demonstrators or have negative attitudes toward them will be aroused to greater condemnation. It is likely that the former segment of the public will find evidence either in the personalities of the demonstrators or in the complex demonstration event to support their prior views and will blame the police for the suffering. On the other hand, the latter segment will readily interpret the demonstrators' actions as provocations of the police, and otherwise find fault with the demonstrators, thereby liking them less and blaming them for their own suffering, which will be construed as deserved.[4]

How are those who inflict the suffering likely to react toward the victims? Up until now I have been discussing the probable reactions of the observers of suffering, not the persecutors themselves. I would assume that people have a belief in their own justness; indeed, rationalizations often serve the purpose of defending that belief. In a demonstration, the police, for example, might actually increase their rejection and devaluation of the demonstrators after attacking them, in order to justify the attack to themselves and thereby maintain the belief in their own justness.

Derogation of the victim by a person following his own harmful act has been demonstrated in a number of experiments (e.g., Davis and Jones, 1960; Davidson, 1964; Glass, 1964; Walster and Prestholdt, 1966; Lerner and Matthews, 1967). If one feels oneself responsible for the victim's suffering, one is more likely to derogate him than when one does not consider oneself responsible (Lerner and Matthews, 1967). Also, a person who has caused harm will attempt to deny his responsibility and minimize, in his own mind, the suffering that has occurred, as some experimental evidence suggests (Brock and Buss, 1962).

The picture presented thus far is not encouraging. But given the varying probabilities that people with differing prior beliefs and attitudes and with different relations (observer or persecutor) to the victim will react to the suffering by rejecting the victim, we can ask what factors in general might serve to decrease the likelihood or severity of rejection.

There are certain components of social action carried out in the spirit of nonviolence that are likely to facilitate its effects on others and to elicit respect rather than condemnation. Nonviolence theorists stress the sincerity and earnestness of the sufferers, and of suffering for a belief or ideal. Lakey (1968, p. 20) claims that the voluntary nature of the suffering "is most likely to communicate the bravery, openness, and goodwill of the sufferer." It is in the context of such positive qualities that suffering is presumably to have a positive effect.

Some of what Solomon and Fishman (1964a) point out and claim are basic and recurring features of the behavior and attitudes of activists (based on their interviews of 19 experienced Negro civil rights workers) are: the maintenance of a group ideology and discipline that forbids violence, an outward display of fearlessness and dignity even in the face of obvious threat to life and limb, and a show of friendliness toward opponents.

Solomon and Fishman (1964a) state: "This display of fearlessness wins respect and sympathy from many onlookers and the national and international community." Frazier (1968) states:

> As was the case in the Montgomery boycott, the feature of the sit-ins which most captured the public sympathy was the discipline of the demonstrators. Sometimes, in spite of unbelievable provocation, they remained nonviolent and even, at times, smiling.

In regard to their study of sit-in participants, which I cited earlier, Pierce and West (1966) noted:

> The influence of the entire group of young sit-in demonstrators upon the adults in their own families and upon the community at large has been extraordinary. Because they were able to maintain self-control through the bitterest days of the demonstrations, a growing degree of admiration towards them evolved. The police developed such a remarkable degree of rapport with the demonstrators that at times their interactions resembled a mutually considerate minuet. Many adults, both Negro and white, were moved by the willing and cheerful sufferings of the children to take a more active part in the civil rights movement.

They add that even some formerly bitter antagonists became supporters and made financial contributions to the movement.

Kelman (1968, pp. 256–258) points out that nonviolent action provides new information to the adversary and general public about the concerns and intentions of the activists and about the character of the activists themselves. The activist communicates his commitment and determination, his readiness to strive toward a mutually satisfactory resolution, and his unwillingness to harm the adversary. Kelman claims that nonviolent action thus induces the adversary to take reciprocal action and it induces bystanders (particularly those who were already somewhat sympathetic) to engage in supportive action. The adversary is not likely to respond as violently and ruthlessly to nonviolent action as he would to violent action. For one thing, nonviolent action does not provide the justification for a violent response that violent action does, both in terms of the adversary's own values and in terms of the bad impression it might create for the general public. Nonviolent action might even "lock in" the adversary to reciprocal positive responses (i.e., it might invoke the norm of reciprocity), which might induce consistent positive attitudes toward the activist—a case of behavior change inducing attitude change.

Moreover, there is often an inclination on the part of observers to try to alleviate the suffering of a victim or to try to compensate him for it. In the Lerner and Simmons (1966) study, it will be recalled that when the observers were given a chance to vote to place the victim in a situation in which her suffering would be ended and she would be compensated, almost all did so. One of the findings of the Lincoln and Levinger (1972) study indicated that observers who thought that the attack was unjustified tried to help the victim if given a chance. Also, there is some evidence that those who have recently witnessed misfortune are motivated to perform altruistic acts (Regan, 1971).

In regard to the harm-doer himself, Walster, Berscheid, and Walster (1970) suggest that the more difficult the conditions make it for him to derogate his victim, attribute responsibility to him for his own suffering, and deny responsibility for the victim's suffering or minimize it, the more likely he will be to compensate the victim.

Perhaps, too, I have dwelt too much upon attitudes toward the activists rather than toward the issues themselves. After all, protests are launched to call attention to issues and not to induce liking for the participants. I have already noted that civil rights protests might have been responsible for favorable attitude change toward civil rights issues despite the fact that they were not generally liked by the American public. Protest might draw attention to issues and arouse consciences even if it generates reflexive resistance. The voluntary suffering aspects of protest might aid in drawing attention and stirring consciences, whether one's immediate reaction to the suffering is sympathy with or condemnation of the activists. However, we cannot expect a complete separation of the activists and the protest action from the issues in the minds of others, and the generating of more resistance than is necessary is likely to be detrimental to eventual attitude change. Thus, the offsetting of resistance through the conveyance of the positive qualities noted above is important.

However, in regard to the sit-ins in the South, Miller (1964, p. 311) concludes that "opponents were seldom if ever won over to the side of justice as a result of voluntary suffering or Christian love on the part of the demonstrators." Instead, he feels that it was the economic pressure and the merchants' desire for stability and civil order that made the sit-ins successful. But he adds: "Particularly among white students, liberals and churchmen, dormant consciences were stirred" (1964, p. 313).

It would seem then that nonviolent action is likely to draw the attention of the general public to the issue and, in some cases (such as racial injustice in our country) constitute a sufficient appeal to conscience in itself that it arouses latent inconsistencies in the attitude-value systems of some of the general public. The voluntary suffering that nonviolent action often involves is likely to arouse and mobilize the sympathy and support of those of the general public who are already somewhat sympathetic toward the activists or the views they represent. The sight of police attacking demonstrators with dogs in Birmingham probably did much to arouse the indignation of white liberals.[5]

But, as for the adversary and those who are initially negative or hostile toward the activists and their cause, nonviolent action may succeed only through the coercive pressures of noncooperation, which will be the concern of the next chapter. (As Kelman [1968, p. 250] notes, attitude change is more likely to follow rather than precede institutional changes.) The very least that the experiments reported above in regard to the effects of suffering suggest is that any sweeping general statement about it "melting the hearts" of others is a gross oversimplification.

Nonviolent protest by itself can succeed against the adversary in certain situations. It can cause him embarrassment in the face of a third party, much the same way as informational exposure can. The suffering of the activists might add to the adversary's embarrassment. But in the case of such deep-rooted prejudices on the part of the adversary which were demonstrated in many of the civil rights campaigns, the adversary might be too enraged and committed to his attitude to feel embarrassed. Yet, as noted before, an adversary might be indirectly pressured by nonviolent protests through a fear of adverse economic or political reactions from the general public.

However, I wish to emphasize my conclusion that nonviolent protest, together with the suffering often involved, has a *direct* positive effect upon only the general public and often only a certain segment of that public. In many cases, such as the civil rights movement, such effects can be important in and of themselves. But nonviolent protest is likely to have only an *indirect* effect upon the immediate adversary by way of the general public. When such indirect effects fail to move the adversary, nonviolent noncooperation—which *directly* affects the adversary (and which also has indirect protest aspects)—might have to be resorted to. Sometimes the nonviolent protest is effective because of the direct threat of subsequent mass noncooperation that it presents.

VIOLENCE AS PROTEST

Violence, such as is often involved in rioting, might have stimulated some gains similar to those of the civil rights movement. Also, the trends in the public opinion surveys cited before kept rising or remained steady even after the rioting began in the mid-1960s (Sheatsley, 1966). Violence, after all, can call attention to issues, and it can coerce. But violence can also create the bitterest antagonism between groups. Martin Luther King, Jr. aimed not only for rights for black people but he looked beyond these gains to reconciliation. He was concerned with whether or not a better society in general would result from the movement. He was attempting to build an integrated society. He sought, as much as is possible within the context of conflict and confrontation, to keep bitterness, resistance, and hostility to a minimum. He wished to use conflict in a creative way, to build community, such as could not exist prior to the waging of conflict and could not be achieved through violence, which is more capable of producing a polarized society rather than a reconciliated one.

As Kelman (1968, pp. 254–255) states:

> Violent confrontations are not necessarily and totally ineffective in producing attitude change. For example, the riots in the ghettoes—though they have instigated strong repressive measures—did induce some whites to reappraise their attitudes. The chances are, however, that as such tactics continue to be used, their potential of frightening white Americans will far outweigh their potential of challenging white attitudes. This is particularly likely if the object of rioting were to shift from the ghetto itself to the white neighborhoods. In short, it is to be expected that as violent confrontations continue, more and more segments of the white population will become alienated from Negro efforts to foster social change and will support a repressive approach.
>
> Thus, if our goal is to bring about a thorough re-examination of white attitudes and to open the society to full participation of those who are now excluded, we cannot rely on the tactics of violence. We must find techniques of confrontation that minimize the alienation of whites, and ways of challenging existing power relationships that protect the integrity of the system. It is part of the genius of nonviolent action that it provides precisely such techniques.

Most important of all for the adherent of the philosophy of nonviolence is his belief that violence is immoral. It becomes his difficult responsibility, in every situation, to create and advance effective nonviolent alternatives. If he wants the means that will be employed to be intrinsically moral, it becomes his burden to present effective moral alternatives to violence.

The prevention of outbreaks of violence has always been a difficult task for the nonviolent activist. For, on the one hand, he must arouse people to action and in so doing he must shake them from apathy and stimulate their courage. On the other hand, this very process might embolden them to commit violence. This is why Gandhi and King, even in the heat of a campaign and at the same time that they were arousing their people to action, would admonish them about violence. Gandhi felt obliged to call off his nationwide noncooperation campaign in India in 1922 because of the outbreak of rioting in some areas.

There are some who claim that the nonviolent campaigns of the civil rights movement were effective only because of the violent disorders that occasionally accompanied them. Von Eschen, Kirk, and Pinard (1969) tried to show that, although the movement was itself nonviolent, it depended for its success on disorder (the authors apparently mean *violent* disorder) which they claim frequently followed in the wake of nonviolent actions. They attempt to support their claim that violent disorder on the part of nonmembers of the movement was essential for the movement's success with their study and observation of a few of the civil rights campaigns. They note that, in one case, peaceful demonstrations on Maryland's Eastern Shore had little effect until violent attacks on the demonstrators elicited violent reactions on the part of some black people in Cambridge. It was only then, according to the authors, that rapid desegregation began in Eastern Shore towns following local announce-ments of proposed demonstrations. Similarly, they point out that a drive to desegregate restaurants in Nashville did not succeed for as long as the demonstrations there were peaceful. But progress was made when attacks on the demonstrators, who were picketting, began to elicit violence and rioting on the part of new recruits who were not willing to adhere to nonviolence.

These examples are informative, and I will not attempt to refute the contention that in these particular instances demonstrations gained atten-tion and achieved results only when they appeared to threaten violent disorder. But those who are determined to discover how to wage conflict successfully without even the unintentional assistance of violence or threats of violence seek to learn from such cases.

Nonviolent protests have been known to attract wide attention, if they are novel enough. Violence is not necessary to do that. If the demonstrations in Maryland failed to draw press coverage and public attention, then they obviously fell short of one of their most important functions. If so, they should not have been continually repeated without being made novel and dramatic enough to attract attention, lest they postpone justice and invite violence. If some of the demonstrations did draw attention, then they might have contributed to the general increase in favorable attitudes, registered by the opinion surveys, that took place at that time in the general public. The progress of a nonviolent campaign cannot be judged only in terms of the immediate adversary; as I indicated before, nonviolent protest is not likely to have its *direct* effect on the adversary himself.

As far as the immediate adversary was concerned, violent power was not the only type of power that could have had an effect. The authors state that one of the reasons why violent disorder was effective was because it brought economic and political sanctions. (For example, in Cambridge, tourist trade was adversely affected.) But nonviolent non-cooperation can do that. Noncooperation can bring about the same sanctions that the authors attribute to violent disorder.

The authors point out that in regard to the restaurants in Nashville, as opposed to the lunch counters, a boycott could not be used because the restaurants did not depend on Negro clientele. I would suggest that if this was the case, then other forms of noncooperation should have been utilized. If none could be found that could be used, this might have indicated that a poor choice of target had been made, especially at a time when there was no shortage of potential targets. But certainly two years is a long time to continue demonstrations (as was done in the Nashville case) without success and without switching tactics. It is dangerous not to go beyond protest when it is not being effective, for continued failure will increase the possibility of restlessness and violence on the part of some.

Nonviolent action is not necessarily dependent upon violent accompaniments for its achievements. Nonviolence—through persuasion, protest, and, if need be, ultimately through noncooperation—can successfully confront injustice. Without violence and because of its absence, it can keep bitterness, resistance, and hostility to the minimum that is possible within the context of conflict and confrontation. Nonviolent action has the potential to plant the seeds of reconciliation even in the midst of conflict.

NOTES

[1]See Bondurant (1965, pp. vii–ix, 4–5, 41–45; 1967, pp. 99–112) for distinguishing characteristics of Satyagraha when such tactics are employed.

[2]There are two aspects to the notion of cognitive dissonance. The first is that the individual strives to reduce dissonance, and the second that the individual seeks to avoid information that might increase dissonance. The implication from both aspects is that a state of consonance is itself intrinsically satisfying. Festinger (1957) claims that if little or no

dissonance exists there would be no motivation to seek out new information. But, while there is a large body of evidence in social psychology supportive of the first aspect, the second aspect is in doubt, and we are left with the question of why an individual might sometimes strive to move further from, rather than closer to, the supposed blissful state of balance. While not denying the satisfaction derived from the end-state of balance, the possible satisfaction involved in the dynamic process of reducing dissonance needs to be stressed. That is, while order may be satisfying and sought after for its own sake, the process of ordering, for which dissonant material is needed, is also sought after. It is not only order, but ordering, not only balance, but balancing, not only organization, but organizing that is intrinsically satisfying. As an analogy, the act of eating is in itself satisfying, not just the end result. More relevant, Barron (1958) has attempted to explain the preference of creative individuals for more disorderly, irregular, and unbalanced abstract line drawings by proposing that such individuals find a challenge in disorder—that of constructing order. Within limits, individuals in general may be said to seek out dissonant information and stimulation for the sake of organizing it and bringing it into consonance with prior knowledge.

When we look at insatiably curious, ever-exploring man in this way, from this dynamic point of view, it becomes clear why he would seek out discrepant information. He does it not so much to avoid cognitive balance as to provide himself with new information and stimulation to be cognitively worked and played with, to be brought into balance with and integrated into his prior system of cognitions. Without this peculiar striving of the nervous system, without the spontaneous self-production of cognitive dissonance, learning and the acquisition of knowledge would more often be a matter of drilling and stamping in, or at the very most a matter of cognitive conflict being imposed by others, rather than a matter of meaningful exploration and discovery.

While this extension of cognitive dissonance theory aids in explaining the results of studies on information-seeking, it also leads to a possible explanation of why novel stimulation and puzzles can at some point become too novel or too puzzling—something to be avoided. At some point, it is proposed, it becomes unorganizable to the organism; he does not see a possibility of incorporating it into his system of cognitions in an orderly way. The dissonance and the seeming impossibility of reducing the dissonance, as satisfying as it would be if possible, evokes an avoidance reaction. The dissonant information or stimulation is, in this case, of negative value to the organism. We might predict that studies on information-seeking of the type derived from cognitive dissonance theory would find that information is not avoided up to a certain point of discrepancy, but is avoided beyond that point. The exact point will vary with the individual, but if he foresees very little chance or great difficulty in consistently incorporating the information into his own system of cognitions, he might fear it and seek to ignore and avoid it. The findings to be cited in this chapter might be construed as supportive of this view.

[3]While previous evidence had led psychologists to believe that once exposed to both types of information—consonant and dissonant—information that is consistent with prior attitudes will be selectively *learned* better (e.g., Levine and Murphy, 1943), more recent evidence does not support this hypothesis. Waly and Cook (1966) did not find that pro-segregation subjects learn pro-segregation statements any better than do anti-segregation subjects, nor did they find that anti-segregation subjects learn anti-segregation statements better than pro-segregation subjects. Greenwald and Sakumura (1967) found that attitudes toward United States involvement in Vietnam did not produce differential learning of "pro" and "anti" statements. But they did find that information novelty might enhance

learning regardless of whether that information is supportive of prior attitudes. Statements against United States involvement were better learned than those supporting involvement, and it was found that novelty ratings of these statements by the subjects were positively related to the learning scores. In the research on verbal learning, the von Restorff effect (in which a distinctive item appearing in a list of otherwise homogeneous items—such as a number appearing among a series of nonsense syllables—is better learned than the other items) is well known to experimental psychologists.

[4]Lerner and Matthews (1967) found that derogation of the victim was less likely to occur when the subjects were led to consider the victim as responsible for her own suffering. Presumably, according to Lerner's theory, when one believes that the victim is not "innocent" but is responsible for his own suffering, that the suffering was brought on by something the victim did, then the victim can be viewed to deserve his suffering on that account, and one's belief in a just world would not be threatened. It is only when the victim appears to be "innocent," when we cannot ascribe her suffering to something she did, that the belief in a just world is threatened. It then will be protected by convincing oneself that the victim is inherently undesirable, and thus derogation of the victim will occur.

However, in the case of the demonstration being used here, one's prior cognitions are causing the behavior of the demonstrators to be interpreted in a particular negative way, i.e., as provocations. When conditions allow for the interpretation of the victims' behavior in a strongly negative way, the behavior, thus interpreted, cannot but reflect on the victims themselves and cause them to be derogated. In the Lerner and Matthews (1967) study, the behavior that led to the attribution of responsibility to the victim himself was of such a nature that it was difficult for anyone to view it as intrinsically bad, and thus it could not reflect badly on the victim.

Simmons and Lerner (1968, Study I) obtained evidence that can be construed as support for this position. When conditions were such as to not prevent the subjects from attributing responsibility to the victim for her own fate, she was derogated. But in this case the behavior that could have led to such attribution of responsibility might have been evaluated negatively, and could have thereby reflected negatively on the victim herself, causing the derogation.

In some cases, such as the demonstration, the attribution of responsibility does not determine the reaction to suffering; rather, prior cognitions determine both the attribution of responsibility and the reaction to suffering, and the attribution of responsibility is a part of that reaction.

[5]A special form of self-inflicted suffering that has sometimes been utilized by leaders in nonviolent campaigns as a form of protest is fasting. Such suffering, especially in our culture, is not looked upon as particularly virtuous. Those who are opposed to the cause of the nonviolent activist to begin with might be inclined to regard the fasting activist as "crazy." However, the effects of such suffering upon those who are sympathetic to the cause, or who are already supporters, might be considerable. During the nonviolent campaign of migrant workers in California against low wages and poor living conditions in connection with their work in the vineyards, Cesar Chavez endured a 25-day fast. Chavez himself regarded the fast as "an act of prayer and love for the Union members" and initiated it "as a kind of penitence for the belligerence that had developed in his own union, and a commitment to nonviolence everywhere" (Matthiessen, 1969, pp. 180, 177). There are reports that this act greatly deepened his supporters' commitment to the cause and renewed their determination to wage the conflict nonviolently (Matthiessen, 1969, pp. 182–184). The sincerity and seriousness of their leader, conveyed by his suffering, touched them deeply.

CHAPTER 6

Noncooperation

If all of the relevant facts that are available to us are also known by the opponent, if he has thoroughly thought about them and interpreted them in relation to his self-interests and values, and if his attitude is still opposed to ours, by what means can we hope to persuade him? We cannot invent new information, and any arguments we offer might present no surprises for him. Of course, new facts sometimes do arise. Events can be great persuaders. Even some well-informed political leaders who had favored American intervention in Vietnam were swayed by subsequent events. But a few new facts are often likely to present relatively little challenge to a well-entrenched belief system that is already rooted in many facts.

As implied earlier, sometimes parties to a conflict become deadlocked in that each side's belief system concerning the area of conflict is so strongly anchored to values and self-interests and so deeply rooted in facts interpreted within their context that persuasion of one side by another becomes quite unlikely.

Negotiations might be entered into at this point during which both parties, even without changing global attitudes, could seek out areas of belief similarity, explore mutual interests, weigh the losses that would accrue through continued conflict, and reach agreement on new and mutually beneficial policies. But the adversary might not feel that he has any losses to weigh, he might be quite content with the status quo, and negotiations might soon break down if he ever consented to enter into them to begin with.

If persuasive attempts and negotiations are proving ineffective, nonviolent protest may be initiated. But if even protest and its consequences fail to move the adversary, then procrastination in going beyond such attempts allows the injustice to continue. In some conflicts, such as that between the peace movement and the U.S. government over the latter's role in Vietnam, the continuation of injustice meant more and more deaths. In a conflict such as the one involved in the civil rights movement, it is oppression that marches on as long as effective action is not taken against the injustices of a segregated and racially discriminatory society.

Persuasion, negotiation, and protest are never abandoned no matter how improbable their success might appear to be. But to allow an alleged injustice to continue to take its toll is a violation of the principle of *ahimsa*. It is sometimes necessary to go beyond rational persuasion, moral appeal, and drawing public attention to the issue.

Taking action—any action—against injustice, such as participating in protest, might salve the conscience of the activist and might even be good therapy for him, even if such action is not effective. But while the activist reaps therapeutic benefits from action that is proving ineffective, injustice persists. Action must be *effective* in order to best meet the requirements of *ahimsa*. It must also be intrinsically moral, for the nonviolent activist does not wish to perpetrate one injustice while he is seeking to stem another. The means must be consistent with the end he seeks.

MORAL AND PRACTICAL BASES OF NONCOOPERATION

A number of proponents of nonviolence have struggled with the question of whether or not nonviolent action is ever coercive. Gandhi himself spoke of nonviolent action in terms of persuasion and of appealing to the conscience of the adversary, either through reason or self-suffering. Yet many of his actions, while involving much self-suffering, seemed to be coercive in effect.

Bondurant (1965, p. 9) states:

> Despite the protestations of a few followers of Gandhi that satyagraha is always persuasive and never coercive the method does contain a positive element of coercion. Non-cooperation, boycott, strike—all of these tools which may be used in satyagraha involve an element of compulsion which may effect a change on the part of an opponent which initially was contrary to his will—and he may suffer from the indirect results of these actions.

Can what seems to be required in certain situations—the direct application of coercive power—be consistent with the philosophy of nonviolence? No simple line of moral distinction can be drawn that will neatly separate informational from coercive power. Deming (1968) states: "To refuse one's cooperation is to exert force." Noncooperation is the withdrawal of one's support. It is coercive to the extent that others depend upon our support for their own actions. Noncooperation by the nonviolent activist with what he considers to be evil is nonviolent coercion.

One can, of course, noncooperate with good as well as evil. *Nonviolent noncooperation entails a refusal to comply with what one considers to be serious injustice.* It involves a refusal to obey when that obedience would contribute to injustice. Such refusal can have a coercive effect on others, yet if noncooperation were to be extended beyond the injustice or the unjust system to indiscriminate noncooperation with the perpetrators of injustice, it would no longer be nonviolent. Indeed, noncooperation, to be nonviolent, must be carried out in a context of active cooperation with good. The nonviolent activist cooperates even with the adversary in what is good. He noncooperates with injustice, not people.

Martin Luther King, Jr. (1958, p. 212) claimed a moral basis for nonviolent noncooperation when he said:

> To accept passively an unjust system is to coöperate with that system; thereby the oppressed become as evil as the oppressor. Noncoöperation with evil is as much a moral obligation as is coöperation with good.

One of the dictionary definitions of "moral" is "good in character or conduct." Nonviolence involves not only reasoned moral appeals but also moral *behavior*, which is noncooperation with evil. Nonviolent noncooperation is a moral form of coercive/reward power. We withhold what is ours to grant, but what often is taken for granted. Noncooperation with evil is intrinsically moral—i.e., it does not derive its morality from intended moral ends that presumably lie in the distant future. The morality of behavior to those who accept the means-ends ethic of the philosophy of nonviolence cannot be so derived.

Noncooperation, then, goes beyond moral appeals. As Deming (1968) states:

> One doesn't simply say, "I have a right to sit here," but acts out that truth—and sits here. One doesn't just say, "If we are customers in this store, it's wrong that we're never hired here," but refuses to be a customer any longer. One doesn't just say, "I don't believe in this war," but refuses to put on a uniform. One doesn't just say, "The use of napalm is atrocious," but refuses to pay for it by refusing to pay one's taxes. And so on and so on. One brings what economic weight one has to bear, what political, social, psychological, what physical weight. There is a good deal more involved here than a moral appeal. It should be acknowledged both by those who argue against nonviolence and those who argue for it that we, too, rely upon force.

The practical basis of noncooperation is simple: no man is an island. The interdependence of all people is so pervasive that we seldom stop to think about it or realize its profound political implications.

There is hardly anything I do, or refrain from doing, that does not affect other people or does not depend upon other people. As Martin Luther King, Jr. (1967, p. 69) said (in another context):

> It really boils down to this: that all life is interrelated. We are all caught in an inescapable network of mutuality, tied into a single garment of destiny. Whatever affects one directly, affects all indirectly. We are made to live together because of the interrelated structure of reality.

As the world grows more populous, more urbanized and suburbanized, more technologized, more socially organized and bureaucratized, as it grows smaller due to modern means of transportation and communication, and as one's work becomes increasingly specialized, this interdependence grows in leaps and bounds. With it grows the practical potential of noncooperation.

In the context of this interdependence, one often grants cooperation so automatically, so habitually, that one remains unaware of one's own implication in the acts of others. To the extent that life is interrelated, others depend upon our cooperation; they need our cooperation, for good as well as for evil. The nonviolent activist utilizes this potential base of power by withholding his cooperation from evil.

Noncooperation with what one considers to be serious injustice is looked upon by the nonviolent activist as a moral obligation. As such, sometimes a single nonviolent activist will undertake an act of noncooperation by himself, without regard to whether or not others join him. He might take his individual act of noncooperation to be his moral obligation, regardless of its ultimate effect upon the alleged injustice.

But the nonviolent activist, acting from a moral standpoint, does not misunderstand the nature of social power. He knows that in order to deal effectively with institutionalized evils he must *organize*. While informational power can often be used effectively by even a single individual working on his own, nonviolent coercive power often springs from organization. Gandhi was an organizer; one gets the impression from reading his autobiography that he was forever organizing. While Gandhi's approach to conflict is sometimes said to be a social invention, the principle of nonviolence is at least as old as the world's great religions. Despite his occasional protestations to the contrary (e.g., Gandhi, 1961, p. 33), what was unique about Gandhi's approach was his development and persistent application of *organized*, principled nonviolence on a group and mass level. In confronting institutionalized injustice, one man's act of noncooperation may be moral, but organized mass noncooperation can be both moral and powerful.

Actually, the stages of persuasion/negotiation and protest not only offer the hope of early conflict resolution but are crucial and often necessary steps in the preparation for mass noncooperation. These previous stages serve to inform and arouse people and thus are a part of the organizing that is often essential for effective noncooperation.

Yet the individual act of noncooperation often plays a role in this organization by setting an example. One single example of noncooperation is sometimes so powerful as to break the ice of hopelessness and apathy. It is sometimes enough to give courage to thousands of others who, while seething over an injustice, do not quite see how they might proceed, or feel an illusory isolation in their attitude, or hesitate to dissent in word or deed out of fear.

Perhaps this is one meaning of Thoreau's (1966) famous statement in his essay on civil disobedience:

> I know this well, that if one thousand, if one hundred, if ten men whom I could name—if ten *honest* men only—ay, if *one honest* man, in this State of Massachusetts, *ceasing to hold slaves*, were actually to withdraw from this copartnership, and be locked up in the county jail therefor, it would be the abolition of slavery in America. For it matters not how small the beginning may seem to be: what is once well done is done forever.

The power of example in adult behavior has been demonstrated in the type of obedience-to-authority study reported in Chapter 1. In the presence of two dissenters who refuse to continue administering shocks, the likelihood of defiance of authority on the part of the subject is dramatically increased (Milgram, 1965a). In the same type of situation, the previous observation of one person who refused to continue has also been found to increase disobedience (Mantell, 1971; Powers and Geen, 1972).

FORMS OF NONCOOPERATION

Noncooperation can take many forms. It should be noted that in comparison with the way this term has been employed in other writings on nonviolence I will use it in an unusually broad manner to include such actions as social and economic boycott and strike, and such acts of civil disobedience as nonpayment of taxes. The central thrust of these actions is the withdrawal of cooperation.

Tactics employed during the independence movement in India included resignation from government positions, the boycott of schools and other public institutions, the publication and circulation of legally prohibited literature, a refusal to lend money to the government (a campaign to cash in U.S. bonds was launched in our country during the Vietnam War), the refusal to utilize such commercial services as banking and insurance, *hartal* (the complete cessation of all normal activity, including the withdrawal of labor and the closing of shops and other places of business), and the preparation of salt from the sea in violation of the salt laws.

Each new nonviolent movement brings with it new tactics (or important variants of the old), partially determined by such factors as the cultural setting, the nature of the conflict and the goals of the activists, the nature of the alleged injustice, and the nature of the society's political and social organization. Nonviolence always requires creativity for effective adaptation to new circumstances. A highly modern, technologized, and bureaucratized society, for example, might require or be conducive to tactics never employed in Gandhi's India, and, conversely, some of Gandhi's tactics might not be applicable to such a society. (For an extensive listing of forms of noncooperation which have been employed in the past, see Sharp[1937].)

Perhaps the best known types of organized noncooperation are the strike and boycott. Hiller (1928, p. 12) states:

> The strike, which has been described abstractly as a form of collective or corporate action, may be more specifically characterized as a concerted and temporary suspension of function, designed to exert pressure upon others within the same social unit—industrial, political, or cultural. It is not a mere cessation of work; it is conflict in the form of a corporate refusal to participate. From this collective nature the strike derives its power of coercion, its behavior traits, and, in part, the motives upon which it rests.

Laidler (1913, p. 27) defines boycott as "an organized effort to withdraw and induce others to withdraw from social or business relations with another."

While such tactics of noncooperation as have been mentioned thus far may be used in the course of a nonviolent campaign, they do not conclusively identify a campaign as nonviolent. There have been many strikes in the history of our country that have not been conducted nonviolently. The spirit of nonviolence is manifested, in part, in a positive regard for the adversary, a willingness to negotiate, a conciliatory and constructive approach to conflict, and a refusal to harm the adversary. There is also a reluctance to resort to coercion, but then only that type of coercion that is consistent with the principles of nonviolence.

In speaking of the strike, the boycott, and noncooperation (which he regarded as an extension of the strike and boycott to noneconomic relations), Case (1923, p. 401) states:

> One and the same principle underlies all these various manifestations (of nonviolent coercion), and that is a strategic recognition of the fundamental and indispensible importance of *cooperation* in every form and phase of associated life. More vital even than this is its recognition that this cooperation is necessarily more or less *voluntary* in every social situation and process, not excepting the grossest forms of exploitation, oppression, and tyranny. In the last analysis the victims always gild their own chains, even when they do not help to forge them.

THE SELF-DETERMINATION OF BEHAVIOR

During the civil rights movement, black people came to realize that the locus of change was within themselves, within the sphere of their own volition. They had been oppressed for so long at least partially because they had implicitly *cooperated* with their own oppression. When they saw signs over public rest rooms that said "whites only," they did not enter; when state laws dictated that they ride only in the rear of buses, they obliged by boarding the buses and sitting in the rear; and they did not sit at lunchcounters with white people. In other words, the blacks cooperated with demands, laws, traditions, and regulations that they themselves considered to be unjust, that actually violated their basic human rights and rights as citizens, degraded them, and gnawed away at their own self-respect and self-esteem. Similarly, Indians under the yoke of British imperialism had cooperated with the government by buying British exports to India, by paying its taxes, by attending its schools, and so on. (Similarly, many of us who were against the war in Vietnam, who considered it morally wrong, nonetheless submitted to the draft, nonetheless continued to pay taxes that would support the war effort, and nonetheless continued to buy products from companies that were directly supporting the war effort.)

The philosophy of nonviolence encourages us, as Martin Luther King, Jr. stressed, not only to cooperate with good but also to *not* cooperate with evil. There is the realization that as much as our oppressors are responsible for our oppression, and as much as we can attribute the origin of the injustices that we suffer to forces outside ourselves, even still, we too are responsible in that we have submitted, in that we have cooperated in our own oppression, in that we have cooperated with injustice. If this is in fact the case to any degree at all, then to that extent we shall overcome by refusing to cooperate with evil any longer. Under the circumstances of prior oppression, the noncooperating individual experiences an increase in self-respect and self-esteem; he becomes more than ever "somebody," a significant social force in his own right, by exercising his own power, his own volition, soul power, self power.

Gandhi (1961, p. 110) said:

> A meek submission when one is chafing under a disability or a grievance which one would gladly see removed, not only does not make for unity, but makes the weak party acid, angry and prepares him for an opportunity to explode. By allying myself with the weak party, by teaching him direct, firm, but harmless action, I make him feel strong and capable of defying the physical might. He feels braced for the struggle, regains confidence in himself and knowing that the remedy lies with himself, ceases to harbour the spirit of revenge and learns to be satisfied with a redress of the wrong he is seeking to remedy.

In one sense, noncooperation is a unilateral act of emancipation from injustice which, in order to be successful, need not force the adversary into doing anything at all and need not depend upon any kind of response from him. Rather, it puts the adversary in a situation in which he will have to decide whether he will openly coerce *us* in order to obtain our obedience. But even if he decides to use open coercion, the control of the conflict need not shift to the hands of the adversary. The nonviolent activist can maintain control by refusing to submit even in the face of coercion. Shridharani (1939, p. 13) put it clearly when he said that "the tyrant has the power to inflict what we lack strength to resist."

Refusing to submit to coercion involves suffering. During the period of oppression, there is a certain reasonableness in obeying authority in order to avoid additional punishment and in order to accrue certain short-term gains. Even the strange force of legitimate power and obedience as a habit is not easy to overcome. Obedience to the existing norms of a social system, even if such norms are unjust, come effortlessly and "naturally" after a while. For these reasons, an oppressed group's refusal to submit any longer might elicit our admiration far more readily than its continued submission will elicit our scorn. Noncooperation sometimes takes great courage and determination.

Thus, although at first glance it might appear outrageous to attribute to the oppressed any responsibility at all for their own oppression, it should be noted that responsibility and the degree of courage needed to act upon that responsibility are two different matters. To say that the oppressed have cooperated with their own oppression is not to imply a callous or derogatory attitude toward them. The greater the coercion they face, the greater will their courage have to be in order to overcome it. But a realization of their responsibility does point the way to effective action: to the extent that they have cooperated with their own oppression, noncooperation can be a force for social justice that lies well within their reach. The realization of this power can itself embolden them, and indeed the outcome can be controlled by the oppressed alone. The extent of this control is dependent upon the degree of suffering that they are willing and able to endure.

Thus, while acknowledging the external forces that have determined and shaped oppression and the coercion that the oppressor applies, it would seem that the philosophy of nonviolence emphasizes the self-determination of behavior. In a paper highly critical of modern social scientists for what they are *not* studying, Chadwick (1971) maintains that they have neglected the capacity of an individual as a causal agent of social change. Indeed, social power is often analyzed from the perspective of the influence that one individual can have over another and that a social system has over an individual within that system. Perhaps more attention should be given to the ability of the individual to actively resist the forces of social power during the course of pursuing a goal that he has set for himself. Such resistance and persistence might sometimes cause changes of the social system itself. A psychology of social control should be balanced by a psychology of social resistance.

One gains the impression from studying the life of Gandhi that he was forever making *vows*. At one time or another he vowed to abstain from sexual relations, not to eat meat, to eat only fruit, not to eat after dark, to fast, to go barefoot for a year, etc. He asked others to take vows, and his first large-scale Satyagraha campaign in South Africa began with a meeting of Indians in Johannesburg at which all present took a solemn oath to resist a proposed law that would require a humiliating registration procedure for Indians.

What can be made of Gandhi's propensity for vow-making? Is it relevant only to an understanding of Gandhi as a person or might a study of it contribute in some way to our understanding of the philosophy of nonviolence and even psychology?

Gandhi's adherence to vows admits of multiple and multilevel explanations, especially when they are looked at one at a time. For example, vegetarianism can be seen to have relevance for the principle of *ahimsa* when that principle is applied to all living things. On at least one occasion, to be discussed below, Gandhi fasted in order to demonstrate his sincerity to his followers. His going barefoot was an act of mourning for the death of a beloved friend. His vow of celibacy might have stemmed from his particular view of the sexual act as a dehumanized relation in which the woman becomes the object or victim of the man's lust; or it could have been taken for the purpose of birth control. One explanation makes much of an early event in Gandhi's life in which, after having been watching over his ill father one night, he left the side of the sick-bed and had intercourse with his wife, during which time his father died.

These and other explanations have been offered; while I can accept many of them, the vows taken together indicate a life-long experiment in self-discipline. Gandhi endured voluntary suffering in the process of experimenting with, and perhaps as a means of strengthening and demonstrating, the mastery of mind over body. "The importance of the vow is being more and more borne in upon me. ...The brute by nature knows no self-restraint. Man is man because he is capable of, and only in so far as he exercises, self-restraint" (Gandhi, 1954a, p. 387).

In organizing the Ahmedabad textile workers' campaign of 1918 (the industrial dispute that serves as the focal event for Erik Erikson's fascinating book, *Gandhi's Truth*) Gandhi asked the workers to take a pledge that they would not resume work until their demand of a 35% increase in wages had been met, and that they would behave nonviolently throughout the struggle. He said to them:

> Whether you seek my advice or that of somebody else, you can succeed without any help from me or anyone else. I and a hundred thousand more cannot bring you success. Your success depends on yourselves, upon your sincerity, upon your faith in God and upon your courage. We are merely your helpers. You have to stand on your own strength. Stand by the pledge you have taken without any writing or speech, and success is yours. (In Desai, 1951, p. 11.)

When the determination of the workers began to falter, Gandhi, "not unmindful of what I had realized during my widespread travels in India that hundreds of persons take an oath and break it at the very next moment" (in Desai, 1951, p. 25), said: "I cannot tolerate for a minute that you break your pledge. I shall not take any food nor use a car till you get 35 per cent increase or all of you die in the fight for it" (in Desai, 1951, p. 25). It is reported that this oath to fast shook the workers deeply and renewed their determination (Desai, 1951, pp. 25–26).

Gandhi then said to the workers:

> You took an oath relying on my advice. In this age the oath has lost its value. Men break their oath at any time and for any reason.
> I am grieved to see this. *There is no other tie but an oath to bind the common man.* The meaning of an oath is that with God as our witness, we decide to do a particular thing. People who are advanced, or are on a higher plane can perhaps do without oaths,

but we who are on a lower one cannot. *We who fall a thousand times cannot lift ourselves without oaths.* You will admit that had we not taken the oath and repeated it daily, many of us would have fallen long ago. You yourselves have said that you have never experienced such a peaceful strike. Starvation is the cause of your falling from your oath. *I should advise you to keep your oath even if you have to starve.* At the same time my co-workers and I have taken an oath that we will not allow you to starve. (In Desai, 1951, pp. 27–28, italics mine.)

The human mind is capable of generating vows and goals and more general principles such as ideals and moral values. These are or can be self-generated autonomous principles or rules through which the mind can influence, govern, or control human behavior. There is a clear distinction to be made between the motives that stem from bodily tissue needs and rules such as vows that stem from the mind alone. The ability to generate such self-governing rules is unique to the human being; it separates man from animals. Rules such as vows can be forces that determine human behavior, just as such motives as sex, thirst, and hunger are. They have characteristics of motives in that they can initiate, direct, and sustain behavior and make it purposeful. Sometimes they conflict with bodily needs, but there is no assurance that they will always become subordinate to such needs. I believe that Gandhi could have fasted unto death. People throughout history, relatively few though they may be, have died because of their vows or ideals. Hedonistic explanations, such as behavioral reinforcement theory, have to be stretched to the point of incredulity or circularity in order to account for this fact. There is no question but that from time to time individuals manage to subordinate their immediate physical needs to mental principles. Furthermore, although some might wish to consider adherence to self-generated rules to be reinforcing, the concept of reinforcement obscures the important distinction between self-control and external control.

Some experimental psychologists have so emphasized the *external* determination of behavior that they have tended to ignore in their research the behavioral forces whose origin lies within the acting individual himself. They have been overly concerned with the manipulation or direct control of *others'* behavior, primarily through the use of reward and punishment. Noncooperation, as I have said, is a form of coercion. But it can be said that the nonviolent activist, through the use of noncooperation, controls *himself* primarily. To the extent that an individual can control *himself*, he can exert influence on the behavior of others. In the face of promises of reward and threats of punishment, such self-control may entail suffering and sacrifice. An individual controls himself when he refuses to indiscriminately respond to reward and punishment with compliance. The ability and willingness to suffer is redemptive—it frees one from the manipulative attempts of others. Without this concept of self-suffering, no psychology of reflective resistance is possible.

This concept of willful suffering is absent from modern American experimental psychology which, still strongly influenced by behaviorism, has been more concerned with the compliance that reward and punishment *may* bring about rather than with the capacity of the individual to resist such pressures. We must consider the potential of an individual to resist the coercive/reward power, group pressures, and societal forces that supposedly determine his fate; to avoid succumbing to them at times by pitting his will on the side of his vow and against even coercion, and thereby maintaining freedom of choice even under coercion. Indeed the *will* to adhere to a vow can become a resisting force to external pressures, even when such pressures are directed at one's own bodily needs. The will of a noncooperating individual becomes an additional resisting force to coercive/reward attempts to end the noncooperation.

One of the premises of modern experimental psychology is that behavior is determined and therefore lawful. But it would be no violation of any known scientific evidence to postulate that some of the determining forces of human behavior originate within the human mind rather than outside of it. Man is not a machine. A stimulus does not always automatically elicit a particular response from him. Habits are of course a part of human functioning, but man does not always respond reflexively. He is conscious, and *reflectively* conscious, a fact that is readily available to introspection. Man's behavior is often not habitual but purposeful. It is often not reflexive but reflective. Cognitive reflection takes behavior out of the realm of habit and reflex and frees one's behavior by giving rise to alternative potential responses to the same stimulus.

When someone delivers a sudden painful blow to my body, I reflexively strike back without cognitive reflection. If someone had physically restrained me at that moment, I might then never strike back. Cognitive reflection will leave me with alternatives.[1] But the behavioral products of reflection often resemble the products of reflexive behavior. Punching someone in the nose can be a reflexive response to his punching me or can be a thoughtfully considered response to his action. Cognitive reflection does not necessarily *eliminate* as an alternative that which could have arisen reflexively.

However, when psychological laws that may be appropriate when describing habitual, reflexive behavior are applied to reflective behavior, they become skeletal, probabilistic, only roughly predictive laws that can only be superficial and situational because they do not directly pertain to the more fundamental cognitive processes of the mind.

For example, the behavioristic laws of reward and punishment can be defied by any person who so wishes. There is nothing immutable about such laws. They do not describe the nature of the cognitive processes that intervene between stimulus and response but merely general trends of behavior at certain times and places. They are predictive so long as people do not make the cognitive decision to rebel. They are predictive so long as people do not exert a will to resist. They are predictive so long as individuals such as Gandhi and King do not come around to stir up resistance and to "break" such "laws." (Chadwick's[1971] paper on the individual as a causal agent of social change is relevant.)

When behavior is studied in terms of gross input and output (stimulus and response) and reward and punishment, with relative neglect of such processes as the interpretation of stimuli, thinking, reflection, and volition, and of the capacity for the self-generation of goals and principles that can determine the course of one's own behavior, superficial and roughly predictive laws are developed that tell us nothing about the *potential* of human beings. Active resistance is not studied and its manifestations are merely regarded as part of the "error variance." When the more fundamental cognitive processes that give rise to much of our behavior are neglected, current trends and fashions in behavior can be described but exceptions from those trends cannot be understood. The study of external conditions surrounding behavior can yield a psychology of behavioral fashions, of norms and averages, but not of active resistance. Note that I am not here advocating a psychology of individual differences. The exceptions to behavioral trends are merely different manifestations of the same cognitive processes that exist in everyone. We need to study the more fundamental cognitive processes of the mind from which both compliance and noncompliance spring.

In an era of bureaucracy, an individual can easily feel unimportant and irrelevant to the workings of the world. Nonviolent noncooperation offers him the opportunity to positively assert himself. An individual can for once decide not to be thrown to and fro by outside and impersonal forces, like a ball upon the ocean waves. He can refuse to lend his self to social systems when such systems perpetrate injustice. He can say "I refuse" and thereby become a significant social force in his own right. He can transform himself into a significant and meaningful individual or, rather, he can discover just how significant he can be by not indiscriminately conforming to the forces outside himself. He can become a new and significant social force by acting on his own will rather than that of others.

When our cooperation is no longer taken for granted, when our cooperation is not blindly given, and when we even refuse to be bullied into granting it, others will find that their only resort is to enter into negotiation with us on an equal footing.

But if one believes that his fate is wholly determined by external social forces that are so overwhelming as to make ridiculous any attempt to combat them, one can wind up in a state of inactive self-pity. Such self-pity can derive from the self-defeating belief that one is an insignificant being who cannot possibly take any action that will affect society in any way at all. Social science has played no small role in promoting the belief that we are but the hapless victims of societal forces.

CONSTRUCTIVE WORK

Nonviolent noncooperation is not a negative concept. It does not imply an indiscriminate defiance of authority or defiance for its own sake. Rather, it entails noncooperation with injustice, which is in itself affirmative. Moreover, not being intended to provoke chaos, such noncooperation is accompanied or preceded by constructive work, which is an integral part of nonviolent action.

In initiating the Indian noncooperation movement of 1919–1922, Gandhi called for the boycott of British courts, schools, legislative councils, and cloth. Noncooperation entails the withdrawal of support and when carried to its limit can lead to the downfall of institutions or governmental structures. Gandhi advocated not only noncooperation but the simultaneous development of parallel structures.

> "Non-co-operation" was an incomplete and in certain ways a misleading description of a movement which was intended not only to dismantle some institutions but also to replace them with others. The students and teachers who walked out of schools run or aided by the government were invited to join "national" schools and colleges; the lawyers and the litigants who boycotted the courts were to take their briefs to the arbitration boards; those who resigned from the army and the police were to become Congress or Khilafat volunteers. The boycott of imported cloth was to be accompanied by the promotion of hand spinning and hand-woven cloth to clothe the people in villages and towns. There was thus to be no vacuum as a result of these boycotts. . . . (Nanda, 1958, p. 204.)

Bondurant (1965, p. 184) states:

In the course of satyagraha during the Indian independence struggle, parallel public
service organizations were actually set up in districts where non-cooperation had
paralyzed the government.

Constructive work need not always be accompanied by noncooperation. During the Champaran campaign (1917–1918) on behalf of the
peasants on the indigo plantations, Gandhi initiated constructive work in
the form of starting primary schools for the children, sanitation work,
instruction in hygiene, and treatment of skin disease (see Sharp, 1960, pp.
34–37). He brought in doctors and other assistants to give medical aid and
to do sanitary work. Gandhi believed that the peasants' exploitation was
partly due to their ignorance, and that securing the redress of their
immediate grievances would not in itself insure that the peasants would
not be exploited in the future. The peasants themselves would have to be
uplifted through education, improved living conditions, increased social
awareness, and increased self-respect (see Rajendraprasad, 1949,
pp. 194–203; Nanda, 1958, pp. 161–162).

During the Ahmedabad conflict, Gandhi advised the workers on how to
spend their time away from their jobs: they should clean and repair their
houses, increase their education, and engage in other types of work, such
as weaving or farming (Desai, 1951, pp. 42–43). Out of the conflict arose a
textile workers' union that is still strong today. Gandhi often tried to
initiate constructive work that would have a lasting impact upon the
people.

Gandhi's constructive program designed specifically for Indian
independence included the following items: communal (Hindu-Muslim)
unity, the elimination of untouchability, the domestic production of
cloth, village sanitation, basic and adult education, women's liberation,
education in health and hygiene, and economic equality (Gandhi,
1941).

Nonviolence entails building community *now*—not "after the revolution" nor in the distant future. It does not destroy now with hope of
building later, but is constructive from the outset. It does not offer people
abstract ideals to be realized at some later date, but immediate attention
to human needs. It does not involve brooding over our present condition
or the self-pity that proclaims that all of our troubles are due to the
adversary and that everything would be fine if only he would leave us
alone. Gandhi believed that internal reforms must not wait for after

independence. He even suggested that the self-development involved in his constructive program could in itself lead to independence.

Indeed, constructive work and noncooperation can sometimes be viewed as two sides of the same coin. If the Indians were to make their own cloth, they would have no need for British cloth; if they were to set up their own schools and courts, they would have no need for British schools and courts. In short, to the degree that they take care of their own interests and needs, they are not dependent upon the British; to the degree that they govern themselves, they have no need for British government.

However, to the extent that the British try to force their institutions upon them, resistance is necessary. But it is then merely a corollary of self-help and self-government. In other words, in setting up their own government they are in the process of casting off the government of their oppressors. Then, on an equal footing, two independent peoples—the Indians and the British—could cooperate with each other on other matters, although only such interdependence that can exist between equals could then flourish.

But nonviolent resistance involves risk and sacrifice. It must be prepared for through the development of group unity, strength, and determination. Constructive work could lead to independence by providing such preparation for subsequent nonviolent resistance, if such resistance should indeed become necessary. Gandhi (1961, pp. 100–101) believed that constructive work should be done for its own sake, and yet would provide training for civil disobedience. Thus, constructive work (which does not necessarily involve noncooperation) served more than one function while being carried out even during periods when noncooperation was not being employed.

> Constructive work ... has an important role in developing resistance. It turns satyagrahis into local leaders and invests them with public trust; and some of this confidence is transferred to their methods of action. The effects of improving conditions should also be remembered. These are likely to include a decline in apathy and an ever widening belief in the possibility of effective action as well as a greater willingness to accept the risks which open resistance must involve. Constructive work can also do much to convince opponents of one's sincerity and goodwill, clearing the way for that change of heart which is the prime object of a satyagraha campaign. It is therefore the most vital aspect of all the resister's immediate preparations for satyagraha, and it is not surprising that Gandhi insisted that unless it is carried out on a sufficient scale mass civil disobedience is impossible. (Horsburgh, 1968, p.72.)

Constructive work can increase the cooperation and solidarity or cohesiveness of the group and can build self-respect. Such constructive work is an integral part of nonviolent action and is compatible with its goals of building community and serving human needs. It makes nonviolence positive, life-affirming, and constructive throughout.

Although Gandhi's concept of constructive work, in practice, seemed to be applied primarily to the nonviolent activist's own group, its extension to the adversary is consistent with the philosophy of nonviolence. Services could be provided to the general public and to the adversary, as well as to one's own group, as Bondurant (1965, p. 43) has indicated. Naess (1962) has advocated international service as part of a nonviolent national defense policy. He has suggested such service as emergency help in cases of natural catastrophe or famine, aid to refugees, and technical assistance. He had also suggested that a service corps be organized on an international basis so that nations may benefit from working together on peaceful projects.

Indeed, as I implied earlier, nonviolent action is characterized by a constant willingness to seek out opportunities to cooperate with others in constructive activity. Kumarappa (1961, p. iv) stated it well:

> Satyagraha may take the form of non-cooperation. When it does, it is not non-cooperation with the evil-doer but with his evil deed. This is an important distinction. The Satyagrahi cooperates with the evil-doer in what is good, for he has no hatred for him. On the contrary, he has nothing but friendship for him. Through cooperating with him in what is not evil, the Satyagrahi wins him over from evil.

Cooperation with good includes an active concern for the welfare of others, even the adversary and his agents. The ability and determination, even in the midst of conflict, to carefully differentiate between issues and people can be illustrated by an interesting case reported by Shridharani (1939, p. 22). He records that a protest procession of Satyagrahis was once stopped by armed police on one of Bombay's main streets.

> About 30,000 men, women and children sat down wherever they were on the street. Facing them sat the police. Hours passed but neither party would give in. Soon it was night and it began to rain. The onlooking citizens organized themselves into volunteer units to supply the Satyagrahis with food, water and blankets. The Satyagrahis, instead of keeping the supplies for themselves, passed them on to the obstructing policemen as a token of their good will. . . .

It is perhaps not difficult to distinguish between issues and people when it comes to the cooperative aspects of nonviolence: we can find ways to cooperate with people who are perpetrating injustice on matters not intrinsically related to the injustice. The fact that the nonviolent activist cooperates even with the adversary in what is good makes "noncooperation with injustice, not people" an intelligible concept. However, noncooperation has its coercive aspects, and the referent for coercion is necessarily people, not issues. This means that in one way or another noncooperation coerces other people.

To the extent that others depend upon our cooperation for their own acts, noncooperation is coercive in that it violates others' expectations, limits their freedom of action, and perhaps prevents them from gaining for themselves something that they had wanted. However, it is important to note the very narrow and limited sense in which noncooperation, to be nonviolent, can be permitted to coerce the adversary.[2] Not only is physical injury to the adversary forbidden, but "the primary necessities of the opponent's life" must be left unscathed (Shridharani, 1939, p. 294).

Nonviolent action is not coercive in the sense of doing harm to the *person* of the adversary in any way. Ideally, the nonviolent activist will take steps to insure that his actions in no way upset the basic well-being of the adversary and his family. It is the nonviolent activist's duty to *protect* the adversary from harm.

In some situations, the possibility of such harm to the adversary is not present at all. For example, an organized refusal to pay a war tax might, if successful, prevent government leaders from carrying on the war, but would in no way harm the leaders themselves. In South Africa, the organized refusal of Indians, under Gandhi's leadership, to register as Asiatics as ordered by a discriminatory law, could not have harmed government officials. Thus, in some cases noncooperation merely prevents the adversary from carrying out an act that we consider to be unjust and for which he needs our support.

But suppose that the adversary is the owner of a business enterprise and the alleged injustice is a racially discriminatory business policy. Suppose also that after all other channels of influences are exhausted, an economic boycott is launched. But the adversary still refuses to budge from his policy, and the boycott forces him out of business, or at least severely cuts his profits. His very means of livelihood is affected. Under such conditions, I believe that it would be the obligation of the nonviolent activist to try to provide adequate food, clothing, and shelter to the adversary and his family. Noncooperation might cause the adversary hardship relative to the perhaps luxurious standards that he has been used to, but it should not be allowed to violate the basic necessities of his life.

The difficulties involved in trying to approximate the ideals of nonviolence multiply when we consider not the adversary but other people whose activities or well-being are in some way related to the adversary. It is a fact that the Indian boycott of foreign cloth had left jobless a large number of workers in England's cotton industry

(Shridharani, 1939, p. 25; Nanda, 1958, p. 317). Because life is so pervasively interrelated, the consequences of noncooperation, which is based upon this interrelatedness, do not always stop where the non-violent activist would like. Indeed, a mass refusal to pay a war tax might be followed by a decision of the government leaders to finance the war through funds that had been reserved for services to the needy. Or the business owner mentioned above might have found it necessary to dismiss his employees.

These examples point to the tremendous difficulties involved in trying to put theory into practice. Nonviolence is an ideal that the nonviolent activist seeks to approximate in action as best he can. The perfect attainment of an ideal is always elusive, yet only those who strive for it in action will have any chance of coming close to it. Noncooperation must be planned with foresight. If adverse consequences to others (such as joblessness) cannot be avoided, the action must be reconsidered. But, if upon further reflection, the action is still believed to be necessary, preparations must be made to attend to the well-being of those who would otherwise suffer from the indirect consequences of noncooperation.

Lest I overstate these potential difficulties, I must quickly add that they are not inevitable and have often been avoided. The Indian refusal to register in South Africa, noted above, could not have brought suffering to people other than those who had noncooperated. The boycotts and sit-ins of the civil rights movement seemed to aid in moving our society closer to racial justice with a negligible amount of hardship for anyone other than the participants themselves (who sometimes suffered greatly). When conflict will entail suffering, the nonviolent activist strives to take the suffering upon himself rather than inflict it upon others.

When noncooperation entails self-suffering, as it often does, participation is difficult to obtain except under very grave circumstances. Self-suffering is a safeguard against precipitous action, in that its prospect prevents the activist from entering into noncooperation too lightly. Because his action is likely to involve self-suffering, the activist will be inclined to be deeply committed to and confident about the rightness of his cause and to have a strong belief in the seriousness of the injustice in question before he embarks upon noncooperative action. The prospect of self-suffering safeguards the activist from callously deciding upon a course of coercion that might be disproportionate to the injustice he seeks to overcome. He will not take drastic action over a minor irritation. He must consider the issue important enough that he is willing to suffer the consequences.

Furthermore, the success of noncooperation often depends upon the organized involvement of large numbers of people. Nonviolent persuasion and nonviolent protest can often be effective when engaged in by small numbers, but it is in the nature of nonviolent action that when conflict becomes severe—when the stage of noncooperation is entered—the nonviolent campaign often depends for its effectiveness upon the participation of at least some considerable fraction of the people who are aggrieved.

In analyzing the civil rights movement, Von Eschen, Kirk, and Pinard (1969) state that one advantage of violent disorder was that it could be created by small numbers of people. But the frequent need of large numbers of participants for noncooperation can indeed be viewed as a virtue of nonviolence. For at a time when the going is getting rough and when the use of nonviolent coercive power is being contemplated, this need acts as a safeguard that insures that the leadership will not get carried away with itself into independent action that it might allege but does not really represent the will of its people. It insures that the leadership, before utilizing coercive power (with all of its risks and dangers of disruption of the status quo), must have the clear support of its people. If the people do not support their leaders' proposal of noncooperation, the leaders must first employ persuasive power in order to gain their support. But if their persuasive attempts are not successful in winning their people over to noncooperation, then the leaders will have no coercive power to employ. Martin Luther King, Jr. could not have boycotted Montgomery's buses by himself. The boycott had the impact that it did only because the overwhelming majority of the black citizens of Montgomery refused to ride the buses.

While the need for mass participation insures that the leaders truly represent their people, this is not its only virtue. Perhaps the most important potential accomplishment of a nonviolent campaign is not the correction of the immediate injustice but the lasting impact that it might have upon the people who had suffered the grievance. The campaign can set an example that will motivate them to stand up to injustice in the future and that will educate them in how to nonviolently confront a social system that perpetrates injustice.

To change an injustice is not necessarily to change people. A nonviolent campaign that has not increased the possibility that the people will be able to resist other or future injustices leaves something to be desired.

But this cannot simply be a matter of learning by observed example. In order to rid themselves of their fear of coercive power and of their unreasoned obedience to legitimate power, the people must themselves participate in the campaign. For any lasting change to take place, they must change themselves. The courage for nonviolent action can be stimulated by example but must, through participation, be hardened for permanence.

The need for the participation of many people is important, then, because of the effects such participation might have on the people themselves. Saul Alinsky (1971, p. 123), the noted organizer of the poor and disadvantaged, wrote:

> We learn, when we respect the dignity of the people, that they cannot be denied the elementary right to participate fully in the solutions to their own problems. Self-respect arises only out of people who play an active role in solving their own crises and who are not helpless, passive, puppet-like recipients of private or public services. To give people help, while denying them a significant part in the action, contributes nothing to the development of the individual. In the deepest sense it is not giving but taking—taking their dignity. Denial of the opportunity for participation is the denial of human dignity and democracy. It will not work.

CIVIL DISOBEDIENCE, NONVIOLENCE, AND DEMOCRACY

Those forms of nonviolent noncooperation that happen to violate laws can be referred to as civil disobedience. A strike, for example, may be illegal in certain situations. Tax resistance is always illegal. However, other forms of nonviolent action (such as protest demonstrations) may at times be declared illegal and thus may also involve civil disobedience.

Gandhi (1954a, pp. 575–576) claimed that only those who have willingly and scrupulously obeyed the laws of a society (perhaps out of an intelligent appreciation for their necessity in promoting the common good) have the right to engage in civil disobedience of certain laws in well-defined circumstances. While the nonviolent activist ordinarily obeys the law, he believes that morality does not necessarily coincide with law. Some people perpetrate injustice in our society without violating a single law. There are some instances in which justice has been advanced by breaking laws. Laws are made by human beings. It would generate little controversy to say that some laws have been made by the elite to protect the luxuries of the elite to the detriment of the self-interests of others.

It is noteworthy that Dr. Daniel Ellsberg, the man who released the "top secret" Pentagon Papers to the press in 1971, construed his famous action as one of noncooperation. Ellsberg, who has studied the philosophy of nonviolence and who once claimed that his action was inspired by the example of the life of Martin Luther King, Jr., said that he could no longer cooperate with concealing the information contained in the Pentagon Papers from the American people. (He also claims to have been influenced by the example of a young draft resister he had once met who proudly went to prison for his beliefs.)

This far-reaching act is an interesting one to analyze as a form of noncooperation. Ellsberg believed that by having knowledge of the information contained in the Pentagon Papers and not releasing it, he was being, in effect, an accomplice to the act of concealment. He believed that the American people, in whose name the Vietnam War was being fought, had a right to have this information. By participating in the *withholding* of the information, he believed that he was cooperating with injustice. His act of noncooperation was one of civil disobedience in that it is allegedly against the law to reveal information labeled "top secret" by the Pentagon, and Ellsberg had stated on a number of occasions that he was fully prepared to face the consequences. His act was not a directly coercive one but was a unique form of noncooperation that combined civil disobedience with informational power. Furthermore, perhaps because its main thrust was informational in nature, here was a noncooperative act that could be carried out without the need for the participation of large numbers of people.

It is sometimes argued that nonviolent action (beyond the first stage of persuasion and negotiation), and especially civil disobedience, is unwarranted in a democracy such as ours. Indeed, in a democracy there are many established and conventional channels available for resolving conflict, and the nonviolent activist will try to avail himself of them. But I believe that both the plight of the black minority in the United States and the effects of the civil rights movement have demonstrated that nonviolent action is an important, necessary, and healthy supplement to the established channels of democratic processes.

One of the predominant characteristics of our democratic society is majority rule. But what is to become of a certain minority group when, at times, the majority (acting in what it believes to be its own self-interests) intrudes upon the rights and self-interests of that minority group? What if it makes laws to serve the purpose of maintaining this intrusion? In the interest of what the minority group considers to be justice, nonviolent action—including civil disobedience—may become necessary. However, in order to prevent majority rule from becoming tyranny by the majority, certain constitutional laws were established that would protect all of the people, right down to a minority of one. These laws can be regarded as the embodiment of the underlying premises of our society. Such premises can be viewed as a prescription for a just society in which the many will not tyrannize the few.

The task of the Supreme Court, established separately from the elected branches of government, is to safeguard the constitutional rights of the people. But the constitutional laws are abstract and general, as they have to be if the constitution is to be a living and lasting document, for those who originated the constitution could not foresee every specific instance in which the laws would be applied. As applied to any given specific situation, they are necessarily interpreted in the context of the prior beliefs, values, and self-interests of those individuals who are entrusted with the duty of making decisions based upon those laws. While certain provisions have been made to decrease the influence of the judges' self-interests, we cannot, and indeed would not want to, abolish their prior beliefs and values, which are a source of their wisdom. The judges, moreover, are appointed by a president elected by the majority, and surely *somebody* has to appoint them. Furthermore, the majority has the indirect power to amend the constitution and to make new laws.

Be that as it may, it was the Supreme Court judges who, in their necessarily subjective interpretation of the constitution, handed down decisions that assisted the black minority in its ongoing climb from the depths of racial oppression. Yet many of its gains had to be made outside of the court and could not have been achieved by law alone. And it can even be argued that some of the gains made through the court were stimulated by nonviolent action, which served to bring the court's attention to the urgency of certain social problems.

Moreover, we have seen in our society that while the legal and established channels of democracy are, in theory, equally available to everyone, such is not always the case in practice. For example, depriving black people of the right to vote for many years in certain parts of our country is well known. And the injustices that poor people suffer within our court system are just beginning to receive widespread attention.

The perpetration of injustice does not coincide with the violation of laws. Nor does it necessarily end with the establishment of new laws. Nonviolent action concerns injustice more than it concerns law. Morality goes beyond law. The nonviolent activist nonviolently confronts what he considers to be injustice, even when that injustice is legal. Moreover, his means are moral even when they are illegal.

Democracy is presumably government by the people. To the extent that this is so, the government's actions are the people's actions. Indeed, if I consider some of the government's actions to be unjust, then my act of cooperating with that government in those acts is unjust. If I considered the destruction of Vietnam to be unjust, then noncooperation with that injustice would have necessitated such acts of civil disobedience as tax refusal and draft resistance. When the only choice is that between allegiance to law and allegiance to conscience, the nonviolent activist will choose the latter. The case of Nazi Germany is perhaps the definitive argument for the occasional moral necessity of civil disobedience in any society.

NONVIOLENT RESISTANCE AGAINST TOTALITARIANISM AND INVASION

The criticism is often heard that nonviolence can be employed only within or against a society of "humane" or "enlightened" people. Probably the two most famous cases of mass nonviolent action are the long struggle for Indian independence led by Gandhi against the British and the more recent American civil rights movement. The critic will quickly point out that the British and Americans are humane people.

I find it difficult to judge, however, whether the people of one nation are more or less humane than those of another. The historical factor of British imperialism gave rise to many conflict situations through which the British perpetrated much violence and inhumanity. Within the past century, they have participated in more wars than any other modern nation. American people have killed—as disturbing as it might be to face this fact—hundreds of thousands of people, perhaps even a million, in Vietnam. And today, less than 30 years after the German atrocities, many of us acknowledge the Germans as being among the family of "enlightened" peoples. What has happened—are all of the present Germans new people? Were all of the Nazis killed off? Have they all died? And is there no possibility at all of a repetition of the Nazi horror in Germany or, say, the United States?

War is a social system *through which many individuals carry out inhumane acts.* Nazi Germany was another such social system. We *can* say that people at times are cruel and inhumane in their *actions*, such as many are during war and such as Germans were in Nazi Germany. When we look deeply into the matter, we meet with the startling possibility that (as I indicated in Chapter 1) the greater part of the massive slaughter of our times can be only superficially attributed to the supposed viciousness and cruelty of large numbers of people. More profoundly, it can be attributed to factors that may, at first glance, seem to some individuals to have nothing to do with inhumanity or immorality. Such factors are obedience to established authority, under certain conditions and to certain authorities, and the calm, well-intentioned problem-solving activity that leaders often engage in prior to their often reluctant decision to go to war.

The perpetration of violence by people who do not harbor inhumane or vicious intent is one of the most serious and difficult problems of social interaction facing mankind.

Conflict, of course, does not always give rise to the social system of war and need not always lead to violence. It is important to note that although the factor of British imperialism gave rise to conflicts (and hence problems for the British leaders to solve) through which violence was perpetrated, the extent of that violence was partially influenced by other factors. The very form of resistance can partially determine what a government's response will be to conflict. Deming (1968) points out that although during the Indian independence struggle the British were responsible for the beating of thousands and killing of hundreds of people—such as in the Amritsar massacre of 1919 in which at least 379 people were murdered (Nanda, 1958, p. 176)—they were far less restrained when dealing with the Mau Mau, who employed violence in attempting to get the British out of Kenya. Although the American civil rights movement encountered much brutality, we should consider what the consequences might have been if the black people had employed organized violence in trying to further their cause.

Of course, the lack of violence, for the most part, on the part of the Jews of Europe did not seem to have any restraining effect upon the Nazis. If some have claimed that nonviolent action is unwarranted in a democratic society, others have argued that it cannot work against a totalitarian government; they have referred to the tragedy of the Jews as a case in point.

The contention that nonviolence cannot work against a totalitarian regime avoids the difficulties involved in trying to distinguish between humane and inhumane people. It refers to a social system through which violent repression is often perpetrated or becomes necessary in order to maintain the system as it is. However, there are a number of misconceptions that often underlie such a criticism (although the difficulties of nonviolent resistance against totalitarianism are indeed great).

One such misconception is that nonviolence works *only* through appeals to the conscience of the adversary. As I have emphasized in this chapter, special forms of coercion are often an integral part of non-violent action. It is the principle of noncooperation that makes it at least thinkable to talk about nonviolent action against totalitarian regimes or for that matter, against invasion. Nonviolence involves not only moral appeals but moral behavior, which can be very powerful when carried to its limits. It is the refusal to cooperate with injustice even in the face of coercion.

Another misconception is that the case of the European Jews is a relevant argument. It is grossly erroneous to think that the Jews employed nonviolence against the Nazis. The absence of the implementation of violence on a massive level does not in itself herald the presence of nonviolent action, which is a planned strategy for waging conflict. I do not know whether the Jews even could have—by themselves—employed either prevalent violence or nonviolence in the situation that they were in, facing, as they were, a governmental policy of extermination. Furthermore, *organization* is necessary for both effective violence and nonviolence. An occasional armed resister here and there firing a gun will not overcome the oppressor, nor will a few scattered nonviolent resisters overcome oppression by acting on their own. Without the possibility of organization, there can be no effective action at all against an organized oppressor.

It is, however, sometimes possible to organize resistance even while under the heel of totalitarian repression. The fact of the matter is that nonviolent struggles have been waged against the Nazis and also in Communist nations, although they were not led by people who necessarily believed in and expounded the moral philosophy of nonviolence. They did, however, involve the strategy of noncooperation. To cite a few cases, such action was employed to a significant extent in both the Danish and Norwegian resistances against Nazi occupation. It was used in the East German uprising of 1953, during the 1956 Hungarian revolt, and in Soviet political prisoner camps (Sharp, 1968).[3] More recently, nonviolent resistance was employed in Czechoslovakia against the Soviet invasion of 1968.

The campaigns against the Nazis and Communists met with varying degrees of success (or failure) in achieving their goals. None could be called completely successful. However, the Danes, for example, did succeed in saving thousands of Jews from the gas chambers in one of the most courageous campaigns of the Nazi period. The Czechoslovakian resistance, which seemed to be imbued with a nonviolent attitude toward the adversary, did not succeed. But it is not likely that the resistance would have succeeded had it been violent, in which case it would probably have elicited a swift Russian repression that would have cost the lives of many people.

The fact that such nonviolent resistances did take place proves that they are at least possible in a wide range of situations and against a variety of adversaries. Having acknowledged that, we can study such cases, analyze the possible causes of their shortcomings, and learn how to increase the effectiveness of nonviolent action, as Sharp (1968)—who has compiled a long list of past cases of nonviolent action—has recommended.

Certainly nonviolent resistance cannot often be launched, much less be successful, against totalitarianism. But the same holds true for violent resistance. To be fairly evaluated, the efficacy of nonviolence must be compared with that of other forms of resistance in similar situations. The Warsaw Ghetto Uprising did not end in victory for the resisters.

The prerequisite (although not a guarantee) of effective resistance, be it violent or nonviolent, is that people who hold common interests communicate with each other, encourage each other, and plan concerted action. There might be some situations in which repression is so complete that organized resistance of any sort becomes impossible, but it is a fact that from time to time very repressive regimes have ended in revolution.[4]

Even when resisters can and do organize violence, their capacity for violence is often, at the outset, or *before* the revolution, no match for that of the government. Perhaps it can be said that every revolution has relied upon a strong dose of noncooperation. When noncooperation is pervasive, it *is* the revolution. In fact, although popularized accounts of revolutions of the past have emphasized their violent aspect, the importance of its role can be seriously questioned in many cases. (See also Arendt, 1969, pp. 48–49.)

Gandhi (1961, pp. 14, 116, 157) had often said that no government could exist without the cooperation of the people. He proclaimed:

> Even the most despotic government cannot stand except for the consent of the governed which consent is often forcibly procured by the despot. Immediately the subject ceases to fear the despotic force, his power is gone. (In Shridharani, 1939, p. 29)

Shridharani (1939, p. 29) comments: "In the final analysis, co-operation of the people at large is the only reality for political authority." The nonviolent resister must, of course, be willing to take risks and endure suffering, but the same is true for the violent resister. What is always in question is the ability to resist, and the possibilities for organizing resistance against the pressures of coercive, reward, and legitimate power, even in the face of suffering and death.

Sharp (1968) states:

> Military action is based largely on the idea that the most effective way of defeating an enemy is by inflicting heavy destruction on his armies, military equipment, transport system, factories and cities. Weapons are designed to kill or destroy with maximum efficiency. Non-violent action is based on a different approach: to deny the enemy the human assistance and co-operation which are necessary if he is to exercise control over the population. It is thus based on a more fundamental and sophisticated view of political power.
>
> A ruler's power is ultimately dependent on support from the people he would rule. His moral authority, economic resources, transport system, government bureaucracy, army and police—to name but a few immediate sources of his power—rest finally upon the co-operation and assistance of other people. If there is general conformity, the ruler is powerful.
>
> But people do not always do what their rulers would like them to do. The factory manager recognizes this when he finds his workers leaving their jobs and machines, so that the production line ceases operation; or when he finds the workers persisting in doing something on the job which he has forbidden them to do. In many areas of social and political life comparable situations are commonplace. A man who has been a ruler and thought his power secure may discover that his subjects no longer believe he has any moral right to give them orders, that his laws are disobeyed, that the country's economy is paralysed, that his soldiers and police are lax in carrying out repression or openly mutiny, and even that his bureaucracy no longer takes orders. When this happens, the man who has been ruler becomes simply another man, and his political power dissolves, just as the factory manager's power does when the workers no longer co-operate and obey. The equipment of his army may remain intact, his soldiers uninjured and very much alive, his cities unscathed, the factories and transport systems in full operational capacity, and the government buildings and offices unchanged. Yet because the human assistance which had created and supported his political power has been withdrawn, the former ruler finds that his political power has disintegrated.

Noncooperation can often be expected to be met with direct and severe repression, which will involve suffering on the part of the resisters. In the face of coercive and violent retaliation, noncooperation can be carried on only to the extent that the suffering can be borne. Repression can either crush or strengthen a nonviolent movement: it is the moment of truth for nonviolent resistance. How the resisters react to it—what they *do* with it—might determine whether or not it works to their advantage. For the use of repression, while it causes the resisters to suffer, is also an indication that the adversary is being affected and is in danger of losing control of the situation.

Gandhi (1961, p. 67) said: "He who has not the capacity of suffering cannot non-co-operate." It is often the case that social change or the correction of injustice requires that there be people who are willing to take risks and to suffer.

There are, in fact, many instances in history in which repression has strengthened resistance. Sharp (1968) states:

> Instead of confronting the opponent's police and troops with the same type of forces, non-violent actionists counter these agents of the opponent's power indirectly. Their aim is to demonstrate that repression is incapable of cowing the populace, and to deprive the opponent of his existing support, thereby undermining his ability or will to continue with the repression. Far from indicating the failure of non-violent action, repression often helps to make clear the cruelty of the political system being opposed, and so to alienate support from it. Repression is often a kind of recognition from the opponent that the non-violent action constitutes a serious threat to his policy or regime, one which he finds it necessary to combat.
>
> Just as in war danger from enemy fire does not always force front line soldiers to panic and flee, so in non-violent action repression does not necessarily produce submission. True, repression *may* be effective, but it may fail to halt defiance, and in this case the opponent will be in difficulties. Repression against a non-violent group which persists in face of it and maintains non-violent discipline may have the following effects: it may alienate the general population from the opponent's regime, making them more likely to join the resistance; it may alienate the opponent's usual supporters and agents, and their initial uneasiness may grow into internal opposition and at times into non-cooperation and disobedience; and it may rally general public opinion (domestic or international) to the support of the non-violent actionists; though the effectiveness of this last factor varies greatly from one situation to another, it may produce various types of supporting actions. If repression thus produces larger numbers of non-violent actionists, thereby increasing the defiance, and if it leads to internal dissent among the opponent's supporters, thereby reducing his capacity to deal with the defiance, it will clearly have rebounded against the opponent. (See also Sharp, 1973.)

Hence, although in itself a coercive force, noncooperation, together with its attempted repression and resultant suffering, operates on other levels as well. It has all of the characteristics of nonviolent protest, as described in the previous chapter, but in greatly magnified form. More strongly than mere protest, it attracts the attention and stirs the consciences of some and might draw sympathy and support from others. While, as with protest, these protest characteristics of noncooperation are not likely to directly affect the adversary in this manner, even a despotic regime must make its way in a world of other people and other nations, and must pay heed to their indirect pressures to some extent. Moreover, those in the service of the adversary who carry out his orders more through compliance than conviction might be moved to join the resisters. During the Russian Revolution, soldiers refused to fire at the workers and many came over to their side (Brinton, 1952, p. 96).

The despot's use of repression raises his costs in a number of ways. It exposes his brutality to others and causes some of them to turn away from him. (Recall the finding of derogation of the agent of brutality in the Lincoln and Levinger[1972] study, reported in the previous chapter.) When the nonviolent activist resists even in defiance of punishment, the despot does not win the cooperation he sought; in failing, the hand of others in his government is strengthened. The adversary (and if not he, his supporters) must sooner or later come to weigh the potential costs and gains of his actions. Repression, as we have seen, already entails considerable costs. And any gains ultimately depend upon the cooperation of the people.

Much of what has been said here in regard to the theory of noncooperation applies to nonviolent defense against invasion (or, more accurately, occupation). An invasion is motivated by the hope of some kind of gain on the part of the invader. But any gains—whether they be political, economic, or militaristic—will often depend upon the cooperation of the people whose territory is invaded, no matter how that cooperation is obtained or whether it is willingly or reluctantly granted.

The economic exploitation of a country has often required not only the political control and domination of the populace, but its labor. In such cases, the need for cooperation is obvious.

However, it is conceivable that in some instances the invader might be able to further his own ends without any need for the cooperation of the people. Expulsion of people from their territory and mass extermination by the invader are events that are not unknown in human history. This occurred during the European conquest of the Americas. This problem and its implications for nonviolence will be discussed in Chapter 7.

In regard to possible strategies of nonviolent resistance to occupation, at least one writer has advocated general strike or total noncooperation with the invader (Hughan, 1963).[5] Indeed, during Ghana's struggle for independence Nkrumah led a general strike that probably contributed to or hastened independence (see Miller, 1964, Ch. 19). In this chapter, however, I have been developing the concept of noncooperation with injustice, which does not necessarily come down to total noncooperation with one's opponents. A number of nonviolent defense theorists have argued against the notion of total noncooperation on practical grounds.

In speaking against a strategy of total noncooperation as well as that of a general strike, Roberts (1968) has made the point that the resisting society would have to operate without communications, sewage, transportation, and power, against an opponent who would have external lines of supply. In short, such strategies would threaten the society and its way of life far more severely than they would threaten the occupation. Roberts states that a general strike would undermine a resistance policy in a number of ways. He suggests that a more selective strategy would be superior.

He suggests that noncooperation should take the form of "a determined continuation of existing patterns of behaviour, in defiance of the opponent's orders, threats and interventions." He stresses the importance

> of maintaining, as far as possible, the social, political and economic order, and of expressing in the resistance the issues about which the struggle is waged. . .
>
> This type of non-cooperation need not necessarily be total; the occupying forces might, for example, be provided with food supplies and other human necessities. But it would involve a refusal to obey the occupier's orders in all important areas of national life—particularly, of course, in those areas where the occupier's challenge was greatest. (Roberts, 1968)

In short, a number of writers have suggested resistance at key points. I mentioned before that nonviolent action entails not only noncooperation with injustice but the simultaneous development of parallel structures. In this case, it involves maintaining the structures we have as best as possible even in the face of occupation.

Gandhi's strategy in India was to focus resistance on certain key issues. Gandhi very carefully selected his targets for organized nonviolent action. For example, the Indian civil disobedience movement of 1930–1931 centered upon resistance to the Salt Tax which, as Roberts (1968) points out, provided the opportunity for dramatic action (such as the march to the sea to make salt), generated much popular support because the tax affected all the people in their daily lives, and caught the opponent off balance because many English people supported a repeal of the tax. Bondurant (1965, p. 89) comments:

> The Salt Acts were chosen by Gandhi for contravention in a general civil disobedience movement because they not only appeared to be basically unjust in themselves, but also because they symbolized an unpopular, unrepresentative, and alien government.

I have briefly touched upon nonviolent resistance to invasion or to a totalitarian regime (which can result in a nonviolent revolution) in order to indicate that the principle of noncooperation makes it at least thinkable to explore nonviolent alternatives to violence on *every* level of social conflict. Especially in regard to invasion, the problems involved, even in theory, are enormous, and many have yet to be satisfactorily worked out. The difficulties may even be insurmountable. Undoubtedly, only those who are thoroughly convinced of the necessity of finding alternatives to violence in all conflict situations will accept such a formidable challenge, but only those who do accept it will have any chance, as minimal as it might appear at present, of overcoming it.[6]

BEYOND NONCOOPERATION

The principle of noncooperation, in the context of nonviolence, can be actualized as a tactic in far more ways than already mentioned or, for that matter, yet discovered. The possibilities for generating tactics from the principle of noncooperation are limited only by the activist's creativity and resourcefulness, his regard for the spirit of nonviolence, and, of course, by the number of ways that he has been cooperating with injustice, either explicitly or implicitly and either actively or passively, within a given situation. The ways in which we have been cooperating with injustice are often not immediately apparent to us. Deep and thoughtful reflection is required in order to bring to conscious awareness forms of our cooperation that have been often granted so automatically that they have become, if they have not always been, nonconscious.

As I hope has already become apparent in this chapter, noncooperation is not necessarily a passive act involving a refusal to do something physically. It can take the form of physically doing something that one has been legally forbidden to do or coercively threatened not to do. Thus, during Gandhi's South African Satyagraha, Indians marched across the border between Transvaal and Natal, a border they had been forbidden to cross by a government that, through harsh and discriminatory laws, was attempting to drive the Indians out of South Africa. Noncooperation can be more active than cooperation. In a situation in which all that one's cooperation entails is lack of physical activity, one can refuse to comply with injustice—or noncooperate—only through physically assertive action.

Moreover, it is difficult to say that a refusal to do something is passive rather than active. A protest demonstration is very physically active and yet it often represents a milder step than the nonpayment of taxes or an economic boycott. For the latter tactics, many need hardly go out of their way physically (although the organizing that mass noncooperation involves might call for much physical activity). Noncooperation sometimes presents a serious threat to the very existence of institutions. It is active in the sense that it can be a grave assault upon alleged injustice.

The lunch-counter sit-ins of the civil rights movement constituted a very physically assertive form of nonviolent action. The sit-ins went beyond merely refusing to buy in stores that adhered to a policy of racial segregation. Yet, insofar as it was a segregated pattern of social behavior that was being challenged, a refusal to buy would have (temporarily, at least) increased that segregation, even though the goal of such action would have been integration. The sit-ins were an attempt to directly replace a segregated pattern with an integrated one by acting out integration within the means itself. They were a refusal to participate any longer in segregation, even in the context of temporary nonviolent action; in this sense, they could be considered to fall within the bounds of nonviolent noncooperation. Similarly, Miller (1964, p. 305) has suggested that an alternative to the bus boycott in Montgomery would have been to board the buses and to sit in an integrated pattern. Such tactics constitute, at least in a physical sense, a more direct confrontation with segregation.

Through such actions as sit-ins, activists are setting up the parallel structures that they believe are just; they are being constructive in their noncooperation. Their very means of waging conflict is constructive and does not allow them to lose sight of the issues involved in the conflict. So, for example, they are combating segregation by building integration in their very act of noncooperating. It is apparent here that in such action the ends are intrinsically related to the means; the ends *are* the means. There is a maximal fittingness between the action and the alleged injustice.

As Kelman (1968, p. 235) puts it:

> Wherever possible, nonviolent action confronts a specific practice or law or institutional pattern that is unjust, and consists in a direct or symbolic enactment of an alternative pattern that corresponds to the desired state of affairs. This effort to give concrete expression to the desired state of affairs—to bring into reality, even if only in symbolic and rudimentary fashion, a pattern consistent with social justice—represents the most characteristic and most dramatic feature of the "classical" nonviolent action campaign. Thus, participants in lunch-counter sit-ins or in Freedom Rides refused to accept the established pattern of segregation and—by sitting where they were not supposed to sit—acted out the new pattern with which they hoped to replace it.

Kelman (1968, pp. 259–260) also states that:

> through the direct or symbolic enactment of an alternative pattern that corresponds to the desired state of affairs, nonviolent action provides a model of how the system might ideally work.

He points out the constructive, *as if* quality of nonviolent action: "Participants in sit-ins and Freedom Rides acted *as if* facilities were integrated."

The fact that noncooperative action can sometimes be more symbolic than coercive reminds us once again that it can operate as nonviolent protest and have similar effects. Noncooperation, in the context of the massive obedience that is ordinarily so readily given, is certainly novel. In addition, it directly dramatizes the injustice being confronted and can raise doubts and can provoke thought about the alleged injustice and compliance to it. Nonviolent action can do this with regard to the general public even while it might be having a coercive effect upon the immediate adversary.

Other aspects of nonviolent action are manifested in circumstances surrounding the original noncooperative act. So, for example, in reaction to the noncooperative self-assertion of the nonviolent activist, the adversary might employ violence. To this, the nonviolent activist responds by refusing to submit to such coercion, by continuing his noncooperation with injustice, and extending his noncooperation with evil by refusing to respond to violence with violence. Instead he suffers the violence of the adversary. As indicated in the previous chapter, such nonviolent self-discipline was exhibited by sit-in participants. Amazing examples of such discipline were witnessed in the salt raids that occurred during the Indian civil disobedience movement of 1930–1931. Satyagrahis who marched on the salt depots, ostensibly to occupy them or to seize salt, were severely beaten but did not retaliate in kind. Those who fell were immediately replaced by other marchers (see Shridharani, 1939, pp. 38–39; Sharp, 1960, pp. 137 ff.).

The possibility of construing the sit-in as noncooperation, as I do, raises the problem of interpretation. More generally, in regard to many acts that involve the withdrawal of support by doing something that might be more physically assertive than one's support was, consistency with the principle of nonviolent noncooperation as described in this chapter can be quite debatable. Many students of nonviolence have constructed an additional category of action that they refer to as nonviolent intervention or nonviolent obstruction, under which they subsume a number of forms of action that seem to go beyond noncooperation. I will discuss this classification shortly.

I have so greatly stressed the concept of noncooperation in my treatment of nonviolent coercion partly because of my quest for a consistent moral underpinning for the tactics of nonviolence. Thus, I have said that noncooperation is a *potentially* moral form of coercion because it rests on the individual's right to refuse to participate. *Nonviolent* noncooperation can be viewed as being based upon the individual's moral obligation not to participate in what he considers to be injustice.

If I were to carry the concept of noncooperation to very loose extremes, there is the danger that I might construe any act that goes against the wishes of certain others as nonviolent. Of course, many possible acts would be immediately excluded from consideration by the requirement that they be consistent with the overall spirit of nonviolence. Yet this requirement still leaves a wide range of potential action open to question. The incident of the "napalming" of draft records by Rev. Daniel Berrigan and his associates—the Catonsville Nine—is a case in point.

What are the limitations of nonviolent action? We must be cautious lest the nonviolent activist, anxious to achieve his ends, become a verbal acrobat, managing to interpret and rationalize almost every act aimed at achieving certain of those ends as nonviolent. Such a situation would bring to mind the ease with which, as mentioned in Chapter 2, modern leaders are able to interpret their own calculated violence as defensive. While it would obviously be difficult for the nonviolent activist to rationalize violence in the context of his philosophy, he is in danger of construing as noncooperation acts that might violate the human rights of others. There is much room for debate here as to what the "outer limits" of nonviolent action should be; while I can offer no set solution to the problem, I will discuss some important considerations and possible guidelines below.

As I have said, the philosophy of nonviolence does not specify a set of tactics that are to be used in every situation. Rather, it contains principles, such as noncooperation with injustice, that when thoughtfully applied to particular situations can aid one in creating novel tactics that will be consistent with the philosophy. As with any principle, there is a gray area: in this case, the gray area consists of tactics in regard to which judgment is difficult as to whether they fall within or without the boundaries of nonviolence.

Recently in our country, groups of anti-war activists have blocked entrance ways to draft induction centers by sitting down in front of them. Such sit-down obstruction occurred during the Indian independence movement and was referred to as *Dhurna*. The participants would invite those who wanted to get by them to step on their bodies—if their consciences allowed them to. Gandhi was against *Dhurna* and often asked his followers to refrain from it (Shridharani, 1939, p. 22).

Such tactics of intervention require smaller numbers of participants than strikes or boycotts. They are often unnecessary when large numbers of people have been organized. If large numbers of young men refused to be drafted, the blocking of induction centers would not have been contemplated. The virtues of the need for large numbers, spoken of earlier, are lost in intervention.

When intervention is not sustained for long periods of time (as it often is not because of the difficulty of doing so), it serves more of a protest function rather than being directly coercive. The salt raids mentioned above were designed by Gandhi not really to obtain the salt but to dramatize the injustices of British rule and thus to draw international attention and support, thereby placing indirect pressures upon the British, which the raids did to some extent (see Sharp, 1960, pp. 117, 150–151).[7]

Intervention often creates a volatile situation in which emotions run high. Such tactics as strikes and boycotts do not necessarily involve the grouping of people in one place, while intervention often does. When a situation is already highly charged, perhaps even protest demonstrations (which also involve the grouping of people in one place) present an unusually dangerous prospect. The massive anti-war demonstrations and rallies on campuses throughout the country in the spring of 1969, touched off by the Cambodian invasion and the Kent State killings, presented the danger of a repetition of the Kent State tragedy. A less dangerous anti-war alternative at that time would have been the organizing of noncooperation, such as economic boycott, draft resistance, and tax resistance. These tactics are potentially coercive, and yet do not require grouping together. The demonstrations were not coercive and yet involved greater danger of violence. The reason why efforts at boycott and resistance on the part of some at that time did not catch on is another matter. Massing together at rallies and demonstrations provided the emotional outlet and direct feedback of solidarity that many students desired. What might pass as good therapy, however, is not always the wisest nonviolent strategy.

Let us now look at intervention and, once again, at noncooperation on moral grounds. Noncooperation involves my personal refusal to participate in what I consider to be injustice. I do not thereby violate anyone else's freedom of action, except insofar as he needs my cooperation for the action he chooses. Deming (1968) states:

> The man who acts violently forces another to do *his* will—in Fanon's words, he tears the other away from himself, pushes him around, often willing to break him, kill him. The man who acts nonviolently insists upon acting out his *own* will, refuses to act out another's—but in this way, only, exerts force upon the other, not tearing him away from himself but tearing from him only that which is not properly his own, the strength which has been loaned to him by all those who have been giving him obedience.

Intervention or obstruction, however, involves imposing upon the freedom of action of others. Recognizing this, Deming nonetheless accepts what she calls nonviolent obstruction. Referring to such actions as blocking access to buildings and blocking traffic and shipments, she states that:

> some freedoms are basic freedoms, some are not. To impose upon another man's freedom to kill, or his freedom to help to kill, to recruit to kill, is not to violate his person in a fundamental way. (Deming, 1968)

She considers the distinguishing or limiting factor of nonviolent action to be that "the person committed to nonviolent action refuses to injure the antagonist."

The difficulty that I find with this interpretation is that it moves us away, however minutely, from an ethic of means. This interpretation leads us to interference with the intended actions of others on the grounds that those intended actions are immoral. Here we are primarily acting not upon our judgment of our own behavior but on our judgment of others' behavior. In other words, strictly speaking, my action (or interference with another's action) must be considered on its own grounds as moral or immoral. My argument, of course, does not settle this complicated issue. It is questionable whether interference with another's action is *intrinsically* immoral.

My personal feeling is that the gray area—the debatable area—of nonviolent action lies *between* noncooperation as an active refusal to participate in an alleged injustice, even where such nonparticipation involves more physical activity than participation (such as the crossing of the Natal-Transvaal border, the Freedom Rides, and the sit-ins), and the very minimal limitation of the refusal to injure the adversary. Within those boundaries of questionable nonviolent action lies nonviolent intervention and obstruction. In this area I include such actions as those that interfere with the freedom of action of others (beyond those actions, of course, that require *our* cooperation). I include such actions as blocking entrance ways to buildings, attempting to take physical possession of something (ostensibly the aim of the salt raids), and destroying property (such as the Catonsville Nine's burning of draft records).

I believe that not enough critical discussion has thus far appeared in the literature on nonviolence concerning the moral aspects of this gray area and its relation to the philosophy of nonviolence. Such discussion would be enlightening and worthwhile. I myself find it difficult to as yet form a firm attitude in regard to this area of tactics.

Even if we were to accept only a very minimal moral requirement for nonviolent action—that of the refusal to injure the adversary—we would still have to consider the fittingness of acts of intervention and obstruction. The plan of the Congress of Racial Equality (CORE) to block traffic on roads leading to the World's Fair in New York City in 1964 had only a remote connection, if any at all, to the alleged injustices of concern to that organization. It involved a blatant violation of many people's freedom of action. It would have been an intervention that would not have replaced one pattern of social behavior with a new and more just one (such as the lunch-counter sit-ins did) and it would not have been directly linked to the prevention of immoral acts. On the other hand, the act of the Catonsville Nine was almost humorous (if the event being protested were not so tragic) in its symbolic and dramatic fittingness.

The World's Fair action noted above would have generated a great deal of anger and hostility on the part of those people whose freedom of action would have been violated. Interference with others' freedom of action is likely to generate more polarization, resentment, and hostility than noncooperation. As we go from noncooperation to intervention or obstruction, and as we go from more to less fitting actions, greater degrees of hostility are likely to be generated. The possible psychological basis for this statement will be discussed in the next chapter.

In any event, it should be clear that nonviolent action is not fully definable through an abstract statement of tactical guidelines. Whether one tends to accept the more stringent or looser of the limitations on tactics discussed above, and whether one interprets any particular tactic as falling within one or the other limitation, it would not be an adequate description of nonviolent action to say merely that it stops short of violence. Nonviolent action always entails a positive regard and respect for the adversary; even when it is coercive, it is not coercive in the sense of threatening or doing harm to the *person* of the adversary. Such a positive, nonviolent attitude must manifest itself in all action said to be nonviolent.

There are many strategists of the waging of conflict (from veterans of the American labor movement to young radical revolutionaries) who have contended that the polarization of conflict through the portrayal of the adversary as completely evil and our side as completely good, and through the scoffing at any signs of tolerance on the adversary's part, is a necessary psychological tactic or prelude for a successful struggle. It has been assumed that conveying the impression that the conflict is between the television caricatures of "good guys" and "bad guys" is necessary for organizing and gaining the commitment of one's potential supporters. In order to strengthen this portrayal, these strategists have sometimes treated the adversary in accordance with it and provoked him into actions and postures that would reinforce his "bad guy" image. When this process of polarization is intentionally initiated as a tactic of organization, it involves a cynically dim view of the mentality of one's potential supporters.

However, if one is trying to prepare his side for *violent* action, such portrayals of the adversary and polarization of the conflict might indeed be useful. Violence without feelings of guilt is more easily performed against an adversary who is viewed as being of completely vicious intent, devoid of rationality, and incapable of moral behavior.

Short of this goal of paving the way for guilt-free violence, the belief that the polarization of conflict through a dehumanized portrayal of the adversary is necessary is simply not in accordance with historical fact. The campaigns led by Gandhi and King showed that it is not necessary. People can be aroused to action over injustices and yet not be reduced to holding a dehumanized view of others.

Refusing to act inhumanely toward others even in the midst of conflict might elicit reciprocation on the part of the adversary and might pave the way for reconciliation, as will be discussed in Chapter 7.

NOTES

[1]If, barring the physical restraint, the entire situation could have been anticipated and my cognitive reflection done beforehand, and if I had practiced a particular nonreflexive response to the situation, then again it might have been possible for cognitive processes to influence my response. (Such is the value of sociodrama, to be discussed in note 6 of this chapter.)

[2]See Shridharani (1939, pp. 291–294) who prefers the use of the term *compulsion* rather than coercion in describing Satyagraha.

[3]For brief accounts of these events see Jameson (1963), Scholmer (1963), Sharp (1963), Miller (1964), Bennett (1968), Ebert (1968a), and Skodvin (1968).

[4]While the organizing activity that went into some of the great revolutions is well known, the organization that had gone into others has been obscured in popularized accounts. Then, too, the organization of revolution has sometimes occurred in an exceedingly short span of time.

[5]For more extensive discussions of what has been called civilian defense, see King-Hall (1959), Liddell Hart (1960), Naess (1962), Hinshaw (1963), Hughan (1963), Miller (1964), Horsburgh (1968), and Roberts (1968).

[6]Some of the European nonviolent resistances mentioned above suffered from lack of adequate preparation and organization, which are essential to a nonviolent campaign. I will mention a few miscellaneous considerations in this note, but for more extensive

discussions of preparation and organization for nonviolent resistance see Shridharani (1939), King-Hall (1959), Miller (1964), Ebert (1968b), and Horsburgh (1968).

Since the leaders of a nonviolent campaign are likely to be among the first to be arrested, a decentralized organization and prearranged chain of leader replacement is necessary, so that when one leader is arrested a predesignated person will take his place, another will substitute for him if he is arrested, and so on.

One kind of preparation for confrontation with the adversary that can be very useful and that has been employed by a number of anti-war groups is the role-playing session, sometimes known as sociodrama. In this, a hypothetical situation is enacted with persons improvising various roles. So, for example, confrontations with police or military officers at a protest demonstration or on a picket line can be rehearsed, as can being insulted or physically assaulted by people during a sit-in at a restaurant. In these role-plays, one person might take the role of the nonviolent activist, another of a police officer or unsympathetic citizen, etc. After each enactment, constructive critical analysis and discussion should take place. The value of such role-plays is that by preparing ourselves for situations before they actually arise we, to some degree, eliminate the element of surprise that often allows our emotional, impulsive inclinations rather than our rational inclinations to dominate or determine our behavior. Through rehearsal, we can increase our potential cognitive control of ourselves and thereby of the situation and make it more likely that we will be able to respond in a nonviolent manner, without profanity or ridicule of the adversary, without violence, and, for that matter, without running from the situation. The training of marshals in the control and guidance of the people on their own side during organized actions can also be assisted by role-playing.

One of the most important aspects of maintaining the organized support of the people is the willingness of the leaders to lead by example. The great nonviolent leaders of the past have not asked their people to do what they were not willing to do and, in fact, did themselves. Good military leaders have also possessed this quality. Lieutenant Colonel Anthony Herbert, the most decorated American soldier of the Korean War, once expressed his dismay at officers in Vietnam who would direct their men engaged in ground combat from helicopters hovering overhead. Colonel Herbert indicated that the great respect he gained from his men was in no small part due to his willingness to expose himself to the same or greater risks than they. Gandhi had been known to engage in menial work that others would shy away from doing, and to suffer in his physical being the hardships of his people and then some. During the Ahmedabad struggle, some of the workers—lapsing into discouragement and bemoaning their hardships—criticized Gandhi for allegedly living better than they did. It was soon after that that Gandhi decided to fast. He said to the workers: "I wanted to show you that I was not playing with you" (in Desai, 1951, p. 29). There are numerous instances in the lives of Gandhi and King that show that these leaders were willing to put their own bodies on the line, to suffer imprisonment, and to do what they would ask of their followers to do. Such leadership by example is likely to generate trust in the leaders. (The widespread distrust of our political leaders might be stemmed if they did not acquire and maintain great wealth or live in greater material comfort than the vast majority of their constituents. For that matter, they might consider exposing themselves to the dangers of the wars that they draft others to fight.)

Perhaps a sensitivity on the part of the leaders to the mental readiness of their people for various actions might contribute to effective organizing. An understanding of this readiness would have to include more than a knowledge of attitudes toward the issue. In Chapter 3, where I discussed the relation between attitude and behavior, I pointed out that different kinds of considerations might underlie the various actions that can stem from the same issue-oriented attitude. In regard to the Vietnam War, a person who was willing to demonstrate against the war might not have been willing to resist the draft because of fear of imprisonment. On the other hand, it is conceivable that a person who was willing to resist the draft might not have been willing to demonstrate because of his belief that the latter action is a waste of time. Therefore, we cannot necessarily assume that only one type of consideration will determine the ordering of behavioral priorities. The fact that a certain number of people participated in anti-war demonstrations did not necessarily mean that no more than that number would have participated in a boycott or draft resistance or tax resistance movement, for each action would have involved different kinds of considerations. The money that went into advertising demonstrations in Washington and chartering buses could have been spent in organizing noncooperation.

It is not inconceivable that a national group could have mailed out questionnaires to sympathizers with the anti-war movement (many of their names and addresses were available). Such a questionnaire could have assessed existing "threshold levels" of potential action (although such a term might be inappropriate in the light of the present discussion). For example, it could have assessed the extent of the willingness of an individual to participate in publicly counseling against the draft, refusing induction into the armed forces, refusing to pay the telephone federal excise tax, a Washington demonstration, a home-town demonstration, refusing to buy a particular corporation's products, etc. The usefulness of such a questionnaire would have been to get at least *some* idea of how many people could be counted on for participation in any particular action. Such findings might help one to decide which of the actions should be called for and where money should be spent, although this would not be the only consideration. Of course, it cannot be expected that all those who indicated a willingness to participate in a certain action would actually do so.

One might argue that the fact that boycott, draft resistance, and tax resistance groups were formed, but did not seem to draw as many people as the calls for demonstration, shows that the people were not ready for mass noncooperation. However, much depends on organization and publicity, and it could be argued that if the national groups and leaders who had been organizing the demonstrations had advocated noncooperation instead, things might have been different.

Once we have decided on a particular action, especially if it is a form of noncooperation, it might be helpful to solicit pledges from the potential participants indicating that they will carry out the action. On a number of occasions Gandhi elicited public pledges from his followers. One such occasion, at a mass meeting of Indians in South Africa, marked the birth of Satyagraha. Publicizing the pledge and even the number who have taken it might have an effect on others who have not yet committed themselves. It might also be useful to get periodic recommitments or pledge renewals from the participants. It can be said that Gandhi's announcement of his fast during the Ahmedabad campaign induced many of the workers to renew their commitment.

[7]Gandhi explicitly stated that he expected the salt raids to draw out the violence of government troops so that the whole world could see the true colors of the British. In other words, his aim was to draw international attention and sympathy. Yet he knew that he was "locking in" the British to a violent response that would injure many of his followers. Indeed, there are radical leaders in our country today who, knowing full well the benefits of ensnaring the government into a clumsy repression, have on occasion made a conscious strategy of evoking repression in the hope of "radicalizing" the young. Going out of one's way (beyond merely exerting one's human rights) to provoke violent repression might

unnecessarily "lock in" the adversary to violence and harden his position. It can have the effect of brutalizing the adversary. To meet repression in the course of carrying out a nonviolent protest or act of noncooperation aimed at correcting a specific injustice is one thing, but to design a strategy with the main purpose of eliciting repression is something else again. I have doubts about the salt raids because I do not believe that it is in keeping with *ahimsa* to commit one's followers to an action whose main purpose is to bring violent repression down upon them. In such a case, the leader is not being nonviolent toward his own followers.

However, there is a thin line between standing up to repression and eliciting it. The nonviolent activist is well aware of the attention-compelling and support-drawing effects of suffering. In Birmingham in 1963 people were arrested and beaten merely for marching. The nonviolent activist does not retreat in the face of repression and, indeed, march after march was staged. Such demonstrations are to be distinguished from ones in which the participants deliberately taunt and insult the authorities, thereby evoking repression. While the participants in the salt raids did not do that, it can be asked whether or not it was necessary for the cause to set up the situation that was bound to have developed as it did at the salt depots. The protest value of confronting repression may be lost when one elicits it by, for example, taunting the adversary. But standing up to repression as was done in Birmingham, and refusing to be deterred by it from confronting injustice, not only has practical protest value but is also in keeping with the moral implications of nonviolence.

CHAPTER 7

Toward Reconciliation

Conflict is not intrinsically destructive. As we know, it pervades nature and life itself. Conflict involves the opposition of forces, either physical or psychological, but the clash of forces does not necessarily beget chaos. There are many examples in nature of the order and symmetry that can emerge through the dynamic self-distribution of forces.

The dynamics of interacting forces are an important source of development and change. Intrapersonal conflict of one form or another has been postulated by various psychologists to be at the root of thinking, problem-solving, creativity, curiosity, attitude change, and intellectual and personality development.

In social conflict the interaction of opposing forces can lead, at its worst, to destructive chaos or to the dominant suppression of one force by another. At its best, it can lead to a new structure of social interaction that is satisfying to both of the parties, with the emergence of mutual benefits not possible before the conflict.

Bondurant (1965, p. 195) says of nonviolent action:

> The immediate objective is a restructuring of the opposing elements to achieve a situation which is satisfactory to both the original opposing antagonists but in such a way as to present an entirely new total circumstance.

I have said that the opposing forces at the root of social conflict can be needs, wants, values, attitudes and beliefs, or actions that stem from them. I refer to the opposition of psychological forces as latent conflict, and the manifestation of those forces in action as manifest conflict. It can be said that the nonviolent activist sometimes tries to develop manifest conflict out of latent conflict in the belief that only in its manifest form can conflict be resolved. He might, for example, try to bring the sources of the dissatisfactions of an oppressed people into articulated awareness, thereby paving the way for action. Stimulating manifest conflict is, however, a delicate and dangerous affair for the nonviolent activist, for it is one thing to arouse people to action and another to direct their actions into constructive and nonviolent channels. That is why, even in the midst of arousing people, Gandhi and King ceaselessly preached nonviolence and offered nonviolent means of action.

To call social conflict the opposition of single forces, such as those I have mentioned, would be somewhat of an oversimplification. Social conflict involves the interaction of *people*, not merely that of one belief about self-interest with another, one ideology with another, or one action with another. A single issue might be at the root of a conflict, but the forces in conflict are not, so to speak, limited to two (i.e., not limited to the single issue) but involve organizations of forces—people—in confrontation.

Because social conflict does involve people and not the blind clash of isolated forces, it is subject to reflective cognitive control. Conflict itself is not evil; it is the waging of conflict and its end-product that are open to moral judgment. But how conflict will be waged and for what purpose is subject to cognitive control.

Social conflict can be waged destructively and can end in chaos. But it can also be waged constructively; it can be creative and can eventuate in a new and more harmonious and encompassing social organization than existed prior to its initiation and resolution.

One of the great questions facing humankind is not how conflict may be eliminated but how it will be waged. As long as there are people, there will be different loci of self-interests, beliefs, and actions; as long as people find it necessary to interact with each other, conflicts will arise. But what will be *done* with conflict? Will it be waged humanely and constructively and be used to further the satisfaction of human needs, or will it contribute to destruction and chaos?

An understanding of the psychological processes involved in the destructive waging of conflict might better prepare us to explore the constructive possibilities of conflict. It should be noted at the outset that because, as I have emphasized in Chapter 1, violence is often rationally planned by decision makers in response to a problem that they saw no other way to confront at the time, the deterioration of conflict as will be described below is not essential for the destructive waging of conflict.

However, those aspects of deterioration that will be described—especially the spiral of distrust—often help to bring conflict to a point at which violence is viewed by decision makers as the only rational alternative at hand.

THE DETERIORATION OF CONFLICT

In Chapter 1 I spoke briefly of the game mentality—a perspective from which conflict is waged through which the issue comes to be relegated to the background as one party sets out to beat the other party, to make it submit. Conflict has its root in issues, often in grave social injustice, but it is between two opposing parties. Thus, it is inevitable that, as attitudes toward the issues generate attitudes toward the people who are involved in the issues, to some degree each side will regard the conflict in terms of beating the other or losing to it. But to the *extent* to which the original issues are lost sight of, the people themselves come to be viewed as the issues.

As I noted in Chapter 2, the individual constructs his world. He strives to understand his world, which necessarily means that he organizes it and seeks to relate aspects of it. But organizing is a simplifying process. Although constructs such as theories, belief systems, and stereotypes may involve the obscuration of perceptual differences, inference beyond perception, and the generalization of such inferences, they are unavoidable and intrinsic aspects of man's structuring of his world, of his need to organize and stabilize his world in order to make it meaningful and predictable and to avoid a "blooming, buzzing confusion."

Self-interests, wants, goals, and emotions (such as fear) can activate and direct the development of belief systems and what I call self-interest-oriented attitudes. Conflict stimulates the development of such self-interest-oriented attitudes toward the adversary. Perceptual facts are interpreted within the context of belief systems. Perceptual facts relevant to a conflict, agreed upon as such by the opposing parties, will nonetheless be interpreted differently by them, as I indicated in Chapter 2. Conflict involves the opposition of belief systems (which include beliefs about one's needs, wants, and self-interests), and so in conflict we can expect this state of affairs to arise.

As was also noted in Chapter 2, the very process of the interpretation of facts often necessitates inference in the form of the attribution of motives and characteristics. In Heider and Simmel's (1944) study, out of the perception of caused movement arose the attribution of intent (hitting,

chasing, wanting something) and characteristics (bully, villain). Once we
have attributed certain characteristics to an individual or group, it is
natural to attribute to them motives consistent with those characteristics,
or vice versa, and to interpret new facts accordingly. (Recall the example
in Chapter 2 about believing someone to be a selfish person and
interpreting what potentially could have been construed to be a generous
act as due to an ulterior motive, thereby rendering the new fact as
cognitively consistent with prior beliefs.)

The development of belief systems involves the interpretation of
perceptual facts through inference and generalization. In the realm of
social relations, perceptual facts can be organized through prior beliefs,
self-interests, goals, wants, values, and emotions such as fear, and
through the attribution of motives and characteristics to individuals. As
the process moves from issues to people, we generalize about sets of
people and form stereotypes of groups.

Constructs can be predictive and adaptive. However, prejudicial thinking (see Chapter 2) always accompanies them to some degree, although
the relative extent of cognitive differentiation is subject to reflective control. What is often involved in the deterioration of conflict is the
generalization of our constructs from issues to people along with the
unwillingness or inability to maintain differentiations within those constructs. (Constructs such as stereotypes can, of course, be transmitted
full-blown from one individual to another without the latter being
cognitively involved in the formative stages of that construct.) Thus, we
tend to move toward an unmitigated black-and-white picture of the
conflict as a whole and of the parties involved.

What we will find to be more relevant to the understanding of conflict
than whether or not a particular stereotype is valid—conflict involves the
clash of *subjective* realities—is the question of whether a particular
stereotype is positive or negative. As Sherif (1966) has indicated, the
functional relations that exist between ourselves and others will partially
determine the nature of the images that will arise. When others are viewed
as coworkers toward shared goals, positive stereotypes may develop, as
they often do in regard to our *own* group in conflict. When others are
viewed as obstacles to one's own goals, negative stereotypes may
develop, as they often do in regard to an *opposing* group in conflict.

A number of psychologists interested in intergroup conflict have
described what White (1966) has referred to as the diabolical enemy image
(see Osgood, 1962; Frank, 1967; Stagner, 1967). Their examples come
mostly from the realm of international conflict but apply to conflict

between smaller groups as well. The adversary comes to be viewed as unmitigatingly evil, cruel, unfair, unjust, and out for its own interests at the expense of others. By contrast, we come to view (or perhaps have always viewed) ourselves as kind, virtuous, just, and humane. These images of ourselves and the enemy have been called mirror images because representatives of each group believe the other group to be wicked and their own group to be virtuous.

It is, in a sense, quite natural to believe that one's cause is just. It is difficult, by contrast, not to view the adversary's cause as unjust, because it is in conflict with ours. But what is involved in the deterioration of conflict is the generalization of our constructs from causes to people and then to a polarized black-and-white picture of the conflict as a whole and of the groups involved.

This polarization of images arises in the course of conflict and can be seen to have its antecedents in the perceptual facts that arise in conflict. Each group responds toward the other in a manner consistent with its image of the other, and its very act elicits behavior on the part of the other that further serves to confirm the image. Thus, the self-fulfilling prophecy: if Group A suspects Group B of hostile intent, it might start to arm itself, which will be construed by Group B as preparation for violent action against it, and it in turn will begin to arm itself, confirming Group A's suspicions (see Frank, 1967, pp. 145–146). Sherif (1966, pp. 25–26; Sherif and Sherif, 1969, pp. 280–281) has emphasized that group stereotypes are products and not initial causes of intergroup conflict, but once formed they do have an effect on the course of conflict.

There is nothing intrinsically abnormal or irrational about the processes I have been describing thus far in this chapter. They are even, in certain respects, adaptive. By inferring the characteristics and intent of the adversary, we are able to predict his future behavior. (Unfortunately, in order to prepare for the predicted behavior—and this preparation is, in a sense, adaptive—we might take action that actually helps to elicit what we have predicted. This is the self-fulfilling prophecy.) The spiral of distrust is difficult to stem once it begins. As constructs become stabilized and *verified* through perceptual facts, suspicion turns to hostility. As this happens, one's construct or stereotype of the other group becomes increasingly less difficult to verify. The ultimate degenerative stage of conflict—war and violence—supplies abundant verification of the evilness of both sides. We readily find justification for our own acts within the context of our belief system and noble ends; the other's violent acts do not stimulate us to seek justification for them, but merely confirm the other's evilness. Our stereotype at this point might have become so simplified that even if we sought it, which we do not, we could not find justification for the other group's violence. In this sense, our violence becomes justified by our ends, while the other group's violence stands without justification and serves to strengthen our stereotype.

Trust always involves risk, however small. In a conflict situation, the risk of trust is considerable. Granted the initial clash of beliefs of self-interest, the resulting fear is adaptive and the resulting distrust is rational. For I have repeatedly pointed out that strong self-interest is an important determinant of behavior and that behavior is easily rationalized. We can fully expect that if those of the other group view our self-interest as incompatible with theirs they will come to view us as hostile or evil if we offer resistance to them, and will self-righteously pursue their own self-interest even in a manner that blocks ours. Even if it were not for the dynamics of the self-fulfilling prophecy, the conflict could deteriorate in a manner similar to that which I have described, although perhaps less rapidly.

Trust can be defined as a confident expectation that someone will behave in a certain way or that a particular thing will happen. We usually take it to mean an expectation that the behavior or event will be positive for us. In the context of conflict, however, a situation often develops in which we tend to expect the worst from the adversary. In time we come to expect, not without cause, that without considering our best interests at all he will stop at nothing to fulfill his. It is difficult to place trust in the adversary for any part of our well-being under these conditions, for the best we can hope for is that some good will come to us only as a by-product of the adversary's pursuit of his own interests, a prospect that is plausible but nothing we can place our faith in. To the extent that the adversary's self-interests coincide with ours, we can also trust that some good will come to us through the actions of the adversary. However, the conflict arose through a *clash* of self-interests. Thus, these are feeble hopes for those who believe that the adversary will pursue his self-interests even in a manner that is detrimental to them. Indeed, since in a conflict we often do find that we can best predict the adversary's actions by postulating that he acts always in his self-interests, such a belief is quite adaptive. This theory or inference, this attribution of intent, is a belief that proves itself to be predictive and therefore valuable and functional for us. Subsequent events confirm it.

As a matter of fact, our past experience in other conflicts has so strengthened our theory that we often do not wait for new information relevant to the new conflict to confirm it as specifically viable in the new situation; instead, we enter the conflict with it: we do not trust the adversary.

The theory is workable and helps us to predict the adversary's actions and so to prepare for them. It is not, however, particularly anxiety-reducing, as constructs often are, because the very construct induces us to fear the worst from the adversary. This fear, of course, coupled with the preparation for the expected actions of the adversary, which might entail our taking the first actions, reinforces our theory through the self-fulfilling prophecy in that our actions confirm the adversary's expectations of us and induce him to belligerent actions. Nonetheless, the self-fulfilling prophecy merely contributes to the deterioration of conflict, but is not essential for it. It would be difficult to dispute the notion that the actions of parties to a conflict will be guided predominantly by their own self-interests.

To trust means to let down our guard somewhat and run the risk that our trusting behavior will be taken advantage of by the other group acting in its self-interest. And the act of ours that we consider to be trustful might be interpreted by the adversary as not of our own choosing but unavoidable, a mistake, or ulteriorly motivated. Trust is always risky and, *in the context of the immediate conflict system*, behavior motivated by distrust is often adaptive and rational. I will return to this discussion later in this chapter.

When a conflict deteriorates to the point of mutual violence, events occur that take on a certain rationality within the context of the conflict itself, although they would otherwise appear to be irrational. Let us consider some aspects of the social system of war.

Sergeant Michael Bernhardt, the man who refused to fire at Mylai, reported that in a discussion about whether or not it is ever reasonable to shoot children, one officer argued that within a few years they might be carrying guns for the Viet Cong (in Lelyveld, 1969). This claim, in the context of the Vietnam War, cannot be dismissed as untrue or absurd. Indeed, some children *did* grow up to carry weapons and shoot at American soldiers. Children who had barely entered their teens have done so. I grant that what would allow a soldier to kill a child without guilt is often the somewhat irrational process of psychological dehumanization, a topic that I will discuss shortly. But such a process can serve a purpose that can feasibly have some rational basis with the context of war. When such inhumane acts as killing children come to take on a certain rationality within a particular social system, the morality of the system itself is called into question.

Within the war system, even the killing of civilians, without any

198 Toward Reconciliation

conceivable rational basis, can come to take on a strange normality. Sergeant Bernhardt found that at Mylai *he* seemed to be the crazy one. Within the context of Mylai it was he—the one who refused to kill—who was indeed abnormal. The abnormality within a particular social system of the refusal to kill is an indication of the inherent evilness of the system itself.

Yet, often, as observers of war we become horrified *only* when we learn that women and children, or civilians, have been killed. Thinking in the context of war, and amidst the most massive slaughter, we become caught up in the rationality of the battlefield—i.e., in the *rationality* of soldiers killing other soldiers *who are about to kill them.*

The war system is recognized as immoral when evaluated according to absolute, not relative, moral principles. From the point of view of a philosophy through which killing is regarded as intrinsically immoral (not subject to moral approval through reference to purpose), moral interpretations are not relative.

The internal consistency of the war system comes to be recognized as absurd only when reflected upon from a cognitive distance—when one steps back and evaluates the social system as a whole. Behavior that can be considered *in the context of war* as rational and adaptive can be viewed within a larger context as irrational and maladaptive. Thus, the massive slaughter of Americans and Vietnamese, and the destruction of the land of Vietnam, is the senseless outgrowth of a rational process.

We are faced here with the strange predicament of humankind that threatens to destroy it: that human beings acting rationally, not stupidly, lock themselves into conflicts in such a way that those conflicts sometimes involve mass destruction and death to both sides.

Only from afar and in retrospect (and when the combined behaviors of both parties to the conflict are taken into account) does the entire interaction appear irrational. The interaction of rational behaviors motivated by self-interest can lead to irrational results in terms of self-interest. This, indeed, is the nature of the prisoner's dilemma game, described in Chapter 1: out of the rational behaviors of two individuals, each acting in his own self-interest, arises a result that did not benefit either one.

As Deutsch (1958, 1960) showed, this negative result can be avoided if each individual in the prisoner's dilemma game is instructed to cooperate and is led to believe that he can trust the other individual. But intense conflict is often not amenable to the mere assurances of a third party. The cycle of distrust, if broken at all, would have to be broken by one of the parties to the conflict not just saying but *acting*, unilaterally, by taking the risk of exhibiting trusting behavior. Yet trusting behavior *by itself* was shown to beget exploitation, at least in the prisoner's dilemma game. (Recall my discussion of the results of experiments employing "pacifist strategies.") Nonetheless, the risk of trust is essential, and I will elaborate on trusting behavior soon.

The rational waging of conflict must be informed by a greater rationality derived from an understanding of the nature of social conflict. Behavior that appears to be rational, or that we can say *is* rational, within the midst of conflict can be seen as irrational when reflected upon from outside of the conflict, within the context of a larger, more encompassing system, and from a vantage point that is informed by a discernible pattern that emerges from knowledge of many conflicts.

Before I move to a discussion of those aspects of nonviolent action that may serve to inhibit the degeneration of conflict and to contribute to constructive conflict, I wish to consider the somewhat irrational process of dehumanization.

DEHUMANIZATION

The psychological process or phenomenon sometimes referred to as dehumanization often attends, results from, and facilitates the degeneration of conflict. Although thus far I have been describing processes that I prefer to consider strangely rational, I am hard put to find rational aspects of the process of dehumanization. Yet, as I previously stated, the rather irrational process of dehumanization can be regarded as sometimes serving rational purposes within the context of war.

The causes and functions of dehumanization are perhaps more diverse and complicated than we suspect at present. Nonetheless, it is so often observed as an aspect of violent conflict that some attempt must be made here to describe it and speculate about it.

Violence stands in need of justification. Sanford and Comstock (1971, p. 7) state:

It has often been remarked that because most cultures prohibit killing people or enslaving them, the process of defining some people as subhuman (lacking will or feelings) is necessary in order to justify what would otherwise be murder or involuntary servitude. From the annals of social destructiveness we may glean an enormous catalogue of names people have been called in order to strip away their humanity. Whether people are seen as devils or monsters, germs or vermin, pigs or apes, as robots, or as abstract menaces, they are thus removed from the company of men and exposed to the defenses we employ against those threats.

Yet perhaps to the extent that an individual finds justification for violence in his understanding of the conflict itself, no special effort at dehumanization is required for guilt-free killing, although dehumanization may result through the degeneration of conflict. For example, although there may be (through the rational processes I have already described) an attribution of evil intent and the like to the Arabs on the part of the Israelis, I doubt whether many Israeli soldiers have a need to regard Arabs as less than human, or subhuman, in order to kill them without guilt. In the course of fierce combat, however, the dehumanization of the enemy may arise.

In other words, to the extent that an individual believes in the righteousness of the cause he is fighting for, or to the extent that he believes that his group's vital self-interests have been threatened, that the adversary is out to destroy his group, and that his violence is necessary for group defense, he has justification enough for his violence. He has enough justification to be able to carry out his violent action without guilt (unless he has internalized an absolute principle against violence, such as conscientious objectors and pacifists have). During the course of mutual violence and war, however, dehumanization may result from the enemy image becoming increasingly bad as, for example, the enemy comes to commit atrocities (as do we). Dehumanization in this case merely constitutes an irrational leap to the extreme, from "bad human" to "subhuman"; it is the irrational outgrowth of the rational processes described previously that led to the diabolical enemy image. Dehumanization in this case is arrived at via this "bad human" image. I will confine the construct of dehumanization to "subhuman" and "nonhuman" images.[1] Opton (1971) states:

> Usually the dehumanization of the Vietnamese has little intellectual or ideological content; the shift from human to subhuman is easiest if not thought about.

Events occurring in Northern Ireland and conditions prevailing there among the Catholics have probably been enough to instill in a number of people there the sense of a righteous struggle in which the killing of Protestants or British soldiers might under certain circumstances be viewed by many Catholics as justified. When anger and hostility have been aroused in people, dehumanization may result but may not be a crucial factor in the perpetration of guilt-free violence.

Sometimes the leaders of a group try to inculcate in their people beliefs about the righteousness of their cause, the evilness of the enemy, and the desirability of violence. They try to stir up their people for violence by arousing anger and hostility; under these conditions, the conveyance of a dehumanized image of the enemy might help to pave the way for violence by further lowering inhibitions against it. Again, however, dehumanization may not be necessary for guilt-free violence.

But violence, as I have stressed, is often perpetrated through obedience. Violence in this form can proceed without hostility. Violence in this form does not even need dehumanization to help pave its way. Furthermore, it can be argued that violence through obedience can proceed without feelings of guilt about its consequences, for responsibility can be deferred to the authorities who are giving the commands. However, as will be pointed out below, this displacement of responsibility may not be enough. The process of dehumanization may be needed to overcome guilt and shame associated with obedient violence, although not for the perpetration of the violence itself. Perhaps it is mostly when belief systems about the enemy that would serve as justifications for one's violence are not developed or successfully inculcated, when obedience becomes the primary factor for one's behavior, that irrational dehumanization takes on its heaviest burden of relieving feelings of guilt.

I have indicated that obedience alone is sufficient for violence. Yet obedience alone cannot elicit the enthusiastic, or at least efficient, autonomously motivated behavior that is often desirable in warfare. The soldier is given orders, but he does not have someone standing over him at every moment giving specific orders for every move he makes. As we shall see, American soldiers in Vietnam carried out many acts of violence for which it is not likely that they received *specific* orders.

It is where obedience was the primary call to action that special efforts must be made by military leaders to instill justifications for violence and feelings of anger and hostility in their soldiers, because autonomous motivation or, at the very least, the reduction of inhibitions against violence is desirable. These purposes are served when military leaders convince soldiers of the justness of their cause. The inculcation of a dehumanized image of the enemy aids in reducing inhibitions.

There are times, however, when rational justifications or hostility toward the adversary (which can stem from beliefs of justification) have not been developed sufficiently to motivate the violence of soldiers. There are times when obedience has been the primary call, and yet has not been sufficiently undergirded by rational beliefs and hostility. It is then that acts of violence depend solely on obedience. It is here that dehumanization, present in many destructive conflicts, takes on an increased burden of reduction or elimination of guilt. I do not mean to imply that even at such times dehumanization is *necessary* for violence. Obedience alone is sufficient. But dehumanization develops and might serve to alleviate feelings of guilt attending acts of violence stemming from obedience not supported by rational justification. Furthermore, once dehumanization evolves, it takes the agent of violence beyond obedience, permitting the violent behavior to become autonomous, allowing him to commit atrocities just for the "fun" of it or over minor irritations. It permits him to commit violent acts not specifically ordered by anyone.

I believe that dehumanization—not merely as a product of anger or hatred or of a deep belief in the righteousness of the war effort but as a primary "justification" for violence needed to reduce feelings of guilt—had been the case for many American soldiers during the Vietnam War. When soldiers find themselves in the midst of a war that they find senseless, when they can find no satisfactory reasons for the war, and when they find it hard to believe in its necessity, dehumanization must serve as "justification" or, rather, must take the place of justification.

Lifton(1971) has referred to the prevalent dehumanizing of Vietnamese people carried out by American soldiers. The Vietnamese were viewed as animals or some kind of subhuman species. In a report of the justifications used by American *civilians* in encountering the fact of the Mylai massacre, Opton (1971) noted that regarding the victims as members of an inferior race was *not* often employed. Not having directly participated in the killing themselves, they perhaps had no need for dehumanization. Significantly, in contrast, he reported that in Vietnam, among those Americans actually engaged in the fighting, he found dehumanization to be very common. "The Vietnamese are turned into debased abstractions—gooks, slopes, dinks—or are spoken of in zoological terms."

While obedience to legitimate authority is enough to elicit violent action, I have argued that the belief in the authority's responsibility for the violence is sometimes not enough to completely relieve feelings of anxiety and guilt. This was apparently the case in Milgram's (1963) study of obedience. Subjects who nonetheless obeyed every command to administer what they believed to be painful electric shock to the "victim" were observed to perspire and shake, and some exhibited nervous laughter. Such strange laughter was observed in a group of American pilots in Vietnam (in Opton, 1971). Sergeant Bernhardt (in Lelyveld, 1969) reported that during the Mylai massacre one soldier laughed every time he pressed the trigger.

Acts of violence that apparently went beyond obedience, and I would assume were permitted by dehumanization allowing violent behavior to become autonomous, were told to Lelyveld (1969) by Sergeant Bernhardt.

> In one village, an old Vietnamese was dumped into a well; then a hand grenade was dropped in after him. In another, some soldiers were interrupted as they were attempting to hang a villager for no apparent reason. In another, an old man dogged the path of a machine-gun crew that had just ransacked his hut, bowing with folded hands and pleading for the return of some keepsakes the foreigners had pilfered—until one of the soldiers became exasperated and gunned him down.

Lelyveld (1969) reports that in some of these and other incidents, civilians who were shot down seemed to be victims of only a soldier's whim. Bernard, Ottenberg, and Redl (1971) state:

> Dehumanization ... facilitates the tolerating of mass destruction through bypassing those psychic inhibitions against the taking of human life that have become part of civilized man. Such inhibitions cannot be called into play when those who are to be destroyed have been divested of their humanness. The magnitudes of annihilation that may be perpetrated with indifference would seem to transcend those carried out in hatred and anger. This was demonstrated by the impersonal, mechanized efficiency of extermination at the Nazi death camps.

Dehumanization can sometimes be the result of anger and hatred generated through violent combat. It can sometimes be the irrational outgrowth of rationally developed belief systems that culminate in anger and hostility. Or it can accompany obedience alone. In any case, it might not increase anger and hostility but merely lower inhibitions to violence still further, allowing it to be carried out with less guilt and shame than otherwise. It serves to lower inhibitions to violent action, and not to generate anger. After all, animals do not necessarily elicit our hostility and violence. We are often kind to animals. It is just that we have less inhibitions against the killing of animals than we do against the killing of humans. I would point out that, when hostility accompanies dehumanization, the latter is merely a result of the former but is not really generating hostility. The function that dehumanization serves is to reduce inhibitions against violence. It *decreases* feelings ordinarily attached to the taking of human life.

Thus far in this chapter, I have described the rational processes that contribute to the degeneration of conflict and that, on occasion, result in the establishment of the temporary social system of the battlefield. This resultant system, which possesses a self-contained rationality of violence, may be attended by irrational processes. Dehumanization, which lowers inhibitions against violence, can be the irrational outgrowth of the anger and hostility generated by the rational attribution of characteristics and intent. It can derive from such processes prior to violence, thereby helping to pave the way for it, or it can be instilled by others. It can also derive from the anger and hostility generated on the battlefield. Or it can arise from a specific need to alleviate the guilt feelings that attend the obedient carrying out of orders to kill human beings. Once generated, dehumanization may permit acts of murder that go beyond obedience.

We must be careful not to over-emphasize the role of dehumanization in the deterioration of conflict. I have described how rational processes can take conflict to the threshold of violence and beyond. It is sometimes just prior to this threshold, and often only during the violence itself, that dehumanization plays an important role. And then it is not necessary for much of the violence itself, but only perhaps for the psychological well-being of those who perpetrate the violence. For at the time that that threshold is approached through rational processes, obedience alone can often be relied upon to carry the conflict through the violence ahead.

The acts of violence described above that seemed to go beyond obedience and be due to whim can account for only a small percentage of the deaths in the Vietnam War. In war, death is far more often the result of planned violence, such as is perpetrated when a pilot carries out his orders to drop bombs on a predesignated location.

REDUCING PSYCHOLOGICAL RESISTANCE

It is primarily the nonviolent action that can be considered to be aimed at the rational processes that lead to the deterioration of conflict that I will address myself to in the following pages. Perhaps by preventing prolonged systematic violence, such action can indirectly serve to inhibit the irrational process of dehumanization.

Prior to describing some of the processes involved in the deterioration of conflict, I cautioned that because violence is often rationally planned in response to a problem that the decision makers saw no other way to confront, the deterioration of conflict is not essential for violence. However, I said that aspects of deterioration, such as the spiral of distrust, often help to generate the view in the minds of the decision makers that violence is the only alternative they have. Similarly, I will argue that those aspects of nonviolent action to be described below decrease the likelihood of prolonged systematic violence by increasing the rationality (for the adversary) of alternative actions.

Nonviolent actions aimed at reducing psychological resistance pave the way for trust, friendship, successful negotiations (assuming that noncooperation has impressed upon the adversary the fact that there is something to negotiate), and perhaps ultimately attitude change. Perhaps nonviolent action works best not by confronting violence on the battlefield but by preventing the adversary from choosing violence in the first place or by inducing him to revoke such a decision. Reducing psychological resistance does not directly inhibit violence but prepares the ground upon which the adversary can find alternatives more attractive to himself. It creates the atmosphere in which alternative policies, which did not seem feasible to the adversary when he believed that his opponent was violent and untrustworthy, become feasible. Furthermore, decision makers, far more so than those who obediently carry out the violence, have to be able to justify that violence to themselves and *others* in order to decide on it. By preparing the ground from which alternatives can arise, nonviolent action decreases the ease with which the adversary can justify a decision of violence.

Before I describe those aspects of nonviolent action that may serve to stem the deterioration of conflict and contribute to constructive conflict, we must consider the psychological potential for such conciliatory action within the nonviolent activist himself. I mentioned earlier in this chapter that social conflict has its roots in issues but involves the interaction of people. Attitudes toward issues generate the attribution of characteristics and intent toward the people involved in those issues and, consequently, attitudes toward the people themselves. To some extent, the conflict will come to be viewed from the perspective of beating or losing to the other people. It will be even more so when, in the course of conflict, actions are directed against people, or in being directed toward issues have their effects on people, and attitudes toward the people involved become more intense.

When, in the course of conflict, attitudes incorporating intense feelings of dislike are generated toward the adversary, one might ask if it is humanly possible to simultaneously entertain positive inclinations toward him. How is it possible for the nonviolent activist to overcome his *own* psychological resistance and to maintain a conciliatory stance and a positive regard for the adversary in the midst of conflict?

The answer lies in the potentialities of reflective consciousness. Reflective cognitive control can of course be used to feed the fires of hatred or to calmly plan actions that will contribute to destructive conflict. But cognitive reflection can also produce alternative responses to the adversary and to the conflict itself, even in its midst.

Martin Luther King, Jr. has eloquently described the distinction between liking and the meaning of the Greek word, *agapē*, or between what perhaps can be called reflexive liking and reflective love:

> *Agapē* is understanding, creative, redemptive goodwill toward all men. *Agapē* is an overflowing love which seeks nothing in return. Theologians would say that it is the love of God operating in the human heart. When you rise to love on this level, you love all men not because you like them, not because their ways appeal to you, but you love them because God loves them. This is what Jesus meant when He said, "Love your enemies." And I'm happy that He didn't say "Like your enemies," because there are some people that I find it pretty difficult to like. Liking is an affectionate emotion, and I can't like anybody who would bomb my home. I can't like anybody who would exploit me. I can't like anybody who would trample over me with injustices. I can't like them. I can't like anybody who threatens to kill me day in and day out. But Jesus reminds us that love is greater than liking. Love is understanding, creative, redemptive goodwill toward all men.... (1967, pp. 73–74)

He has described how nonviolence combines firmness with love, toughness with gentleness, and morality with practicality:

> Somehow we must be able to stand up before our most bitter opponents and say: "We shall match your capacity to inflict suffering by our capacity to endure suffering. We will meet your physical force with soul force. Do to us what you will and we will still love you. We cannot in all good conscience obey your unjust laws and abide by the unjust system, because noncooperation with evil is as much a moral obligation as is cooperation with good, and so throw us in jail and we will still love you. Bomb our homes and threaten our children, and, as difficult as it is, we will still love you. Send your hooded perpetrators of violence into our communities at the midnight hour and drag us out on some wayside road and leave us half-dead as you beat us, and we will still love you. Send your propaganda agents around the country, and make it appear that we are not fit, culturally and otherwise, for integration, and we'll still love you. But be assured that we'll wear you down by our capacity to suffer, and one day we will win our freedom. We will not only win freedom for ourselves; we will so appeal to your heart and conscience that we will win you in the process, and our victory will be a double victory. (1967, pp. 74–75)

Nonviolence does not require the impossible: we are not required to always like the adversary. But reflective love is within the reach of all those who possess reflective consciousness, which permits human beings to go beyond the reflexive. And that is what nonviolence requires.

Perhaps part of what is required is an ability to empathize with the adversary. In order to understand another, we must put ourselves in his place and, so to speak, try to momentarily appropriate his belief system or his particular construction of the world. To understand the meaning ascribed to a perceptual fact by another individual one must grasp, if only momentarily, his network of interrelated beliefs, values, and self-interests pertaining to that fact. This might not, and perhaps should not, produce liking. To understand is not to condone. But such understanding might eliminate hatred on a reflective level.

Nor does nonviolence require that we not be angry. Often only those who are angry over an injustice rise to initiate action against it. Nonviolence does not require the elimination of certain emotions (if that were possible) or even the suppression of certain emotions (which, in a number of psychological respects, would be undesirable). Some of those people who have been angered by injustice have allowed that anger to steer them into violence; certain others have reflectively channeled their anger into constructive nonviolent action. Nonviolent action may entail cognitively controlled anger.

Perhaps conflict can be constructively waged to the extent that the focus of opposition can be limited to the issue itself while, at the same time, positive bonds between the people involved in the conflict can be established or strengthened. This ideal cannot be perfectly attained because of the attribution processes already mentioned and because actions directed toward issues affect the people involved in those issues. Yet, within this limit, the confrontational aspects of social conflict can be relatively more or less issue-oriented. Because such confrontation, even when confined as narrowly as possible to the issue, will tend to generate negative attitudes toward the people involved, sources of positive bonds between the people must be explored even in the midst of the conflict.

Ideally, the stance of the nonviolent activist is both firm and conciliatory. In regard to the issues it leaves no room for appeasement or the compromising of principles, although the activist is always open to persuasion or negotiation. In regard to the adversary, it is always conciliatory. Noncooperation with the evil deed but not with the evil doer, as Kumarappa has put it, while cooperating with him in what is good, can be viewed as an attempt to meet these criteria of the constructive waging of conflict.

Limiting actions and words of an oppositional nature to the issue itself can serve to keep the focus of conflict on the issue, where it belongs, and can serve to abort many of the rationales for initiating violence against us that the adversary might have otherwise developed.

Refusing to injure the adversary might go a long way toward breaking the spiral of the self-fulfilling prophecy, and thus serve to hinder the degeneration and widening of the conflict. It may serve to minimize the adversary's fear, which is often a source of hostility and planned violence.

Deming (1968) says of nonviolence:

> Because the human rights of the adversary are respected, though his actions, his official policies are not, the focus of attention becomes those actions, those policies, and their true nature. The issue cannot be avoided. The antagonist cannot take the interference with his actions personally, because his person is not threatened, and he is forced to begin to acknowledge the reality of the grievance against him.

She speaks of the two hands that the activist puts upon the adversary, one "making it impossible for him to operate within the system as usual" and the other tempering his response to this disruption.

I pointed out in the last chapter that Gandhi's movement suffered fewer casualties than the Mau Mau movement in Kenya, although both were against the British. Referring to the violence that the British did perpetrate in India, Deming (1968) states:

> There was a limit, nevertheless, to the violence they could justify to themselves—or felt they could justify to the world. Watching any nonviolent struggle, it is always startling to learn how long it can take the antagonist to set such limits; but he finally does feel constrained to set them—especially if his actions are well publicized.

She points out that in Kenya, "where the British could cite as provocation the violence used against them, they hardly felt constrained to set any limits at all on their actions. . . ."

Deming insists that one will, in the long run, receive fewer casualties when waging conflict nonviolently. She claims that many people are unable to comprehend this because they are misled by the fact that they are suffering casualties while the adversary is not. But, she says, "they fail to recognize that they are suffering *fewer* casualties than they would be if they turned to violence." Furthermore, Deming points out that people are used to taking greater casualties as an indication of defeat, but that in nonviolent struggle victory is not measured in these terms, for the nonviolent activist was not out to punish the adversary nor to seek revenge in the first place.

Because nonviolent action is, in certain respects, firm and unyielding, it can never entirely eliminate frustration and hostility from the realm of the conflict. Noncooperation frustrates others' self-interests and thereby generates hostility. One of the problems of nonviolent action is how to generate the minimal frustration, fear, hostility, and psychological resistance that is possible within the context of conflict and social change. Because noncooperation does not obstruct others' freedom of action except insofar as that freedom depended upon our support, and does not violate or threaten injury to the person of the adversary, it might generate relatively less hostility than other forms of coercion. But our refusal to carry out the will of the adversary will in itself be frustrating to him, especially if we have cooperated in the past and he expects that as a matter of course we will continue to do so.

There is some experimental evidence to suggest that what is interpreted by the victim of frustration as nonarbitrary would generate less hostility than frustration that is interpreted by the victim as arbitrarily induced. For example, if you have left an article of yours in a repair shop and come to pick it up at the appointed time, you might feel angry and hostile if the repair man informs you that it is not ready but does not give you any reasons for the delay. But if the repair man were to inform you that the item is not ready because of a death in the family, you might not feel irritated at all.

When these and similar hypothetical situations were presented to people in the form of questionnaires, it was found that subjects tend to believe that they and others would feel less angry and hostile in the nonarbitrary frustrating situations (Pastore, 1952; Cohen, 1955).

Some investigators—pointing out that the above findings could indicate either a reduction of hostile tendency or an inhibition of the overt expression of hostility in nonarbitrary conditions—have found evidence for the latter position (Rothaus and Worchel, 1960; Kregarman and Worchel, 1961; Burnstein and Worchel, 1962). In other words, the instigation of hostile tendencies might be similar in both cases, but it might be less socially acceptable to respond with overt hostility in a nonarbitrary frustrating situation.

The reduction of hostile tendencies is, however, not entirely ruled out by these findings. Some support was found for it under experimental conditions of actual frustration in the Burnstein and Worchel study. My personal experience has been so compelling on this point—i.e., while waiting through an unusual delay for something, I have often had the subjective experience of a sudden vanishing of anger after someone had given me substantial and believable reasons for the delay—that I have no doubt that it is a factor in the phenomenon under discussion.

In either case, the findings might have implications for nonviolent action in a conflict situation. It is possible that by fully explaining to the adversary and to third parties the reasons for our noncooperation and our felt necessity for it, we might thereby reduce the amount of the adversary's resultant hostility, or the amount of overt hostility that he will feel capable of justifying to third parties.

Unfortunately, it can be argued that the crucial difference between the arbitrary and nonarbitrary frustration conditions in the above experiments was that in the latter the frustrating agent did not seem to be entirely responsible for the resulting frustration. It would be difficult for the nonviolent activist to maintain that his noncooperation was beyond his control.

However, there are a number of other aspects of nonviolent action that might serve to hold to a minimum the psychological resistance that will be generated. These include the attempt to limit oppositional actions and words to the issue itself and the refusal to injure the adversary—factors that I have already mentioned. They also include employing rational persuasion attempts throughout the conflict, standing always ready to negotiate, and refusing to knowingly exaggerate the justness of our position or the evils of the adversary's position.

Other factors that may contribute to the constructive waging of conflict include the nonviolent activist's willingness to make every effort to resolve the conflict through established channels before taking more drastic action, always allowing the adversary room for face-saving action, and offering or leaving him a way in which he can participate in a constructive solution and thereby even gain in stature in the eyes of the public, rather than suffer humiliation (see Bondurant, 1965, p. 40). It is important to try to alleviate all conditions, such as fear of humiliation, that might hinder the adversary from making conciliatory moves.

When we refuse to portray the conflict in black-and-white terms, when we show a willingness to acknowledge the validity of certain of the adversary's arguments, and when we refrain from taunting or insulting him, we open the door to the possibility that the adversary will begin to trust us.

TRUSTING BEHAVIOR

I said earlier that trust involves risk and that behavior motivated by distrust has its rational and adaptive aspects. We tend to expect the worst from the adversary in conflict in that we anticipate that he will pursue his own self-interest without regard for ours. Indeed such a theory of distrust, such an attribution of intent is, as I have said, often confirmed for us by subsequent events. It is a theory that often proves itself to be predictive and therefore valuable (although our own actions, and thus a self-fulfilling prophecy, may be making a partial contribution to the confirmation of the theory).

Perhaps the only way to break the spiral of distrust in conflict is by exhibiting trusting behavior. But here we run the considerable risk that our trusting behavior will be taken advantage of by the adversary acting in his own self-interest. Furthermore, our actions might not be interpreted by the adversary in the way we had intended them. He might regard our actions as signs of weakness; he might suspect diabolical trickery; or he might find evidence enough that can be interpreted as supportive of a theory that we are out to destroy him. From the perspective of his own theory of distrust, the act of ours that we consider to be trusting is likely to be interpreted otherwise by the adversary.

In fact, when we initially weigh the risk of trust against the rationality of distrust, there is no contest. Only when we step back from the conflict, cognitively extricate ourselves from our immediate involvement in it, and view it in the context of our knowledge of many conflicts in the past, do we find that our distrust-motivated behavior (rational though it is within the context of the immediate situation) is bound to contribute to a descending spiral of distrust and the deterioration of conflict, with resultant losses for both sides. Thus, only when interpreted in a larger context, do we find that distrust-motivated behavior is indeed quite risky. We then discover that distrust-motivated behavior involves a risk as great as, or greater than, trust-motivated behavior.

However, within the context of the immediate conflict, trusting behavior becomes rational rather than foolhardy only when embarked upon from a *base of firmness*. Our trusting behavior, by itself, may be taken advantage of by the adversary. But, when combined with a demonstration of our firmness and our intent and capacity to remain firm (e.g., our capacity to renew a strike that had been called off as an indication of good faith), the adversary may eventually come to realize that his reciprocation of our trusting behavior is in his interests as well as ours. This combination of trusting behavior and firmness, such as the power of noncooperation—the capacity for which is never relinquished—is a part of nonviolent strategy.

In order to wear down the adversary's theory of distrust, our trusting acts need to be numerous and consistent. Although theories do change when they come to be increasingly less predictive and therefore less useful and adaptive, the adversary is not prone to easily give up his theory, which has proved to be predictive in past conflicts and, to some extent, even in the present one. People cling to theories long after they have ceased to be predictive of important events by—with a slight stretching of concepts and acknowledgement of "exceptional cases"—explaining new events in the context of the old theory (see Chapter 2).

Thus, we can expect our initial actions to be interpreted in ways other than we had intended. It is very likely that the adversary will be able to maintain his theory of distrust for some time by interpreting our acts accordingly. Yet, the ability to predict our future actions is of value to the adversary. When we combine our trusting actions with firmness, we might make it advantageous for the adversary to relinquish his old theory or at least to hesitantly take some action of his own on an experimental basis, an action that he considers to be inconsistent with his theory. In other words, we might act in such a way as to make, in his view, the possible benefits that he might gain from taking certain actions that are inconsistent with his theory worth the risk. Once he takes such action, it will be easier for us to change his theory through reciprocation, thereby turning a spiral of distrust into one of trust. Thus, there is some hope that over a long series of consistent actions on our part (but only then) it might be possible to induce the adversary to relinquish his old construct and to evolve an expectation of trust, by inducing in him a self-interest-oriented attitude that points in a different direction than the one that underlies his old construct.

As I have said, if anything is to induce trust, it will be our actions and not our words. The adversary has probably had much prior experience with betrayals of words, or what he interpreted as such, and since everyone *speaks* good intentions, he wants to see them put into action. We will instill trust in our words only by demonstrating that they are consistent with our actions, but this will come about only after we have shown our actions to be consistent in themselves. The spiral of distrust, if broken at all, will be broken by one of the parties to the conflict not just saying but *acting*, unilaterally, by taking the risk of trust.

I have been talking thus far of what I have called trusting behavior. It might be useful at this point to make a conceptual subdivision between what I will call trustworthy behavior and trustful behavior. I will define a trustworthy act as that which involves not taking advantage of the adversary. A trustworthy act can be risky in that it may prolong the hardships we might have to endure before achieving our goals. It may elicit the attribution of trustworthiness. I will define a trustful act as one that involves at least partially placing the responsibility for one's own immediate destiny in the hands of the adversary. In other words, it involves knowingly entering a situation in which the adversary will have the opportunity to take advantage of us. In a sense, the nonviolent activist does this every time he enters unarmed into a situation in which the adversary is armed for violence. In practice, the distinction I have made is not often clear-cut, and an act may have both trustworthy and trustful characteristics.

Gandhi has given us a number of surprising examples of trusting actions. He was often criticized because of them as being naive and inclined to throw away opportunities. Perhaps such criticism has come from a misunderstanding of his strategy. There is much evidence to indicate that Gandhi was a very shrewd and astute political leader; it is difficult to believe that he was naive. Perhaps we can best understand the actions in question and learn something of value from them if we entertain the possibility that taking the risk of trust was an integral part of Gandhi's strategy.

Gandhi took a notable trustworthy action during his South African movement. European railroad workers in South Africa had gone out on strike just at a time when Gandhi's nonviolent campaign, the government's brutal and repressive reaction to it, and the ensuing unfavorable publicity had placed the government in a difficult position in regard to the Indians. Rather than taking advantage of the added difficulties that the unrelated strike had presented to the government, Gandhi suspended his movement until the strike was over—a move that has been said to have positively impressed his opponents and might have contributed to the subsequent settlement (Shridharani, 1939, pp. 78–79; Nanda, 1958, p. 118; Erikson, 1969, pp. 215–216).

On another occasion, in India in 1922, Gandhi suspended a mass civil disobedience campaign (much to the dismay of his colleagues) because some violence had broken out on the part of his people and he sensed that the campaign might degenerate into a violent struggle (Shridharani, 1939, p. 129; Nanda, 1958, pp. 231–232). There were indications that there was some feeling on the part of the British that such a move was a sign of weakness on the part of Gandhi's movement (Nanda, 1958, p. 237).

In order to attempt to break the spiral of distrust that often accompanies conflict, one can also take trustful actions. It should be noted that a trustful act need not stem from a trustful attitude. The nonviolent activist may have an exceedingly low expectation that his trustful behavior will not be taken advantage of by his adversary. He may have much reason to be suspicious of the adversary. But he may take the risk in action anyway. He is not immune from the spiral of distrust, but he can attempt to break it—both for himself and the adversary—with his actions.

In South Africa, Gandhi led a civil disobedience campaign against a registration act that ordered a number of humiliating procedures for

Asiatics. Gandhi then agreed to a settlement offered by General Smuts: the registration act would be repealed if the Indians first registered voluntarily. Gandhi was criticized by his own followers. They thought that they should withhold voluntary registration until *after* the act was repealed. But Gandhi, who once said that a Satyagrahi is born to be deceived, answered that a Satyagrahi should never be afraid of trusting the opponent, even if that trust has been betrayed many times before; that "if the opponent plays him false twenty times, the Satyagrahi is ready to trust him for the twenty-first time" (Gandhi, 1954b, p. 159). He also answered that noncooperation could be resumed at any time in the form of refusing to show the registration certificates to authorities when ordered to do so, if it turned out that the Government did not follow through on its promise. Thus, "to say that in trusting the Government we play into their hands is to betray an ignorance of the principles of Satyagraha" (Gandhi, 1954b, p. 159). This stand subjected Gandhi to attempts on his life by some of his own followers who felt that he had betrayed them. As it turned out, General Smuts did not repeal the law, and Gandhi had to renew the struggle (Gandhi, 1954b; Nanda, 1958, pp. 90–104).

Gandhi had often been accused of settling for too little in negotiations. But, as in the Champaran campaign, he was willing to compromise on matters other than principle in order to show his good faith to the adversary and relieve some of the bitterness that might have been incurred in conflict. In Champaran, he knew that the big gain was the psychological change of the peasants, who now no longer feared the planters, and that the actual extent of the immediate settlement was of secondary importance (Nanda, 1958, pp. 160–161).

There were other instances in which it had been claimed that Gandhi put too much faith in his adversaries and conceded too much in negotiations. But there are indications that in the long run he gained the respect of even those who had deceived him (Nanda, 1958, p. 119).

In contemplating the strange trusting actions of Gandhi, it must again be emphasized that he sought far more in conflict than the gain of immediate objectives. He sought the friendship of the adversary and strove for an outcome in which there would be no hostility or bad feelings between the parties. Furthermore, he did not want merely grudgingly given concessions, but actually sought to ultimately convince the adversary of the justness of his cause! He wanted to convert the adversary. To Gandhi, Satyagraha was a process of conversion. I will return to these themes shortly.

Acts of reconciliation might at first be interpreted by the adversary as insincere, as mistakes, as signs of weakness or admissions of guilt, or as indications of ulterior motivation. In the context of conflict, they will be looked upon with suspicion by the adversary and they might be taken advantage of. But when they are combined with firmness, in the long run the adversary might become aware of his own self-interest in reciprocating such acts. When acts that lend themselves to a conciliatory interpretation occur over and over again, a pattern emerges that is difficult to interpret otherwise, even by the adversary.

The idea of a series of conciliatory acts finally generating reciprocation is behind Osgood's (1962) GRIT (Graduated Reciprocation in Tension-reduction) proposal, designed specifically for reversing the arms race between the United States and the Soviet Union.

Osgood has described the arms race as a tension-increasing spiral of terror. He has offered his proposal as a means of reducing tension levels and mutual fears and suspicions, while maintaining security. His aim is to gradually create an atmosphere of mutual trust within which negotiations between the conflicting parties can then be successfully carried out. He has pointed out that successful negotiations can proceed only when some mutual trust has first been established. Trust must be demonstrated in action before words will be trusted. Trust is more likely to be established by actions rather than by words. It is only after some mutual trust has been established that negotiations can hold much promise and that confidence can be placed in contracts and agreements.

The GRIT proposal directs one party to the conflict to take unilateral initiatives representing a sincere intent to reduce tensions and is designed to induce reciprocation. These initiatives, in regard to risk potential, should begin on a small scale and gradually be increased in risk in accordance with the degree of reciprocation that has been elicited from the other party.[2] In the context of the arms race, early steps might include the closing of an overseas military base or the withdrawal of military troops from an area close to the other nation's border. "The approach to disarmament implicit in GRIT is to give up nuclear deterrents last." The elimination of the nuclear weapons would finally be achieved through negotiation.

The unilateral initiatives proposed are not limited to the military sphere. The initiatives can be carried out in any area of potential intergroup relations. Osgood has suggested such actions as providing urgently needed medical aid, sharing medical and scientific information, eliminating tariff barriers, and reducing travel restrictions on the other nation's tourists in our country.

Recognizing that actions (though possibly less so than words) would be open to various interpretations, Osgood has suggested that the prior announcement and clarification of each act might serve to limit the range of interpretation. Toward this end, they should also be as unambiguous, concrete, and open to verification as possible.

In short, the GRIT proposal calls for a series of unilaterally initiated conciliatory acts that are continued over a considerable period of time, regardless of whether there is immediate reciprocation. The assumption is that eventually the pattern of actions developed will give rise to the adversary's interpretation of our intent as sincere and will induce reciprocation. When the adversary begins to reciprocate, we can steadily increase the magnitude of our acts and engage the adversary in a tension-reducing spiral.

Osgood has stressed that unilateral initiatives should take advantage of mutual self-interests and of opportunities for cooperative endeavors. Unilateral initiatives will work best where reciprocation is in the adversary's self-interest. The GRIT proposal would have the best chance of succeeding where the overall objective is in the common interest of both parties and can be obtained through cooperation. Such is the case in regard to nuclear disarmament. However, the parties must first become aware of the mutual interest that is involved and that would be furthered by reciprocation and cooperation. The best prospect for such action would stem from mutual recognition of superordinate goals. Sherif (1966, p. 89) has defined such goals as "those that have a compelling appeal for members of each group, but that neither group can achieve without participation of the other." As Frank (1967, p. 252) has suggested, survival is a superordinate goal that is threatened by the nuclear arms race.

Trust can conceivably be generated by the superordinate goals themselves. For example, when two groups face a common crisis that can only be overcome by working together, they can trust each other, confident in the knowledge that it is in the best interests of each group to help the other, and that group A will do so because to work for group B's self-interest is the same as working for its own. In such a situation, graduated unilateral initiatives may not even be necessary. However, in regard to nuclear disarmament, although a superordinate goal of survival exists we have a situation in which deceit by one nation can conceivably serve its immediate self-interest to the detriment of the other's. Thus, there are situations in which graduated unilateral initiatives from a base of firmness may be necessary in order to induce reciprocation, reduce tensions, and establish mutual trust.

As Osgood recognizes, GRIT is not limited to use in the arms race or in international conflict. The basic concepts involved are applicable to any level and type of social conflict. GRIT confronts the problem of how to generate trust in the midst of conflict while remaining firm. Those who are familiar with Osgood's proposal as applied to the arms race know that in that context he views nuclear retaliatory capacity "as a security base from which to take limited risks in the direction of reducing tensions," or as the source of firmness, and thus they might wonder what relevance GRIT can possibly have for nonviolent action. But the basic concepts of GRIT do not require that the base of firmness from which risks are taken be military in nature. The source of firmness in nonviolent strategy is nonviolent resistance, the "weapons" of which the activist never relinquishes, and which can be resumed at any time. From this perspective, the nonviolent strategy of combining resistance with unilateral initiatives toward generating mutual trust can benefit from GRIT, is compatible with GRIT, and bears similarities to it.

The efficacy of GRIT has been supported in several laboratory studies. In an Inter-Nation Simulation "game," Crow (1963) found that GRIT moves were initially met with suspicion and hostility, but were eventually reciprocated, resulting in a reduction of tension level (as judged by the participants). In an extended form of the prisoner's dilemma game that allowed for gradations of cooperative response, Pilisuk and Skolnick (1968) found support for the GRIT strategy.

Perhaps more convincing in regard to the efficacy of unilateral initiatives inducing reciprocation, is Etzioni's (1969) analysis of a series of internationally important events that began with a speech by President Kennedy in June of 1963 in which he announced a unilateral halt to nuclear testing in the atmosphere. Kennedy's speech was printed in Soviet newspapers—a conciliatory gesture in itself. In the United Nations, a conciliatory initiative by the Soviet Union on one issue was reciprocated by an act of the United States on another. Then, only a few days after Kennedy's speech, Premier Khrushchev announced that the Soviet Union was stopping the production of strategic bombers. Within a few days, the White House-Kremlin hotline was agreed upon. In August, a nuclear test-ban treaty was signed. In October, Kennedy approved the sale of wheat to the Soviet Union, and an agreement was reached to ban orbiting nuclear weapons. Other conciliatory actions were also made during the period of June to October, 1963. The Russians had reciprocated American initiatives, and had offered their own. Then came negotiations and treaties.

Etzioni (1969) points out that many of the gestures were symbolic in nature and did not represent a risk for either side. Thus, American nuclear experts had determined beforehand that the United States had little knowledge to gain from continued atmospheric testing. The Soviet Union's strategic bombers were about to be phased out anyway. The wheat sale was small and of little economic importance. Perhaps for these reasons, while these events might have contributed to the reduction of international tension, they did not lead to a reversal of the arms race. Bolder gestures that are more than symbolic and that involve risk might be necessary for greater mutual gains.

I believe that the effectiveness of GRIT is dependent upon a willingness to take risks. The deterioration of conflict entails considerable risk. Perhaps we would be deceiving ourselves if we thought that the generating of trust can be accomplished without risk. Gandhi seemed to have been well aware of its necessity.

Negotiations must spring from a common desire to reach an agreement and from mutual trust. The nonviolent strategy can be viewed, in part, as an attempt to foster awareness of common interest while simultaneously generating trust. In the kind of conflicts that Gandhi and King waged, it might be asked how the fostering of awareness of common interest is possible. For what was most beneficial to the adversary from his viewpoint was undoubtedly the state of affairs that existed before the other party began to assert itself and that that party is now unwilling to allow. How then can I speak, as I and other writers on nonviolence have, of a *mutually* satisfactory solution to conflict?

During the time that our cooperation was unconditionally granted to the adversary and taken for granted by him, there was indeed no reason for him to negotiate. His concerns were being maximally served and he felt no compulsion to take our concerns into account. Indeed, he probably conveniently believed that the pursuit of his own interests was completely congruent with a pursuit of the common interest. But noncooperation transforms the situation by impressing upon the adversary that his own interests are dependent upon our interests and that each must take the others' interests into account and seek common ground. Noncooperation is power that puts us on an equal footing with the adversary and reminds him that we are both interdependent and that *now that we do not grant our cooperation automatically* negotiations leading toward a mutual agreement will be mutually beneficial.

Of course the adversary's interests, as he viewed them, were perhaps best served when our cooperation was automatically granted. Once we began to noncooperate, the adversary's "good old days" were gone forever. At that point, the adversary lost some of his power. He lost it when, and because, we began to organize our own power—or, rather, when we organized and therefore gained power. Once we begin to offer noncooperation, the entire situation is transformed. Only in the context of the new situation that has now arisen can we talk about reaching an agreement that will be beneficial to the adversary. That is, it can be judged as more or less beneficial to him only relative to the new circumstance that any agreement must take our interests into account to some extent. It cannot be judged relative to the old situation because that situation no longer exists. When I speak of the possibility of an agreement that is mutually beneficial, I mean beneficial granted the prior limitation that it will have to be somewhat beneficial to us also.

But the very noncooperation that is necessary to transform the situation also disrupts expectations, frustrates the adversary, and arouses fear and suspicion. The conciliatory actions being described in this chapter are necessary to allay fears, generate trust, and move the conflict toward reconciliation and away from bitterness and hostility.

FRIENDSHIP

Prior to my discussion of GRIT, I indicated that Gandhi sought far more in conflict than the rectification of immediate grievances or a negotiated settlement. He sought the friendship of the adversary, perhaps for its own sake. Yet such friendship could of course facilitate the reaching of a settlement. He also sought to ultimately convert the adversary. I will discuss Gandhi's quest for friendship first and then consider the possibilities of attitude change.

Trust is not inextricably tied to liking. I have trusted people whom I did not like. That is, sometimes I have been confident that if, within a certain context, I acted in a positive manner toward a certain person I did not like, he would reciprocate, or that if he said that he would do something, he would in fact do it. It is also conceivable that a person would not trust, within the context of certain situations, some people whom he likes. A person who likes his wife may nonetheless not trust her alone with another man. However, trust often facilitates liking, liking often facilitates trust, and very often they arise together.

Perhaps one way to generate trust and liking is by convincing the other of one's sincere concern for his well-being in general. We often come to trust and like those we believe are concerned about us. Such concern has to be demonstrated to us, and it is difficult to show it from a distance. We often suspect and fear the strange and unknown, and this applies to people as well as to things.

Gandhi seemed to purposefully seek out the friendship of his adversaries. He often sought personal interaction with his opponent. The friendship between Gandhi and the leader of the opposition in the Ahmedabad labor-management conflict is described by Erikson (1969). One is surprised to learn how friendly they were—although they had been friends prior to the conflict—and that they even ate lunches together during the conflict (Erikson, 1969, p. 333).

Gandhi often engaged his adversary on a personal level. While in jail in South Africa, he made a pair of sandals for General Smuts! This is indeed a unique way to wage conflict.

Shridharani (1939, pp. 232–233) has described what he has referred to as Gandhi's personal touch method:

> His first maneuver, when an *impasse* arises, is to cease public utterances and controversy through the printed word. Instead he seeks a personal interview with the opponent or spokesman of the opposition, as the case may be. Being an exceedingly gracious person, his first inquiries during the intimate meeting are after the opponent's health and his family's; he knows and remembers every name of any consequence to his adversary. With the amenities out of the way, he turns to a lengthy review of the past when both of them worked shoulder to shoulder and admired each other—Gandhi's way of emphasizing with all his persuasive power the fundamental unity underlying their temporary differences. But even at this point, Gandhi does not broach the issue; he lets his opponent air his grievances first. It is then that Gandhi lets loose a barrage of logical arguments with all the ease acquired while practicing law.

The outcome, however, often might not have been as inevitable and painlessly smooth as Shridharani (1939, p. 233) would lead us to believe:

> Finally he convinces his adversary that both parties have the same end in view, and their only differences lie in their ways of gaining this mutual objective. The straightening out of these little residual differences Gandhi leaves for the inevitable next interview. But as it is expected, in most cases when the adversary comes to see Gandhi again, he is in fine shape for the final adjustment of minor points.

Gandhi sought personal contact with his opponents to the point of trying to be their house guest. It is amusing to learn from Shridharani that some of his opponents tried to avoid intimate contact with him for fear of being won over.

Such methods are, of course, totally consistent with the nonviolent philosophy of conflict. They can be utilized in a wholly sincere manner by those who have internalized the attitude and concept of nonviolence with all of its many implications. The personal touch method does not violate the principle of noncooperation with evil because the adversary must be distinguished from the alleged injustice. The method is entirely consistent with an approach to conflict through which we sincerely strive to wage conflict without bitterness or a quest for revenge and through which we seek to do whatever possible to limit the conflict to the issue itself. Friendly gestures and expressions of concern for the adversary on a personal contact level can help to increase the differentiation of the stereotypes or constructs that the adversary holds of the nonviolent group. They can serve to break down the diabolical enemy image.

Of course the root of the conflict would still remain. But disputes between friends proceed far differently than disputes between enemies or strangers.[3] In the former case, a dispute represents a disagreement that occurs upon a ground of much mutual agreement and many ties of friendship. In the latter case, the disagreement—being the most salient source of information that one has about the other—can become the primary base of development of inferences and constructs by and about the disputants. Unchecked by information from other sources, they can balloon into undifferentiated negative images that can only generate fear and distrust.

Gandhi sought to break down such images through direct personal contact. But the kind of contact, and what is done within the context of that contact, is important. As we recognized before in discussing the contact hypothesis, the result is not inevitably positive. It is plausible to assume that personal contact can be conducted in such a way that each party merely receives informational reinforcement for its previously un-mitigatingly negative image of the other. Gandhi was determined to unilaterally turn the contact situation into a different kind of experience.

He sought to wage conflict without polarization, and his technique was to try to transform the conflict into a friendly dispute. Toward this end, he emphasized and forged common ties between himself and the adversary. He sought to settle differences on a ground of friendship. All of the methods of nonviolence could be employed in a manner that would not violate these aims.

> The greatest safeguard for peace was the stress he laid on non-violence. Non-co-operation with the symbols and institutions of British rule, ruled out even hatred of Englishmen. Again and again Gandhi declared that he would not do to an Englishman what he would not do to a blood brother. He had, he publicly recalled, non-co-operated even with his brother on matters of principle. (Nanda, 1958, p. 204)

Nonviolence is consistent with love for the adversary and can be used, even to the point of noncooperation, with friends. For the nonviolent activist is against, not people, but what he considers to be injustice.

Gandhi's gestures of trust and goodwill might have been taken advantage of many times. But in the long run his methods of nonviolence, including his personal touch method, probably contributed to the relatively bitterless aftermaths of many of the conflicts he waged. For example, the Ahmedabad struggle ended in a celebration in which both workers and mill owners participated, and goodwill was expressed by both sides (Desai, 1951; Erikson, 1969, pp. 360–362).

ATTITUDE CHANGE

Although one of the goals of Satyagraha, or nonviolence, is attitude change, in many conflicts it would be enough if one's grievance is redressed. It would be so much the better if a settlement is reached with a minimum of lingering bitterness and resentment, as seemed to have been the case in the Ahmedabad conflict.

An interesting case in which Satyagrahis persisted beyond the rectification of the immediate grievance was the Vykom Temple Road Satyagraha in India (see Shridharani, 1939, pp. 89–92; Bondurant, 1965, pp. 46–52). Caste discrimination was involved in this conflict. Untouchables had been forbidden to use a road that passed a Brahmin temple. The Satyagrahis led processions along the road. They did not retaliate when attacked and beaten by Brahmins, and submitted peacefully to arrests. When volunteers came to replace those who had been arrested, the police erected a barricade on the road. The Satyagrahis took up positions opposite the police and confronted them day and night without interruption. They constantly pleaded their case with the police. Even when the monsoon flooded the road, the Satyagrahis maintained their positions, sometimes standing in water up to their shoulders, while the police used boats. After several months, Gandhi helped in getting the State authorities to remove the barricade and police. But the Satyagrahis, now having gained free passage, nonetheless intended to refuse to use the road until they had persuaded the Brahmins. Finally, after persistent persuasive attempts on the part of the Satyagrahis, the Brahmins gave their full consent and said: "We cannot resist any longer the prayers that have been made to us, and we are ready to receive the untouchables" (Shridharani, 1939, p. 92).

In Chapter 3 I discussed the probable relations of various types of social power to behavior change and attitude change. I noted there that coercive power is often likely to produce behavioral compliance without attitude change. The stability of behavior change that is not supported by attitude change is directly dependent upon the continuance of coercion. It rests upon external pressures rather than on internal inclinations. A conflict that results in a continual need to maintain coercion in order to uphold the behavior change that was sought does not result in true resolution. Such a situation does not represent the resolution of conflict; it represents its suppression. The coercion, moreover, continues to generate psychological resistance.

I concluded in Chapter 3 that the probability of attitude change taking place as a consequence of behavior change is enhanced the less resistance and the greater attraction that can be generated in attempting to elicit the behavior change. I drew the practical implication that one should apply the minimal pressure necessary to obtain behavior change if one is also hoping for attitude change.

Noncooperation perhaps represents the minimal pressure necessary. I have noted that although noncooperation is bound to induce some psychological resistance, it is likely to generate less than other forms of coercion. But besides employing minimal pressure there are other ways in which the possibility of obtaining attitude change even with the use of coercive power can be enhanced. The nonviolent activist seeks to offset the psychological resistance engendered by noncooperation with simultaneous friendly, sympathetic, trusting, and helping gestures toward the adversary. Some strategies of such behavior have been discussed above. They may generate attraction to offset the resistance and offer promise of averting, to some extent, the degeneration of conflict discussed earlier in this chapter. They are, in fact, an integral part of *nonviolent* noncooperation. The activist extends the two hands of which Deming (1968) spoke.

While minimizing the psychological resistance generated and attempting to offset that resistance might maximize the possibility of attitude change, it does not produce it. The processes through which behavior change might beget attitude change were discussed in Chapter 3.

Perhaps the wisdom of seeking attitude change lies in the recognition that enduring peace cannot rest upon grudgingly given concessions or upon force. This is especially clear in issues of religious or racial integration where the two parties are going to have to live together and have their lives touch in many ways after the struggle. The long climb out of slavery and oppression did not end for the black people of this country with the passage of civil rights laws. Even when the vigorous enforcement of those laws results in benefits to the black people, a harmonious community does not necessarily ensue. Yet such community is the goal of the nonviolent activist. Blacks and whites might attend the same schools, eat at the same restaurants, live in the same neighborhoods, and work side by side at the same jobs as equals, but if they continue to hold segregationist attitudes, what we will have is contiguity but not togetherness, a conglomeration of peoples but not integration. Such a situation is bound to sporadically ignite racial confrontations. And the minority group is bound to suffer as the spirit of the laws are violated by people who have only grudgingly complied with them.

In such a situation, enduring conflict resolution cannot rest upon forced concessions but must ultimately stem from changed attitudes. Martin Luther King, Jr.'s dream, consistent with the tenets of nonviolence, was of an integrated community of diversity, not of a defiant stand-off of coexisting peoples in a polarized society.

But how can attitude change be attained when we have found it necessary to go beyond persuasion through reason to the coercion of noncooperation? We are faced with a situation in which the nonviolent activist, originally having sought to obtain behavior change as a consequence of attitude change induced by persuasion through reason, has resorted to means which, although nonviolent, have a higher probability of eliciting behavior change than attitude change. In the process of obtaining behavior change, his means have generated psychological resistance to attitude change.

I indicated in Chapter 3 that there are at least two ways in which behavior change might beget attitude change. In the first way, the individual, in the context of the action that he has been pressured to take, might be stimulated to reexamine his attitudinal position. In this process he might reorganize or reinterpret his old information. Due to external pressure, the individual will have to make a decision about whether or not he will comply, and perhaps whether or not he should have complied; the necessity of that decision might induce him to rethink the attitudes supporting his old behavior. But the more external pressure that has been applied, the more likely will the individual be to comply without rethinking his position, because at that moment the matter of avoiding hardship might far outweigh that of the issue-oriented attitude. When minimal pressure is applied (although not so little as to be easily discounted), the individual will be more inclined to take the leisure of reexamining the entire situation, including his attitudinal position, for more doubt has been raised in his mind as to whether he should or should not comply. In other words, inner conflict, which stimulates thinking, will be aroused. The more external pressure that is applied relative to that needed to finally get him to change his behavior, the less inner conflict there will be, and therefore the less rethinking. Moreover, the greater the external pressure applied, the greater will be the psychological resistance that is generated. Thus, even if the individual were to reexamine his position, and even after he has complied, he would be less inclined to entertain potentially discrepant information or to engage in counter-attitudinal advocacy. In other words, he would be less inclined to interpret his old information in a manner discrepant with his original attitude.[4]

However, when the attitudes concerning the issue are deep-rooted, it would be overly optimistic to expect that they would be changed through any of the processes noted above, even if compliance has been gained. In such a case, compliance would only be gained through prolonged pressure that has produced such hardship on the individual that he has reason enough to reluctantly comply without any inclination to reconsider his attitude. After all, if his attitude is strong, he would only comply if there were no doubt in his mind that he can no longer resist the external pressures that have been applied. But rather than rethink his position, one which for him is not at all open to question, he would be more apt to spend his time thinking about how to circumvent the pressures in the future.

Furthermore, perhaps attitude change, if obtained at all, is not so likely to occur within the conflict situation, in the heat of conflict, or even immediately thereafter as it is to occur through the context of the interactional structure that ensues from the settlement of the conflict on the behavioral level. (I have in mind, for example, the racial integration of transportation, housing, or schools as required by a law or agreement established as a result of a nonviolent campaign, or the integration of a restaurant that might arise through a settlement between the nonviolent activist and the restaurant owner.) In other words, attitude change, if obtained at all, is not as likely to occur during noncooperation as it is in the context of the new interactional structure that ensues.

We must therefore look at the second way in which behavior change might eventuate in attitude change: the changed behavior might take the form of immersion into a new social interaction structure (e.g., racially integrated housing) through which the individual is exposed to new information (e.g., about living with members of the other race) that might be potentially inconsistent with his prior attitudes.

However, even *how* this new information is interpreted is likely to be related to the degree of psychological resistance generated in bringing about the behavior change and to the strength of prior attitudes. Psychological resistance and strong prior attitudes might also lead to hostile behavior within the new interactional structure and perhaps to the propagation of a self-fulfilling prophecy. Thus, the conciliatory gestures of the nonviolent activist's party must be kept up and play an important role even after the new interactional structure has arisen.

There are several psychological factors that might facilitate attitude change through the immersion into a new social interaction structure, such as integrated housing. (A number of what might be called structural factors pertaining to social interaction have already been mentioned in Chapter 3.)

The individual might find the new situation satisfying and rewarding. Thus, a self-interest-oriented attitude might develop that will direct him to seek out or interpret new information in a manner consistent with it.

Also, when an individual finds himself committed to further interaction within the new situation, he might try to make the best of that situation for his own well-being. This desire might lead him to seek out and elicit positive information about the attitudinal object—e.g., racial integration.

> Being committed to further association with the object, the person is likely to be open to and to search for new information that would help to make the anticipated association more effective, more comfortable, more rewarding. The nature of this information would typically be such as to lend attitudinal support to the association and to lead to the development or strengthening of favorable attitudes toward the object—in other words, to bring attitudes into line with the action taken and the future action that is anticipated. (Kelman, 1962)

Furthermore, the individual may be inclined to like those toward whom he has acted favorably (Jecker and Landy, 1969). Such favorable behavior might have been induced by situational pressures or social norms present in the new interactional structure. Attitude change through the seeking out of positive information might (in this situation of having acted favorably) be motivated by a desire to reduce negative self-evaluation, such as guilt for having betrayed one's attitude or shame for having not resisted pressure, stemming from one's knowledge that he has acted in a manner contrary to his attitude (see Kelman, 1962).

Finally, such factors as I have described are likely to be operative and facilitate attitude change only to the extent that the individual has previously refrained from the actions he now engages in, not so much out of a deeply held, internalized, negative attitude toward the object (e.g., racial integration) but more because of societal norms and cultural traditions that have generated pressures toward conformity to group standards. What I have just said might be consistent with what Kelman (1962) speaks of when he refers to:

> situations in which the person's avoidance of the object is *not* generated primarily by the characteristics of the object itself, but by *the price he would have to pay in order to enter into closer association with the object.*

It is sometimes the case that many of the people over whose heads a conflict rages have actually had a close-to-neutral internalized attitude toward the issue. In the case of racial segregation, they might have contributed to the original segregated social structure more because their desire to associate with members of the other race was nil (or not nearly as strong as their desire to avoid the social sanctions that would be invoked against them if they failed to conform to group behavior patterns) rather than out of any strong internalized attitude against integration. This is not to say that they do not have negative attitudes, but they might not be as strong as we might at first imagine. And the attitudes of many others might be largely vacuous attitudes (see Chapter 4) even if they are extreme.

There is much evidence of a correlational nature to suggest that conformity to group norms has been an important factor in race prejudice in the South (Pettigrew, 1959, 1961). Changes in interactional structure in such cases, in line with the contact hypothesis, should offer much promise for attitude change or favorable attitude formation. But the new structure cannot be temporary in nature or expected to be temporary.[5] Pettigrew (1961) has stated in regard to the South that:

> violence has generally resulted in localities where at least some of the authorities give prior hints that they would gladly return to segregation if disturbances occurred, peaceful integration has generally followed firm and forceful leadership.

Thus, in many instances segregational structures might be kept intact largely through outward conformity to group norms, through fear of social sanctions, and through vacuous attitudes. In such cases the coercion of noncooperation and the passage of laws might burst a bubble that was unstable to begin with. Many people, once finding themselves in a permanent and pervasive integrational social structure, might gain a positive attitude toward integration through new information and the processes enumerated above. At the least, they might come to find nothing terribly wrong with it.

But we cannot be optimistic about changing through interaction the deeply engrained negative attitudes of others. As for these people, perhaps only their children—being raised within the new interactional structure of integration—will develop positive attitudes toward integration. There are those whose conversion can be little expected; but the new interactional structure, if brought about in a manner that did not stir up bitterness and resentment to an unnecessary degree, might serve to allow future generations to live in harmony. This is a long-term process.

Both the breaking of conformity-induced segregation and the more gradual change that becomes visible only when we look at the attitudes of succeeding generations seem to be operating in our country's continuing climb from racism.

SUPERORDINATE GOALS

Thus far, in regard to the constructive waging of conflict, I have discussed some of the processes involved in the generation of trust, liking or friendship, and attitude change. In discussing attitude change, I used the issue of racial integration as an example. Attitudes toward such an issue are of course bound up with attitudes toward people, although not exclusively attitudes of liking. However, even in regard to conflict issues of a different nature, attitudes toward people may be very important. I have assumed that conflicts waged on a ground of friendship proceed far differently from those waged on a ground of enmity.

When two parties to a conflict hold hostile attitudes toward each other, it often appears to them as if one party's gain will have to be the other party's loss. When such parties hold positive attitudes toward each other, they can often find a solution satisfactory to both through mutual exploration of the issue.

Attitudes of one group of people toward another are partially dependent upon the functional relations between those groups. I have already alluded to the concept of superordinate goals in my discussion of the generating of trust. In much of the remainder of this chapter I will explore this concept more thoroughly. I have already mentioned (in Chapter 6) that Gandhi's concept of constructive work is easily extended to include the adversary, and such an extension is consistent with the philosophy of nonviolence. I indicated that nonviolent action is indeed characterized by a constant willingness to seek out opportunities to cooperate with others, including the adversary, in constructive activity.

Sherif (1966, p. 153) has proposed that "the reduction of hostility must depend on intergroup action to achieve goals that are desired by all parties and that require their cooperation." Such superordinate goals, according to Sherif, provide the motivational bases, common to the conflicting parties, that are the essential conditions for the reduction of intergroup tensions. "All successful solutions to intergroup problems involve a positive base: the cooperative activity of peoples gripped by realization of a common lot" (Sherif, 1966, p. 173).

The significance of superordinate goals in intergroup relations was brilliantly demonstrated by Sherif and his associates in the course of studying the dynamics of intergroup conflict. The study consisted of a series of three field experiments conducted with 11-year-old boys during three-week summer camp sessions in isolated campsites completely at the disposal of the investigators (Sherif, 1951, 1966; Sherif and Sherif, 1953, 1956, 1969). Under experimentally controlled conditions, they were able to observe (among other things) many of the characteristics of the degeneration of conflict spoken of earlier in this chapter.

In every experiment, after the boys were divided into two groups, each group participated separately in camp activities for the next few days. The activities introduced into each group involved all of the members of the group and were highly appealing to the boys. These activities, which required that the boys act interdependently in order to achieve common goals, included cook-outs, hikes, camping out overnight, improving a swimming place, swimming, improving their cabins, improving hide-outs, transporting canoes to the water, and clearing up a field for athletics. Under these conditions, friendships formed and cohesive group organizations emerged along with the development of status hierarchies, group customs and norms, common attitudes, and group pride and patriotism. The groups developed characteristic rituals and ways of doing things, and they standardized sanctions for violations of group norms of behavior. (The groups also took on names: Red Devils and Bull Dogs in the 1949 experiment; Panthers and Pythons in the 1953 experiment; and Rattlers and Eagles in the 1954 experiment.)

In each experiment the two groups were then brought into contact with each other through the introduction of a tournament of competitive intergroup events. Points were to be awarded on a group basis to the winner of each game or contest, and the members of the group that had accumulated the most points were to receive prizes. The events included, among others, baseball and touch football, tug-of-war, a treasure hunt, and cabin inspection.

The series of events started out innocently enough, in an atmosphere of good sportsmanship, but the narrow conflict of group interests that the tournament had created soon degenerated into mutual hostility. In one experiment the members of the group that began to fall into a losing position as the tournament progressed accused the members of the other group of being "dirty players" and "cheats," while attributing fairness to themselves. Members of each group began to refer to those of the other as "stinkers" and "sneaks." The groups made posters exhorting its members to fight on, and each group began collecting green apples in preparation for raids (1949 experiment).

In another experiment, the conflict degenerated into seizing and defiling each others' flags, name-calling, fighting, and raids on each others' cabins (1954 experiment).

> Within six days the intergroup conflict produced such an unfavorable image of the out-group, with accompanying derogatory stereotypes, that each group was dead set against having any more to do with the other. (Sherif and Sherif, 1956, p. 307)

The intergroup conflict, however, greatly increased intragroup solidarity. When the boys were asked to rate the members of both groups on a number of adjectives, the ratings of members of one's own group were almost exclusively favorable (brave, tough, friendly) and those of the other group were predominantly unfavorable (sneaky, smart alecks, stinkers).

The members of each group engaged in justification of their own actions and attributed all responsibility for the hostility and fighting to the other group. In this atmosphere, at the end of the tournament, the experimenters proposed a party to let "bygones be bygones"; but this was actually contrived by them as an additional frustrating situation (1949 experiment). A table of refreshments was arranged in the mess hall. Half of the refreshments were deliberately left battered and crushed, and the experimenters saw to it that one group arrived before the other. Told to take their share of the refreshments, the group took the appetizing half. When the members of the other group arrived and saw what was left, they began to protest, calling the others "pigs" and "bums." The first group justified its behavior with remarks of "first come, first served." After this incident, the hostilities between the two groups became especially intensified and ugly. The experimenters had to intercede to break up violent fights. The next day food and tableware, including knives, were thrown at mealtime, accompanied by a bitter exchange of insults. "Neither group was sure who started the fight, but each was sure it was someone in the *other* group" (Sherif and Sherif, 1969, p. 242).

Apparently becoming concerned that a dangerous situation was getting out of hand, the experimenters decided to immediately conclude this phase of the experiment and to stop the continued fighting in any way possible.

> At this point, the experiment proper was over. The conflict was not over, however. It took another two days of genuine and active efforts by the staff, involving "preaching" and coercion, just to stop the group fighting. The groups planned raids on each other's cabins. Green apples were collected and hoarded by both groups for "ammunition," with the explanation that this was done merely "in case" it might be needed. The Red Devils attempted "sneak" attacks when the other group and counselors were asleep. (The Red Devils had tended to show signs of disorganization after their defeat in the competitions. In this period the group was again united.) This fighting and raiding between groups took on a planned character. They were not merely outbursts upon momentary encounters of individuals. (Sherif and Sherif, 1956, pp. 296–298)

Perhaps the most significant part of this study were the efforts that were made by the experimenters toward reconciliation of the groups. The experimenters stated the problem in this way:

> How can two groups in conflict, each with hostile attitudes and negative images of the other and each desiring to keep the members of the detested out-group at a safe distance, be brought into cooperative interaction and friendly intercourse? (Sherif and Sherif, 1969, p. 254)

A number of measures were tried, but the one that proved to be very effective was the introduction of a series of problem situations that embodied superordinate goals—goals that are highly appealing and urgently compelling for both groups and that cannot be achieved by either group working alone.

Among the situations arranged by the experimenters (in the 1954 experiment) were the following. They secretly created a breakdown in the camp's water supply system and called the groups together to inform them of the crisis. Through cooperative action, the groups located the difficulty and resolved the problem. Next, the campers were told that there was an opportunity to bring one of two films to the camp, but that the administration could put up only half the money needed to get it. The groups met with each other, selected the film by a common vote, and figured out how much money each group and each of its members would have to contribute. That evening, the groups saw the movie together.

Another crisis was produced by the experimenters when both groups were taken to a lake for an overnight camp-out. As lunchtime approached, the two groups looked on while a staff member tried to start up the truck that was to be used to bring the food. As planned by the mischievous experimenters, the truck would not start. The rope that was used for tug-of-war during the tournament was lying nearby. Both groups joined together in winding the rope around the front bumper and pulling. After considerable effort involving the members of both groups, the truck started. When the food arrived, the groups prepared the meal together rather than dividing up the food, as they would have done earlier. That afternoon at the lake, the truck again developed trouble when it was about to be used to bring back the food for supper, and the two groups again successfully cooperated in pulling the truck to get it started. That evening, the meal was again prepared cooperatively (Sherif and Sherif, 1956, pp. 321–324).

A remarkable reduction of hostility was observed. Near the end of the experiment, the boys initiated a joint campfire, at which they entertained each other. Name-calling stopped. New friendships developed across group lines, as confirmed by sociometric ratings. There was a decline in the attribution of negative qualities to the members of the other group. In fact, positive images emerged. They stopped shoving each other in the meal line. They decided to go home in the same bus rather than in separate ones, and the members of one group used their own money to treat the other group to refreshments.

These findings indicate, as Sherif has proposed, that a common motivational base provided by goals that groups desire and toward which they must jointly strive is an important basis for the reduction of intergroup hostility. It is important to note that this reconciliation between the groups did not occur immediately but emerged gradually in the course of the cooperative pursuit of a *series* of superordinate goals.

Superordinate goals arise from the interdependence of groups. This interdependence, when recognized by both groups, can be a strong foundation for intergroup unity and positive attitude formation.

Perhaps one of the most stable and recurrent observations that can be made of group dynamics is that individuals faced with a common enemy increase the solidarity and cohesiveness of their own group. Indeed, Sherif and his associates noted that intergroup conflict tended to strengthen group belongingness, solidarity, and friendships. The existence of a common enemy who can only be overcome by cooperative action not only unifies a group but can pull groups together in common cause. In the first experiment a softball game between an intergroup team elected by all of the boys and a team from outside the camp served to temporarily reduce intergroup hostility.

The interdependence of nations imposed by the existence of a common enemy is perhaps so potent a base for the reduction of hostility between nations that it might account for the otherwise puzzling fact of the rapidly changing alliance patterns between nations in recent years. Thus, we find nations that were engaged in a bitter war against each other, and whom we could expect to enter into a long aftermath of hostility and resentment, manage to quickly "bury the hatchet" and enter into alliances with each other against a new, common enemy.

Common self-interest, commonly recognized, is a potent determinant of interpersonal and group dynamics. But the recognition of interdependence fostered by the threat of a common enemy gives rise to conflict on a more massive level. "Logically, the end result is repetition of the stage of intergroup conflict on a larger scale, with potentially more serious consequences" (Sherif and Sherif, 1969, p. 255).

A common enemy is not the only potent threat to have been observed to unite individuals or groups. From time to time, witnesses have been astonished to observe the solidarity that emerges when individuals are confronted with a common danger or crisis of any sort. Thus, the impersonal clustering of individuals that many believe New York City is has been known to close ranks in cooperative, helping, and friendly behavior when faced with a blackout or unusually heavy snowstorm.

But not even crisis is necessary for this phenomenon. Whenever common interest is involved, there is a potential base for the emergence of a cooperative effort that will involve the harmonious coming together of individuals and groups. This common interest need not involve the specter of the threat of a common enemy, or even a common danger or crisis; it can entail a more positive goal that will merely better the well-being of the people involved or fulfill their desires. The essential component is that of a problem situation that embodies a superordinate goal.

However, it is important to note that alliance is not the same as friendship; cooperation is not love. The alliances formed by individuals and groups in pursuit of a specific goal have often been observed to wither away after that goal has been achieved or after a crisis has passed. People are quite capable of entering into "practical" partnerships even though they dislike each other, working together for the specific gain of the moment, and then going their separate ways. Trust of one for the other need not extend beyond the immediate problem to other areas of interaction. Temporary alliance does not insure enduring friendship. The Soviet Union and the United States were quite capable of cooperative activity in defeating the Nazis, but this massive joint effort did not prevent the "cold war."

Groups have cooperated with their worst enemies at times without that cooperation spreading to friendship. Superordinate goals, which can be either more or less compelling, as will be discussed below, merely furnish the opportunity for cooperative activity. Cooperation, in turn, merely furnishes the opportunity for the reduction of tension and hostility between groups and for the rise of friendship. It is what happens within the context of that cooperation, what is *done* with the opportunities provided by superordinate goals, that determines whether or not enduring harmony will ensue. Conflicts are rooted in clashes of self-interest and its effects sometimes spread to hostility between groups. Cooperative efforts are rooted in common interests and can lead to a "spread of affect." Superordinate goals *can* provide the occasion for intergroup contact under conditions noted in Chapter 3 as conducive for positive attitude formation. That is, they may provide the occasion for noncoerced, intimate, and cooperative contact in pursuance of important goals. But superordinate goals positively structure the nature of human interaction to only a limited extent. How the individuals and groups utilize the opportunities presented will determine whether that interaction will have implications beyond the achievement of immediate goals.

Before Sherif and his associates introduced the ultimately successful superordinate goals into their final summer camp experiment, they tried to reduce the intergroup hostility through a different tactic. They brought the groups together in close physical proximity in a series of situations that were presumably pleasant in themselves. These situations included eating together in the same dining hall, watching movies together, and shooting off firecrackers in the same area.

> These contact situations had no effect in reducing intergroup friction. If anything, they were utilized by members of both groups as opportunities for further name-calling and conflict. For example, they used mealtimes in the same place for "garbage fights," throwing mashed potatoes, leftovers, bottle caps, and the like accompanied by the exchange of derogatory names. (Sherif and Sherif, 1956, p. 318)

The investigators concluded that contact in itself, under pleasant conditions and yet not requiring interdependent activity toward superordinate goals, will not reduce hostility.

It should be noted that the conclusion about the inability of intergroup contact in itself to provide the occasion for the reduction of hostility is inferred from a situation in which intense hostile feelings already existed. Earlier in this chapter, I discussed the possibility that there are situations in which groups that had kept apart did so more through conformity to group norms without necessarily the accompaniment of intense hostile feelings toward the other group. In such cases, contact even in the absence of superordinate goals might open the door to new information, gained through interaction, that might lend itself to favorable interpretations and form the base for favorable intergroup images.

Thus, the nature of the information conveyed about one group to the other in the course of the interaction partially determines whether or not hostility will be reduced and friendship formed. But information, partially determinative of interpretations as it is, is always susceptible to multiple interpretations. Interdependent action toward superordinate goals provides the best opportunity for the reduction of the psychological resistance that works toward the inhibiting of favorable interpretations of the information that arises.

But the nature of the information itself is important. There is no magic to contact in itself. Groups in contact, even if working toward superordinate goals, might sometimes convey information about themselves, or perform actions, that are all too easily and readily interpretable in a manner that gives rise to or confirms a negative group image, even though psychological resistance has at first been reduced. When members of one group find a rise in crime when their neighborhood is integrated by the influx of members from another group, certain negative stereotypes (if previously held) are obviously going to be reinforced.

Thus, the nonviolent activist has a job to perform beyond that of bringing his and the other group into contact or into mutual striving toward a superordinate goal. Within these new interaction situations, his group must put its best foot forward. This can be prepared for through the constructive program. For, through the constructive program, the members of the nonviolent activist's group will uplift themselves from what they had been due to oppression. For example, the degradation of oppression might have induced people to heroin addiction and crime. The other group, even if they happened to be the oppressors, will not look favorably upon this information about the activist's group. This is not surprising, and should not arouse indignation, for it should be realized that such an oppressed group often does not even look favorably upon itself because of these things. Part of the function of the constructive program is to raise dignity and self-respect through constructive work. Often, in the process, the group will gain the respect of others as well, through its own uplift.

The object is to create a situation that reduces psychological resistance and, through the vehicle of that situation, to convey information that can lend itself to a favorable interpretation. The structure of the situation created by superordinate goals promotes the first condition and partially influences the second. An attitude can stem from self-interest and can direct the individual to search for supportive information, and self-interest can influence the direction or manner in which new information will be interpreted. Individuals or groups who have come together in pursuit of a common interest will have to work together, cooperate with each other, and depend upon each other. Moreover, they have come together voluntarily. These conditions are conducive to the favorable interpretation of information about the other and also to the rise of information that will lend itself to a favorable interpretation. Each can let down his psychological guard toward the other because he knows that it is in the best interests of the other individual to help him and that he will do so because to work for his own self-interest is to work for the other's. This interdependence will not only allow for one individual taking actions that will benefit the other but also for the building of trust and for the occasion of rationalization of why one is working with the other: "He's not so bad, anyway." Cooperative interaction, motivated by self-interest, will be rationalized through favorable interpretation of the information that arises about the other. Furthermore, cooperative interaction can in itself provide information of a favorable nature to each about the other.

The striving toward superordinate goals is therefore a foundation for positive attitude formation. Attitudes follow the lines drawn by self-interest and by the functional relations between groups. Thus, superordinate goals provide an important condition—Sherif (1966, p. 130) says essential—for the ultimate effectiveness of such measures as the dissemination of information and intergroup contact. They provide the motivational base for these measures to be used in favorable directions.

A superordinate goal is one that is both urgent and compelling for both groups. The survival of mankind and of civilization as we know it is a potentially very compelling superordinate goal. This goal cannot be achieved by any one nation singly. World nuclear disarmament would be a step toward this goal and will require the cooperation of many nations.

The prisoner's dilemma game paradigm contains within it the ground of interdependence necessary for the rise of superordinate goals. The cooperation of the two parties is necessary for the attainment of a goal that will benefit both of them. Yet, in this paradigm there is also a tug in the other direction. Each party, attempting to act in its self-interest (i.e., that of preventing itself from being exploited and suffering losses) acts in a manner that results in a mutual loss.

The nuclear arms race has similar characteristics. Nations head in the direction of possible mutual destruction. Even in the present, the nations suffer great losses because huge amounts of money are diverted from domestic problems and improvements that are desperately in need of attention. Yet the ground of interdependence exists. Cooperative action toward the potential superordinate goals of nuclear disarmament and human survival, however, has not yet ensued.

In other words, the most compelling grounds of interdependence sometimes do not give rise to cooperative efforts toward superordinate goals. One reason for this is that the compelling tugs of fear that sometimes exist tend to propel the parties in an opposite direction. In the case of nuclear disarmament and human survival, it is not that the potential superordinate goals are not recognized by the nations involved but that there are other compelling factors in the situation.

In characterizing a superordinate goal as one that is both urgent and compelling for both groups, Sherif (1966, p. 88) distinguishes it from a common goal by saying that it cannot be achieved by a single group through its own efforts and resources. He also says that it supersedes other goals each group might have, and its attainment may require subordination of either singular or common goals.

But goals vary in the sense of urgency and compellingness they arouse, and sometimes the most urgent and compelling goals are not the ones most easily recognized; if recognized, they are sometimes not the ones toward which the groups can easily be directed to take cooperative action (e.g., nuclear disarmament). However, some goals may conceivably be obtainable by one nation acting singly and yet furnish the opportunity for cooperative activity through which the reduction of hostility may come about.

The Soviet Union and the United States could have, for example, more easily entered into a cooperative effort in reaching and exploring the moon than in nuclear disarmament. Each nation was capable of reaching the moon by itself. It could be said that each nation had more compelling and urgent problems to attend to, and, in fact, many Americans argued that the money that went into landing people on the moon could have been better spent by the United States government. However, the moon goal, while not necessary to achieve, was highly appealing to many people (both Soviet and American), and this would have been a sufficient condition for a massive, far-reaching cooperative effort, which unfortunately did not occur.

Of course, the Soviet Union and the United States have engaged in a number of cooperative efforts, such as the International Geophysical

Year. But many and more massive cooperative efforts—and by no means such efforts alone—will be required before nuclear disarmament is brought about. Modern technology has provided many possibilities—in transportation, commerce, exploration of the ocean depths, and the exploration of outer space, in the discovery of new sources of food, the long-range prediction of weather, and the combating of the effect of floods and earthquakes, to name a few. But we and they cannot afford to squander any of the opportunities for collaboration that arise.

The actual interdependence between groups—the ground for potential superordinate goals—is rapidly increasing in the modern world. Sherif and Sherif (1969, p. 266) have noted that modern technological development in communication, transportation, distribution, and even destruction ultimately increase the spheres of activity in which group becomes dependent upon group and nation upon nation.

Yet the lack of recognition by groups of their interdependences and the potential superordinate goals to which they give rise is often the obstacle to cooperative efforts between groups.

> To a world accustomed to thinking in terms of the privacy of group and national life, the realization that one group's affairs affect all is not immediate. For many potential superordinate goals to be recognized, the heavy hand of the past must be lifted. The superordinate goal must be singled out from the cumbersome complexity of accustomed practices that enmesh modern life. Ultimately, the successful pursuit of superordinate goals entails a soul-searching examination of the range of human identifications and human dependencies in actual living. (Sherif, 1966, p. 148)

PROMOTING INTERDEPENDENCE AND ITS RECOGNITION

This book concerns a unilateral approach to conflict. The philosophy of nonviolence entails a strategy through which one party can initiate manifest conflict, wage conflict, and initiate conflict resolution and reconciliation. The nonviolent activist takes upon himself the responsibility of attempting to inhibit the deterioration of conflict. He recognizes that it is often up to one party to the conflict to take unilateral initiatives toward resolution and reconciliation. The nonviolent activist's strategy entails constantly seizing and holding the initiatives in conflict. It was already indicated in this chapter what initiatives the nonviolent activist might take toward breaking the spiral of distrust.

What initiatives are open to the nonviolent activist in terms of promoting positive interdependences between groups and nations and the recognition of superordinate goals? It would be possible for the nonviolent activist, even outside of the context of conflict, to help

accelerate the trend of interdependence by, for example, promoting technological development of a constructive nature or increased world trade.
Through the communication of information, he can foster the recognition
of interdependences that already exist and of the potential for
superordinate goals already available. Proposals for cooperative undertakings toward superordinate goals can be offered. One group cannot
"sell" a goal to another group if it has no appeal for the latter. But there
are many potential goals which, if they do not touch on the basic needs of
a group, are highly appealing in terms of its wants and desires. Scientific
and technological developments increase the number and variety of such
goals.[6]

Sherif (1966, p. 147) states:

> Superordinate goals cannot be fabricated or unilaterally proposed. They arise in the
> functional relations between groups, and their possibilities increase with the diversity
> and volume of concerns affecting both groups. With increased contact and a growing
> diversity of concerns affecting both sides, each group in an intergroup system becomes
> more dependent upon the other, so that what happens *within* its bounds is increasingly
> conditioned by its relations with the other groups in the system.

I grant that there must be a ground of interdependence from which
superordinate goals, as they have been defined by Sherif, can arise. This
interdependence, as I have said, can be actively promoted. Yet, beyond
that, out of such interdependence, superordinate goals can be actively
fashioned by one group. It would have been entirely possible in the
summer camp experiments for one of the camp groups itself to have
sabotaged the water supply or to have deliberately disabled the truck that
was to have brought back the food rather than the experimenters who
actually did create the superordinate goals involved. In other words, the
unilateral fabrication of such goals is entirely within the realm of
possibility. I am not advocating that the nonviolent activist (not in keeping
with his philosophy) engage in destructive work for the sake of some
hoped-for good; I merely wish to use Sherif's own examples to make my
point. More positively, it is at least conceivable that one of the camp
groups could have taken the initiative in bringing a movie to the camp by
doing what the experimenters had done: ascertaining that two films were
available and offering to put up part of the money. This could have led to
what in fact did happen: the mutual calculation of how much each group
would have to pay, the intergroup vote for the films, and the intergroup
viewing and enjoyment of the film selected. Moreover, on a larger scale,
movement toward an existing superordinate goal can be unilaterally
initiated: recall Osgood's GRIT proposal.

Sherif and Sherif (1969, p. 266) maintain that where one group is intent on dominating another the conditions for superordinate goals are not present. However, as I have already indicated, when the oppressed group unilaterally emancipates itself from exploitation and is able to stand firm in the face of the ensuing added suffering, then it has put itself, in one sense, on an equal footing with the adversary. The adversary, as intent as he may be on continuing the domination, will be faced with a new reality in which it is possible that he will stand to gain by cooperating with the nonviolent activist in certain areas of common interest. In other words, nonviolent action by an oppressed group, ideally, puts the conflict on a new level, in which the adversary, in lieu of being able to dominate any longer, will be ready to turn to the attainment of goals that now require the participation of the other group on an equal footing. I agree with Sherif, then, that at the time of domination of one group by the other, the conditions for superordinate goals are not present. In such a case, nonviolent noncooperation is a necessary first step and resistance must precede cooperative effort. Noncooperation can confront the adversary with a new reality in which he will begin to recognize common interests. Certain goals that he could have achieved before through domination can now be achieved only through cooperation and negotiation.[7]

Indeed, in a study cited by Sherif (1966, pp. 103–105) involving the analysis of desegregation decisions in ten Southern cities, it was found that organized action during the civil rights movement of the early 1960s achieved results through bringing to others' awareness the common interests involved in reaching a negotiated settlement. Negotiators came together with the superordinate objective of averting the crisis to the city generated by nonviolent resistance, which had brought manifest conflict to a head. The mutual focus of the negotiators was how to achieve the common good of the community.

Noncooperation can bring interdependence to others' awareness. It can impress upon the adversary that there is indeed something to negotiate. Interdependence can exist between functional equals. But it also exists between oppressor and oppressed. The oppressor comes to depend upon his exploitation of the oppressed. The oppressed, in turn, come to rely upon the oppressor. (Thus, the slave comes to rely upon the master for the basic necessities of life.) It is the domination-subordination nature of such interdependence that the nonviolent activist seeks to break through noncooperation. A ground of interdependence still exists, but noncooperation brings it to the full awareness of the adversary and at the same time paves the way for the pursuit of superordinate goals through the cooperation of functional equals. (Even such cooperation will be broken at times by the nonviolent activist when he believes that his cooperation is contributing to injustice to others beyond the two groups.)

INDEPENDENCE AND INTERDEPENDENCE

Thus we see that interdependence is the base for both noncooperation and superordinate goals, for both the waging and reconciliation of conflict. The myriad of interdependences between people that are present are often not recognized. As I indicated in Chapter 6, creativity and imagination are required on the part of the nonviolent activist to bring these interdependences to his own awareness as sources of potential noncooperation. So, too, education and persuasion (and sometimes noncooperation) are needed to bring to others' awareness the interdependences that can serve as sources of potential superordinate goals.

The striving toward superordinate goals can be seen to be a logical component or extension of the theory of nonviolence. It is consistent with the concept of constructive work and is intrinsically tied, together with noncooperation, to the central premises of nonviolence. Nonviolent action includes cooperation with good as well as noncooperation with evil. It entails noncooperation with injustice but not with the perpetrator of the alleged injustice. Working toward superordinate goals is fully consistent with this stand.

Thus what might at first glance be a seeming paradox of cooperation and noncooperation is resolved once it is realized that the nonviolent approach is based upon the differentiation between good and evil—not as attributes of individuals or groups of people but as attributed properties of actions and social systems (or interactions). The nonviolent activist *seeks out* opportunities for cooperation with justice.

Interdependence is the key to the effectiveness of both the cooperative and noncooperative aspects of nonviolence. For there is no power in either approach if our cooperation is neither needed nor desirable to others. The relationship between nonviolence and interdependence was sensed by the foremost advocates of nonviolence. The concept of interdependence was present in the thoughts of Martin Luther King, Jr., as indicated by his acknowledgement of the "interrelated structure of reality" (see Chapter 6).

If our efforts are necessary to achieve a goal or to maintain a system desired by another group, we have the power to grant or to withhold that contribution. Thus, another seeming paradox—that of my advocacy of promoting interdependence on the one hand and the rather firm manifestations of independence that seem to pervade nonviolent action on the other—is resolved.

The interdependence that is to be promoted is not that which exists between master and slave, between oppressor and oppressed, but that which exists between self-respecting equals. Noncooperation can be offered by the oppressed to the extent that they are willing to bear the added suffering that may be involved (which is one reason why self-suffering holds such a central position in the philosophy of nonviolence). Those who seek to dominate others seek to gain something from the efforts of the dominated. Their aim is not to kill them but to use them. In the process they may employ threats of violence or violence. But the oppressed have the power to unconditionally frustrate the aim of the oppressor. They may ultimately have to suffer the violence of the oppressor, but the maintenance of noncooperation, which they even still have the freedom to carry out, signals the complete failure of the oppressor. Freedom always refers to something beyond itself; it is not freedom from death that noncooperation confers, but freedom from the exploitation of others. Slavery necessarily entails obedience, and it is in the above sense that Gandhi (in Bondurant, 1965, p. 30) could say: "The bond of the slave is snapped the moment he considers himself to be a free being."

Gandhi's constructive program was to him a way of building independence and, with it, self-respect. He wanted the Indian people to strive toward self-sufficiency and toward their own spiritual, material, and intellectual uplifting. Independent people are not subservient to others. They are self-respecting people. They are significant forces in human society. What they have to give cannot be taken but is theirs to give or to withhold.

Yet this is not to deny a base of interdependence between peoples. The question is whether or not an individual or group has the capacity to withhold cooperation from the pursuit of a goal that springs from that interdependence. To the extent that an individual or group is able to bear suffering, it has that capacity, and to the extent that the individual or group is self-sufficient, it has that capacity. When the master finds that he can no longer freely take the services of his (former) slave, he may enter into cooperation with him on an equal footing. So, on an equal footing, groups will acknowledge their interdependence and the mutual gains that can come about through working together.

Thus, Gandhi (1941, p. 7), in discussing his constructive program for India, could say:

> Complete Independence through truth and non-violence means the independence of every unit, be it the humblest of the nation, without distinction of race, colour, or creed. This independence is never exclusive. It is, therefore, wholly compatible with interdependence within or without.

The interdependence of independent people or groups is not a contradiction in terms. The growing complexities of modern life increase the interdependence of individuals and groups by increasing the need for specialization of functions. But specialization confers significance on each group's contribution to the whole. The extent of the significance of one group's contribution is the measure of what it has to withhold. Independence is a quality of people who have the capacity for self-control. Where there is a ground of interdependence between groups, independence can be expressed in action by withholding one's contribution, and such action will be powerful to the extent of that contribution's significance. But since a group (or individual) also *gains* from participation in the interdependent system, it cannot withhold without sacrifice. Noncooperation for the nonviolent activist is only an occasional break in his overall pattern of cooperation. The nonviolent activist will cause temporary disruption, but he is checked by the self-sacrifice that such disruption will entail to search his mind and conscience thoroughly before he does so. Nonviolence can be a process through which an increasing independence of individuals and groups will proceed along with the increasingly interdependent societal structure encompassing all of mankind. Nonviolence can insure that independence will accompany the inevitable increasing differentiation and hierarchal integration of the affairs of human society.

Social organizations can arise from a base of interdependence. The rise of nation-states from the union of smaller groupings might have been primarily due to the requirements of military defense. They became stabilized through this continuing need but also through other internal mutual concerns such as transportation, commerce, and communication. Perhaps, still later, from these practical ties emerged emotional ties such as friendship, and love for country, or patriotism.

Perhaps the most stable social organization is not imposed but emerges from interdependence. It arises from the interaction of people with mutual interests. Although there may be exceptions, we have seen in recent history that arbitrarily drawn national boundaries have produced internal strife rather than stability and harmony in certain parts of Africa, where tribes have been artificially tied together into nations. Moreover, the United Nations is a weak body partially because the interdependence of the nations of the world (and their recognition of it) has not yet developed to a degree that will allow a strong world organization to *emerge.* It is true that through the imposition of organization intrinsic interdependence might arise. However, world organization is more likely to be preceded by and emerge from a considerable further advance in interdependence and its recognition.

Those who advise the development of world government as an approach to world peace will not see it achieved through mere advocacy. They would best direct their efforts to attempting to accelerate the already advancing interdependence of the world. But even under world government conflicts will arise. Wherever there are human beings with self-interests, there is the potential for conflict. Nonviolence will become more and more applicable as a means of conflict resolution as mankind's interdependence advances.

Nonviolent noncooperation is a possibility as prevalent as the existence of interdependence. As for the magnitude of violence involved in the calculated extermination of an entire group of people, interdependence may be a partial inhibiting factor. Interdependence between groups by no means terminates the possibility that massive annihilation will be carried out. But where people are interdependent—where people need each other in order to obtain certain objectives—one group is less likely to set for itself the goal of extermination of another group. There are, no doubt, many cases in history (and some painfully recent) in which groups have slaughtered other groups that could have aided them in reaching certain objectives. Yet the slaughter of American Indians was perhaps facilitated by the fact that they were not *needed* by the white settlers. In the minds of the latter, the Indians were probably expendable. (This is not to say that there were not partial inhibiting factors present, such as empathic feelings toward other human beings.) Increased interdependence is an inhibiting factor here merely because the degree to which we need or want something from the efforts of the other people is an obvious factor that has to go into any consideration of whether we can afford to get rid of them and also whether we can afford to incur the displeasure of third parties from whom we also want something. However, it sometimes happens that a group, without setting as its goal the annihilation of another group, employs violence as a means of gaining a certain objective but gets drawn gradually, one step at a time, into committing the unintended deed. My conjecture, therefore, pertains only to interdependence as a potential inhibiting factor of group extermination as an intended goal.

The distinction is important, because whereas it is doubtful that the nonviolent tactic of noncooperation can be at all useful to a group that faces another whose intended goal is annihilation of the former, or for that matter, expulsion from its own territory (although the noncooperation of third parties in this situation *can* be effective in preventing these objectives), noncooperation becomes feasible when the other's objective is exploitation of one form or another. In these latter cases, where one group attempts to subjugate another, interdependence by itself in no way serves to inhibit violence because the oppressor seeks to gain what he wants through a policy of (relatively) limited violence. He seeks to turn interdependence into one of a domination-subordination nature. But in such cases, the methods of nonviolent action, as described in this chapter, that can serve to inhibit the deterioration of conflict are feasible. (Recall the comparison of violent and nonviolent strategies against British domination.) Moreover, noncooperation, which is based upon interdependence, makes violence as a policy of the other group less rational as a means of gaining anything for itself—i.e., less rational to the extent that the intended victims of subjugation have the willingness and ability to maintain noncooperation come what may and can convincingly convey this impression to the adversary. Thus, whereas in a war system, as noted before, acts of violence become rational, violence becomes irrational in an interdependent system in which one group is irrevocably committed to noncooperation.

Increasing interdependence between groups and nations makes forms of nonviolent action other than noncooperation increasingly workable.

As Sherif (1966, pp. 4–5) has noted, the increasing interdependence among nations has already arrived at the point where the policy makers of one nation must take into consideration how the people of other nations will evaluate their actions. Policy makers have come to be concerned about their nation conveying a favorable image to other people throughout the world; and they must justify their actions to others.

Thus, under conditions of recognized interdependence, each group in conflict is subject to the indirect pressures, perhaps in the form of the threat of the withdrawal of cooperation, in one sense or another, by other groups not directly involved in the immediate conflict. Under these conditions, nonviolent protest as a means of drawing world attention to an alleged injustice becomes increasingly significant. Unfortunately, however, the concerns of *national governments* as third parties have yet to go significantly beyond their indirect self-interests that may be involved in a distant conflict. Furthermore, the future potential for the phenomenon noted by Sherif to inhibit policies of violence will have to await a decreased readiness of other peoples—the world onlookers—to accept the justifications of violence conveyed to them by those who employ strategies of violence in conflict. However, even at present, those who confront nonviolence with violence are likely to receive the condemnation of many peoples.

Moreover, already in today's world, every nation and every group is called upon to give some justification, convincing not only to itself but to others, for the use of violence and especially for massive slaughter. Nations that have carried out extensive killing, I know, have been able to find numerous nations around the world who would stand by and accept the justifications offered. But it is difficult to convince others that massive slaughter is justified when the opponent is nonviolent. In India, Great Britain could not have done this; and in fact it restrained its violence there. Local governments within the United States could not have done this, and so although civil rights activists have had to endure suffering and have become victims of violence on occasion, there has been no massive blood-bath. The Soviet Union could not have done this when it invaded Czechoslovakia, and there is a real question as to whether or not it would have unleashed its full capacity for massive violence if the Czechs had continued their nonviolent resistance. As a matter of fact, those Danes and Norwegians who participated in nonviolent resistance against the Nazis were not subjected to annihilation, although some were killed. It is true that the Nazis regarded these people as part of their own "master race" and that their goal was never annihilation in regard to them, and thus it cannot be inferred from these particular situations that if the European Jews had been able to organize nonviolent resistance and had done so their fate would have been different. However, it can be inferred that it would have been possible for groups of German people themselves to save Jews through nonviolent resistance, while escaping their own massive slaughter, just as the Danes had done.

The Nazis, in the end, became victims themselves. Perhaps what aroused other nations of the world to action against them was primarily a desire to protect their own self-interests. In today's world, however, moral indignation can also serve as a stimulant to action for third parties and can be heightened by nonviolent action. And because of the increasingly pervasive interdependence of nations, third-party action can effectively take the form of noncooperation. At any rate, under conditions of interdependence that already exist in our world, the moral indignation of third parties becomes translated into potential practical losses, which those who contemplate massive slaughter as a course of action must take into account as a rational consideration. If the Soviet Union had carried out massive slaughter in Czechoslovakia, the moral indignation already expressed by Communist parties in other nations over the invasion itself would have become a threat to the very unity it was trying to preserve.

Thus, one sense in which nonviolent action can make a violent policy on the part of the adversary irrational is by indirectly, and through moral indignation, inducing third parties to raise the costs of violence for the adversary.

Sherif (1966, p. 173) has indicated that the expansion of interdependence followed by "the recognition of a common predicament leading to transactions to do something about it" are the basic conditions for what he calls a larger sense of "we-ness." These are the prerequisites for the emergence of organizations cutting across group lines, for the development of norms for human conduct applicable to all, and "for the rise of effective morality, ultimately reflected in the conscience of individuals."

A widened sense, in the minds of individuals, of the applicability of moral principles—reaching beyond family, group, and national lines to all human beings—might arise out of a broadened recognized base of interdependence. The expansion of individuals' spheres of love might also ensue.

In this event, nonviolent protest and moral appeals might become more effective means of inhibiting violence. Far more crucial to the establishment of world peace and the abandonment of war and organized violence, however, will be the further development of creative alternatives to violence.

NOTES

[1]Bernard, Ottenberg, and Redl (1971), from whom I borrow these terms, subsume the bad human image under dehumanization.

[2]"In a sense, the *relative* risk potential of our initiatives in any program would remain roughly constant; this is because clear reciprocation by an opponent of an earlier step makes it possible for us to take a larger step with no greater real risk than another small step would have meant before" (Osgood, 1962, p. 95).

[3]In meaning to imply that conflict is waged more humanely between friends than between strangers, I must qualify these and the following remarks. Sometimes social norms might not allow us to be as ferocious with strangers as we, in rare instances, might be with friends. Furthermore, a dispute between friends can, on occasion, overwhelm the friendship. I

should also point out that one should see Coser (1956, pp. 67–72) for the development of a viewpoint that seems to be contradictory to the one being presented here.

[4]Also, attitude change might occur due to strains toward cognitive consistency between the individual's cognition of his behavior that has already been induced and his attitude. Such strains would be greater the less the pressure needed to get him to engage in the behavior was applied, and therefore the more difficult the decision was. This deduction is from Festinger's cognitive dissonance theory and experiments such as those reported in Chapter 3 that may be interpreted as supportive of this theory. I do not believe, however, that such attitude change is an automatic readjustment, as perhaps implied by the theory, but that the individual is induced to rethink his position and in the process might convince himself. The mere decision to comply under minimal pressure might induce him to find attitudinal support for his decision or to engage in counter-attitudinal advocacy.

[5]Perhaps it can be said that attitudes in the South against integration were more often identification-based than internalized. One part of Kelman's (1962) analysis would lead us to believe that induced action would be less likely to lead to change of a segregationist attitude that is based on identification with a reference group than of one that has been internalized. However, this prediction assumes that the individual can easily leave the new situation, and perhaps does not take into account the new information that the individual may be exposed to. As I conjectured in Chapter 3 (where I discussed the distinction between identification and internalization), identification-based attitudes might be less stable than internalized ones.

[6]Moreover, unforeseen events can present opportunities for the initiation of cooperative undertakings. In time of natural catastrophe, for example, the nonviolent activist can and will pitch in to help without making or waiting for proposals of cooperation. Clearing away the damages of a flood, or helping another group to do so, can go a long way toward breaking down polarized images that one group holds of another. In an American college town, for example, it can help to break down the fears and tensions that might exist between students and townspeople. It is consistent with the philosophy of nonviolence, and the principle of *ahimsa*, to attend to the basic welfare of people wherever people are found to be in need, without discrimination in regard to oppressor or oppressed, adversary or friend. Such constructive work is an end in itself, but can help to promote positive attitude formation for each group toward the other.

[7]It is important to allow the adversary full participation in seeking a constructive solution that will move the conflict from the point to which the nonviolent activist has brought it through his noncooperation. Certainly, as I have said, the adversary would often like the situation to be as it was before the confrontation, but our noncooperation has changed the entire situation. Once the adversary realizes that our noncooperation is a fact of life, that he has to recognize our self-interests as well as his own, he will be as capable as we are in suggesting, creating, and implementing solutions in the context of this new perspective, which will move us to a satisfactory reconciliation. For example, once white citizens of an American town realize that they will have to integrate their schools, they might be just as capable as the activists of offering a safe and efficient plan for it. Of course, they might try to avoid or delay the inevitable by offering plans that involve only token integration, but, when they realize that this is unacceptable to the activists, they will get down to business. Safety and efficiency is something that both parties to the conflict would want to maximize in a new plan, and the others would know how to do that as well as or perhaps better than the activists.

The value of involving in the planning of change those who will have to live with it has been demonstrated in a number of studies. Coch and French (1948) showed that when change in production procedures had to be made in a factory, the most efficient group of workers during and after the change-over was the one that had participated in planning the change. Those who had the new procedure imposed upon them by management without being consulted were least efficient and least satisfied with the new state of affairs. People are more likely to enjoy and affirm that which they do for themselves.

CHAPTER 8

Means and Ends

From a psychological perspective, I have explored a philosophy of action that is deeply rooted in both moral and rational thought. I believe that the bold idea of nonviolence presents to humanity a ray of hope that it cannot afford to ignore.

Hasty criticism of an idea sometimes turns our attention from it before we have had a chance to develop it and before we can realize that what has been attacked is merely a caricatured version of that idea. I believe that it is the obligation of the social scientist (or any other seeker after truth) to take an idea and, regardless of the prejudgments that others have made of it, to explore and develop its implications to the best of his ability in order to see for himself what promise it holds and what light it sheds. During this period of exploration, he would be wise to regard thoughtful criticisms of the idea as challenges to overcome, as stimulating aids to the full development of the concept, rather than as terminal roadblocks. It is faith in the beauty of an idea that can sustain him in this endeavor, not reason alone.

Gandhi did not claim to possess truth, but merely to have experimented with it, both in thought and action. But it is often a difficult task to reconcile thought with action.

CONFRONTING SOME CRITICISMS

One of our country's foremost organizers against social injustice, Saul Alinsky (1971, p. 25), wrote:

> The men who pile up the heaps of discussion and literature on the ethics of means and ends—which with rare exception is conspicuous for its sterility—rarely write about

251

their own experiences in the perpetual struggle of life and change. They are strangers, moreover, to the burdens and problems of operational responsibility and the unceasing pressure for immediate decisions. They are passionately committed to a mystical objectivity where passions are suspect. They assume a nonexistent situation where men dispassionately and with reason draw and devise means and ends as if studying a navigational chart on land. They can be recognized by one of two verbal brands: "We agree with the ends but not the means," or "This is not the time." *The means-and-end moralists or non-doers always wind up on their ends without any means.*

It must be said that many of the most prolific contributors to the literature on the ethics of means and ends, such as Gandhi and King, were no strangers to organized action. Gandhi evolved his philosophy through action. Some of the foremost activists for social change in our country have adhered to the philosophy of nonviolence. Moreover, a number of the leaders of the American civil rights movement had studied the literature on nonviolence before embarking upon their historic mission. Martin Luther King, Jr. had been inspired by Gandhi's writings and was well-versed in the literature on nonviolence before his leadership of the Montgomery bus boycott catapulted him to world fame.

Furthermore, a careful study of the philosophy of nonviolence would reveal that one who merely says "I agree with the ends but not the means," and then does nothing, would be out of step with the philosophy. He might perhaps qualify as a "means-and-end moralist," but so does the nonviolent activist. Therefore, I believe that it is erroneous to equate all "means-and-end moralists" with "non-doers." A failure to realize that nonviolence demands action against injustice represents a basic misunderstanding of the philosophy. To advise a brutally oppressed people that their means are unworthy of their ends and then to offer no means, would not only be sheer folly but would be to silently contribute to the injustice that they are presently enduring. Nonviolence is not a passive waiting game.

By claiming that Gandhi merely selected the most practical means at hand and then cloaked them in moral rationalizations, Alinsky (1971, p. 38) seemed inclined to remove the successful nonviolent activists of the past, indeed in this case the originator of organized nonviolence, from the realm of "means-and-end moralists." Thus he could proclaim that all "means-and-end moralists" are strangers to the world of action and are passive non-doers.

It is true that Satyagraha was not conceived of in an ivory tower but was born in thought *and* action. However, to say, as Alinsky (1971, pp. 38–39) did, that Gandhi did not use guns because he did not have them, and that even if he had them, the Indian people were too passive and submissive to use them, is to overlook a number of important considerations. It is often the case, *before* the revolution begins, that an oppressed people do not have guns, or at least not nearly as much capacity for violence as does the government (see Arendt, 1969, p. 48), and also that these oppressed people are, perhaps because of their oppression, weak and submissive. Alinsky (1971, p. xxii) himself quoted John Adams as having implied that the American Revolution took place before the war began, because the real revolution consisted of a "radical change in the principles, opinions, sentiments and affections of the people." The revolution, whether it is accompanied by the use of violence or not, can only take place when the people refuse to be submissive any longer. Looking at the situation of Gandhi's India in the context of similar conflicts in recent history, it would not be unreasonable to conclude that, although Gandhi's choice of means was partially based on pragmatic considerations, the choice of violence was no less open to him than it has been to revolutionaries throughout history.

Alinsky (1971, p. 41) doubted whether the idea of nonviolent action would have ever occurred to Gandhi if he had been faced with a totalitarian regime. Perhaps it wouldn't have. Theories are often born in their most fertile soil and extended to other territory only later. (That is, a scientist might develop a theory by attending to certain data A. The theory might never have occurred to him if he had concentrated on data B. Yet, once the theory is evolved, he might find that he is able to fruitfully apply it to data B.)

Moreover, as I pointed out in Chapter 6, there are cases in which nonviolent resistance, if not the full-blown philosophy, has arisen in totalitarian atmospheres. Furthermore, the fact that it is hard to develop an organized mass resistance while under totalitarian repression is as much a difficulty for the use of organized violence as it is for the use of organized nonviolence.

Alinsky was fond of pointing out that throughout history individuals and groups who have acted expediently in their own interests while expounding self-righteous justifications for their actions have condemned those same actions as immoral when used by others against themselves. He suggested that even some of those who had supported nonviolent tactics in India had reversed themselves once they had gained political control (1971, pp. 39 ff.).

The process of the rationalization of self-interest has by no means been neglected in this book. But we often fail to distinguish between the individuals who have adhered to a particular philosophy or theory, or have even contributed to its development, and the philosophy or theory itself. If Copernicus, for example, after having developed the heliocentric theory, would have renounced it, this action would have had no relevance to a proper evaluation of the theory itself. (I do not mean to imply here that Gandhi ever renounced his own philosophy; he did not.)

To take this example further, it has been suggested that Kepler's quest for supporting evidence for the heliocentric theory was partially motivated by his sun-worship (Burtt, 1932, pp. 44 ff.). We can say, in a sense, that his findings were partially a result of his need to rationalize his belief in the divinity of the sun. Yet this in no way detracts from his findings or from the heliocentric theory that they support. Even if we were to grant that the philosophy of nonviolence could have arisen only under the circumstances in which it did, or that it was the product of Gandhi's rationalization, it would demand evaluation on its own merits. Discoveries are no less profound for being rationalizations.

Alinsky (1971, pp. 26 ff.) regarded his psychohistorical observations pertaining to the conditions under which people have attempted to justify means through reference to ends as indicative of "rules" reflecting the behavior of those who wage conflict. They can be looked upon, however, as referring merely to trends in human behavior, the dangers of which the nonviolent activist seeks to avoid. I believe that the philosophy of nonviolence merits our support not in spite of but partially because of our knowledge of such tendencies toward justification. The nonviolent optimist looks not only to what man has done and to how he has justified it, which he takes fully into account, but also to what he is capable of doing. Man is capable of generating and striving to adhere to new principles of action that reject violence.

Because Alinsky was a very talented organizer and one who exhibited much creativity in developing humane tactics for waging conflict, the nonviolent activist has much to learn from his experience. He was a man of decisive action, who most certainly had great faith in people and a great fervor for social justice. In fact, it seems to me that his overriding concern that led him to a rejection of means-ends morality was his fear that it would lead to inaction or ineffective acton against injustice.

However, I have emphasized that nonviolence *demands* action against injustice. Thus, it becomes incumbent upon the nonviolent activist to search for and find nonviolent means. It is the *faith* of the nonviolent activist that there is always a nonviolent alternative to be found. But what if, in a given situation, he cannot find it? Despite the demonstrations of nonviolent action in the nonhypothetical world of the past, the skeptic is prone to dream up hypothetical cases especially contrived to produce a moral dilemma from which it is seemingly impossible for the nonviolent activist to extricate himself. By way of an intriguing dialogue between the nonviolent activist and the skeptic, Joan Baez (1968, pp. 131–138) has made several important points in regard to the "What would you do if ...?" query, only some of which will be mentioned here. As she has indicated, when the nonviolent activist does offer a way out, the undaunted skeptic proceeds to eliminate it by placing as many additional hypothetical restrictions on the already hypothetical situation as he can, all designed to insure that he has created an air-tight moral dilemma. She also has made the point that although there are certain situations that may present unresolvable moral dilemmas even for the nonviolent activist, this is no ground for discounting the philosophy, which is not thereby proved unworkable. As Martin Luther King, Jr. (1958, p. 99) has suggested, the nonviolent activist is not free from moral dilemmas. Moreover, the great threat confronting mankind is not the hypothetical individual assault on Grandma (one of the skeptic's favorite hypothetical cases) and the reflexive spur-of-the-moment reaction to it but, as Baez indicated, the organized, reflective violence of groups and nations. According to the view that I have presented in this book, it is the rationally planned violence, obediently carried out, that is responsible for the greater part of the carnage of our times. Finally, one of the major problems in our world is that we are willing to accept violence when given "suitable" justifications for it. Instead of unequivocally condemning all violence, we have been inclined to withhold judgment until we have considered the justifications that will inevitably be offered.

But what if? What if the nonviolent activist walked into a room and found a man standing with a gun in the act of killing ten people lined up against the wall? The activist finds, in this amazing world of hypothetical cases, a loaded gun lying on a table near the door. His marksmanship is not good enough to allow him to shoot the gun out of the killer's hand, or to aim to wound, and the only way open to him to restrain the killer is to shoot to kill.

Gandhi once said: "In our ignorance we must kill rabid dogs even as we might have to kill a man found in the act of killing people" (in Erikson, 1969, p. 422). He has also said: "I do believe that where there is only a choice between cowardice and violence I would advise violence" (Gandhi, 1961, p. 132).

At the risk of confusing a man with a philosophy, I accept these statements as relevant to our understanding of nonviolence. How are we to interpret them? While Gandhi would have advised violence over cowardice, he maintained the faith that there is always a third alternative—that of nonviolent action. The ideal of nonviolence permits of neither cowardice nor violence. He believed that it is our (present) *ignorance* that allows us to see only the two alternatives.

The above hypothetical case presents us with a dilemma: we are confronted with a situation in which it appears to us that the only way we can stop an injustice is to commit violence, which in itself involves injustice. Perhaps it can be said that the action that the nonviolent activist might take in this hypothetical situation and Gandhi's statements quoted above are inconsistent with the ideal of nonviolence. They are acknowledgments of the great difficulty involved whenever one tries to wed philosophy with action. They are consistent, however, with the striving toward the ideal of nonviolence, which demands action based on the refusal to do or allow injustice. To kill a man who is in the act of killing other people is the closest that that particular situation allows the nonviolent activist to approach his ideal, given the limited state of advancement of the tactics of nonviolence or given the inability of the activist in that particular situation to devise humane means. But to say this is not to deny that the act of killing, even in this situation, is intrinsically immoral. It is a violation of the sanctity of human life. No amount of justification will make a violent act intrinsically moral. The nonviolent activist strives to avoid killing, but in this situation, granted his limited knowledge, had no way of doing so because not having killed the man would have drawn him into passive complicity with the killing of others.

Of course, it is commonplace today for national leaders on the eve of war to express their sadness and reluctance to enter into it and to proclaim that they have been left with no alternative. They often try to portray (and might very well believe) their situation to be precisely analogous to the moral dilemma of our hypothetical case. It is perhaps true that in *their* ignorance they cannot find alternatives in their situation, just as the nonviolent activist in *his* ignorance could not find an alternative in the hypothetical case. That is why the task of the nonviolent activist is to seek, discover, create, and demonstrate nonviolent alternatives while, although ceaselessly condemning violence, not self-righteously looking down his moral nose at those who turn to violence.

What distinguishes the nonviolent activist is that his ideals pertain to means, to action, and not only to ends. He strives toward moral means and ends, and restrains himself from justifying means in terms of ends. When ideals pertaining to ends gain ascendancy over those pertaining to action, violence is more probable. Often in severe conflict both parties are mindful of the morality of their ends but only of the effectiveness of their means, which they seek to justify in terms of their ends. The nonviolent activist, willing to take risks in order to avoid violence, willing to suffer, and not willing to value his adversary's life less than his own, is more likely to find alternatives to violence. Because he strives to adhere to principles of action that reject violence, he more diligently seeks nonviolent alternatives.

That these abstract differentiations have any bearing on action is testified to by the fact that Gandhi, King, and others who have adhered to nonviolence on moral grounds had, when conventional channels were closed to them, found ways to wage conflict humanely. Moreover, while no two conflict situations are identical, they waged conflict nonviolently in situations quite similar to those in which, at other times, conflict has been waged violently by people who have claimed to have had no other alternative. Those who do not seek creative alternatives to violence are doomed to violence.

Perhaps, however, man is not even capable of ever perfectly attaining nonviolence. Arthur Koestler (1969) has referred to nonviolence as "a philosophy easy to eulogize and impossible to realize."

Gandhi might have agreed:

> *Ahimsa* is a comprehensive principle. We are helpless mortals caught in the conflagration of *himsa*. The saying that life lives on life has a deep meaning in it. Man cannot for a moment live without consciously or unconsciously committing outward *himsa*. The very fact of his living—eating, drinking and moving about—necessarily involves some *himsa*, destruction of life, be it ever so minute. A votary of *ahimsa* therefore remains true to his faith if the spring of all his actions is compassion, if he shuns to the best of his ability the destruction of the tiniest creature, tries to save it, and thus incessantly strives to be free from the deadly coil of *himsa*. He will be constantly growing in self-restraint and compassion, but he can never become entirely free from outward *himsa*.
>
> Then again, because underlying *ahimsa* is the unity of all life, the error of one cannot but affect all, and hence man cannot be wholly free from *himsa*. So long as he continues to be a social being, he cannot but participate in the *himsa* that the very existence of society involves.... (Gandhi, 1954a, pp. 427–428)

From time to time, man has bettered himself by striving toward ideals that he could never attain but only more and more closely approximate. Democracy, for example, is an ideal that our society is founded upon, and yet it can never be perfectly attained. Yet we believe that we will improve our society by honestly striving toward it. It would be foolish to deny the value of striving toward that which cannot be perfectly attained. Gandhi believed that man has the potential to approximate the ideal of nonviolence more closely than he already has. One need only believe that man is capable of moving more closely toward the ideal of nonviolence in order to seriously entertain the philosophy. For the skeptic, ironically, the striving toward nonviolence is not good enough; he wants to see it in its perfect form or not at all. He seems to start with the assumption that nonviolence has been presented as a magic formula and then, strangely, sees reason to reject it upon finding that it is an imperfect instrument. To mock the philosophy of those who have demonstrated with at least partial success that conflict can be waged nonviolently is like mocking the ideal of democracy because it has not been perfectly attained.

The faith of Gandhi was that possessed by any experimenter who has entertained a new theory or hypothesis. One seldom finds that which one does not seek, and it is equally true that one seldom seeks that which one has no hope of finding. It is the duty of the nonviolent activist to seek creative alternatives to those of turning one's back on injustice and violence, so that we may move toward a nonviolent world. It is his faith that we can free ourselves from our ignorance.

The reluctance that leaders often express as they plunge their nations into war is accompanied by their belief that their only choice at that point is between violence and cowardice. If there were another way, they say, they would gladly seize upon it. But, as I have pointed out, nonviolent action has been employed in situations that have appeared to be quite similar to those in which violence had been used. It is interesting, though hazardous, to speculate in retrospect about the Vietnam struggle. Is it not possible that Ho Chi Minh could have led his people in waging conflict nonviolently against the French? I am not knowledgeable enough about the history of Vietnam to be aware of all of the important differences between Gandhi's India and Ho Chi Minh's Vietnam. But one similarity is that both leaders were up against a colonialist power. Furthermore, those who would argue that nonviolent strategy could be employed against the British because they are a humane people would probably be willing to classify the French as humane also (even though *both* nations have been responsible for much violence). Then, too, Ho Chi Minh was probably revered by his people as much as Gandhi was by the Indians. Is it not within the realm of possibility that, if not decades of conflict, at least decades of massive slaughter and destruction could have been avoided? Could it not be that the United States, whose involvement began with financial support to the French and then the sending of military "advisers" to Vietnam, might have had no pretext to enter militarily?

There are those who would object to these speculations because they blame primarily the French and the United States for the years of slaughter in Indochina. But, regardless of the matter of placing blame, an important consideration is whether or not Ho Chi Minh and his people, on their own initiative, could have avoided the violence that engulfed them by waging conflict nonviolently.

PREVENTIVE NONVIOLENCE AND NONCOOPERATION IN FOREIGN POLICY

Through much of this book I have considered nonviolence as a strategy for initiating and waging manifest conflict. In this form, nonviolent action has been employed by oppressed and exploited people and by those in sympathy with such people, as in the case of the anti-war movement in the United States. But nonviolence can also be used to resolve latent conflict before it becomes manifest. Preventive nonviolence is perhaps more available to the unexploited and unoppressed, to the "haves" rather than to the "have-nots," or to those who, perhaps inadvertently, are participants in the perpetration of social injustice.

Undoubtedly, the most rapid movement toward a world of peace and social justice can be made through the use of nonviolence, not by the downtrodden but by the politically and economically powerful.

It is no secret that our government has propped up unrepresentative and repressive military dictatorships in various parts of the world. At the present time, some of its economic policies encourage institutionalized racism, exploitation, and oppression. Our nation's giant corporations, in collusion with our government, have exploited the resources and labor of countries all over the world. Our government has made the world safe for American exploitation by helping to overthrow nonobliging governments, as in Guatemala. It has financially supported institutionalized brutality, as in the case of Duvalier of Haiti. When one reads the startling facts of American imperialism (see, e.g., Oglesby[1967] for documentation) one might conclude that American greed has known no bounds. In the deepest sense, the few have been living off the misery of the many.

The classic example of organized and institutionalized racism is the Union of South Africa. Its national policy and practice are the incarnation of the doctrine of white supremacy in the midst of a population which is overwhelmingly black. But the tragedy of South Africa is not simply in its own policy; it is the fact the racist government of

South Africa is virtually made possible by the economic policies of the United States and Great Britain, two countries which profess to be the moral bastions of our Western world (King, 1968, p. 202).

It is not enough for our leaders to speak out against apartheid in South Africa when all the while we economically cooperate with oppression not only in Africa, but in Latin America, Vietnam, and other parts of the world.

Something is dangerously wrong when economic greed dictates the rationalization of racism and oppression. However, it can be said that it has been our fear of Communism that has either led to or has helped to rationalize—probably both—our complicity in the oppression and exploitation of others. The exact weight of economic factors in shaping our foreign policy can be debated, but the self-interest of national security and fear of its being jeopardized has certainly been a major factor. Especially in regard to Vietnam, it can be argued that our foreign policy has been motivated more by the fear of the spread of Communism than by economic factors.

We have often supported what we ourselves as a nation consider to be evil, out of a belief that it had been necessary in order to protect our national security. The fear of Communism has gained a stranglehold over our foreign policy, with the consequence that that policy has become one of negative and destructive reactions rather than of positive and constructive initiatives.

I believe that fear has driven us to knowingly cooperate with present injustice, and we have considered such action to be necessary in order to obtain the ultimate goal of world peace and justice. In short, I believe that a well-intentioned people guided by well-intentioned leaders have rationalized destructive and unjust means in terms of idealistic ends.

And where has such a policy led? Our stupendous build-up of nuclear armaments has not brought us security, nor has the unspeakable horror that our government has visited upon the Vietnamese people. And our complicity with racism and oppression throughout the world has contributed to the misery of others but not to security for ourselves. We are no more secure today than yesterday, but we do have considerably more blood on our hands. An ends-dominated strategy insures nothing about the future while opening the door to cooperation with evil in the present.

In countries where we have supplied arms to the few that would enable them to suppress the many while extracting the natural wealth of those countries and sharing it only with the few, we have been alienating more friends than we have been making. Ironically, in intending to stop the spread of Communism, we are pushing more and more people toward it.

I realize that a nation such as ours, which has evolved its present foreign policy and military machinery over many years, cannot abruptly reverse its entire policy, fully disarm, and completely embrace nonviolence as an overall strategy. Due to the attitudes toward world affairs that have been built up among the people and their leaders, it cannot realistically be done overnight. Moreover, we have contributed to a world atmosphere in which such a sudden shift would be too unacceptably dangerous to contemplate, although on this point many advocates of nonviolence would disagree with me. But those who advocate nonviolent national defense estimate that it would take from ten to twenty years to prepare and train the citizenry for it (see King-Hall, 1959, pp. 209, 217). Within that time, a nation could attempt disarmament through Osgood's GRIT plan. In other words, the advocacy of immediate unilateral disarmament is not necessary and the dangers of that policy can be avoided. We can move toward nuclear disarmament while we are preparing for nonviolent national defense and while we are engaged in a policy of noncooperation with injustice.

The limited use of nonviolent approaches to world affairs would be feasible at the present time both in terms of domestic public opinion and world effect. It can be strongly argued that the United States would be more secure today if it had adopted a policy of noncooperation with injustice and cooperation with good rather than that of the rationalization of the cooperation with injustice through the false hope of idealistic ends. Perhaps we can begin to avert the evil that is perpetrated when means are divorced from idealistic ends.

Noncooperation with injustice does not mean total noncooperation with another nation. Such would be an overly simplistic policy that would do more harm than good. American companies doing business in South Africa comply with racism if they pay black people less than white people for the same jobs or otherwise practice racial discrimination. If they are willing and able to resist racism, their presence could be a positive force. Noncooperation with injustices perpetrated by a military dictatorship would not mean that we should not cooperate with aid or trade programs that we are sure will benefit the people of that country. If we did not make such distinctions, we could easily fall into the mistake of contributing to the hardships that people of such countries are already enduring. However, there are many instances in which our resources and our aid have contributed to oppression and in which noncooperation is called for.

Furthermore, nonviolent foreign policy would include efforts to eliminate poverty and misery throughout the world. As Martin Luther King, Jr. (1968, p. 206) has pointed out:

> Two-thirds of the peoples of the world go to bed hungry at night. They are undernourished, ill-housed and shabbily clad. Many of them have no houses or beds to sleep in. Their only beds are the sidewalks of the cities and the dusty roads of the villages. Most of these poverty-stricken children of God have never seen a physician or a dentist.

Those people and nations that hoard their wealth while other people lack adequate food, clothing, shelter, and medical attention are not only morally deficient in their actions but court world disaster that will surely engulf themselves in the end.

Nonviolence, through its use by Gandhi and King, has come to be known as a weapon of the oppressed. But it can most rapidly transform the world when employed by the economically and politically powerful. It is precisely the United States, as the most powerful and wealthy nation in the world, whose nonviolent initiatives would have the most far-reaching effects.

The moral force of noncooperation must be employed throughout human society. World opinion is becoming an increasingly important ingredient in world politics. It will become a more potent factor in world affairs when it comes to be backed up by moral noncooperation.

Looking at the world today, it is often not difficult to predict in what areas severe manifest conflict will erupt. It takes no great gift of foresight to know that in a country like Rhodesia, where a few hundred thousand white people economically and politically suppress and exploit millions of black people, there exists an unstable and dangerous situation that sooner or later will explode. White Rhodesians can avoid disaster, both to themselves and the blacks, by relieving oppression, sharing the power, and laying the foundation for an integrated society in which whites and blacks will need each other in order to move toward superordinate goals. Likewise, the white people of South Africa cannot maintain security through repression indefinitely.

But wherever people are oppressed there is a potential for violence and chaos, and in the midst of a world-wide revolution of rising expectations due to advances in technology, transportation, and communication, we need not concern ourselves with such predictions. Moral action for its own sake is bound to yield practical benefits to those who engage in it.

The powerful nations of the world can continue to opt for the short-run material benefits of exploitation and wait for the initiatives for social change to come from the oppressed themselves. But if the American people believe that they would not tolerate injustice to themselves, they should not expect that other people will long tolerate injustice to *themselves. And it would be an understatement to say that we have no guarantee that those initiatives will be nonviolent ones, devoid of intention to turn the tables on the oppressors. On the other hand, those nations can offer the nonviolent initiatives themselves, by noncooperating with racism and exploitation. With a policy of moral concern for others, in which we would apply our ideals to our means themselves, we face a bright future for ourselves as well as others.

PEACE

The elimination of the gross injustices I have been speaking of will not eliminate conflict from our world. There will always be clashes of self-interests. Shridharani (1939, p. 254) has said of Gandhi:

> He takes ample cognizance of man's tendency toward self-interest and, consequently, stresses the necessity of a permanent institution or instrument to deal with the inevitable, though sporadic, social conflict.

There are those who believe that conflict would be absent in a classless society. However, as Shridharani (1939, p. 254) has noted, "the roots of 'interestedness' seem to go deeper than class." Therefore we must find nonviolent alternatives to war.

There are those who ask us to distinguish between the violence of the oppressed and the violence of the oppressors, between revolutionary violence and reactionary violence, between aggressive violence and defensive violence, between violence that liberates and violence that represses, between international and intranational violence, or between political violence and criminal violence. Those who claim that there are inconsistencies in the nonviolent position should consider the inconsistencies involved in decrying the misery wrought by the violence of the North Vietnamese while ignoring or rationalizing the results of American violence in Vietnam, or the inconsistencies involved in deploring the suffering caused by the Vietnam War while condoning violence committed at home in the name of protesting that war, or those involved in denouncing the violence of terrorist groups while tolerating the violence of national armies.

For the countless millions of dead of past wars there is no distinction between the violence of aggression and the violence of defense or between the violence of the oppressors and the violence of the oppressed. For these victims, there has been only one kind of violence—the kind that kills and maims human beings and humanity itself.

Violence can never liberate us from violence. It cannot liberate us from the deadly game of history in which the oppressed and oppressors change places every so often. It cannot liberate those who employ violence from their own repressive means. Those who advocate violence to combat injustice merely contribute to it. Only if one wishes to change places with the oppressors, and throw them down to the depths of oppression, is violence needed. Such a program is not revolutionary but reactionary, for it in itself does not achieve change in the social condition of mankind but only a change in personnel—a change in who will oppress and who will be oppressed. In the long run, there is no advance here, but merely a continuation of the injustice of violence, of the age-old seesaw power game that has been played throughout history and that now threatens to destroy humankind.

Those who advocate violence are not revolutionary, in the sense that they stoop to the adversary's level by playing his game for their own ends. The nonviolent revolutionary seeks to change the game itself. He cannot do so by committing himself to it but rather by foreshadowing the new society by his own actions. The revolution most worthy of the name will be the one from violence to nonviolence.

Granted our tremendous capacity for violence, both psychological and technological, what endangers human life is our willingness to justify violence. We all subscribe to the commandment: Thou shalt not kill. But we often add: "Except when . . .," and the victims of those exceptions are legion. Notwithstanding the most massive slaughter, we are often inclined to withhold judgment until the self-righteous perpetrators of violence come to give us reasons for it. It is not only when we believe that the violence is protecting our self-interests do we excuse it; even when we or our nation are not directly involved in the conflict, we listen patiently to those who come from the scene of conflict to inform us why they have turned to violence. If we are sympathetic to their cause, we shy away from reproaching them for their means. Perhaps we do so out of ignorance because we have not studied or developed other means that we might suggest to them.

If we believe that the destruction of human life is immoral, then it is always immoral. Justifications do not have the power to raise the dead from their graves or to obliterate the evilness of violence. It is easy to refrain from violence when there is no conflict, when there is no *reason* for violence. But a time must come when the peoples of the world condemn violence absolutely, when they refuse to wait for the words of justification, when they no longer accept justifications of violence as excuses for violence. The development of nonviolent alternatives will hasten that time.

The distant future in which the moral ends that are used to justify violence are to be achieved is uncertain. What is certain is the carnage on the battlefields of the world. Violence is not only immoral, but we are finally learning that it is not practical. The moral end of peace, which our leaders promise as they lead us to war, never arrives.

> If we assume that life is worth living and that man has a right to survive, then we must find an alternative to war. In a day when vehicles hurtle through outer space and guided ballistic missiles carve highways of death through the stratosphere, no nation can claim victory in war. A so-called limited war will leave little more than a calamitous legacy of human suffering, political turmoil and spiritual disillusionment. A world war will leave only smoldering ashes as mute testimony of a human race whose folly led inexorably to ultimate death. If modern man continues to flirt unhesitatingly with war, he will transform his earthly habitat into an inferno such as even the mind of Dante could not imagine. (King, 1968, p. 214)

Our capacity for justification is seemingly limitless, and the reasons given for violence are rational in the short run, and only in our ignorance and limited knowledge of the waging of conflict. But as for the long run, we stand in danger of justifying ourselves out of existence.

When our government, in the name of peace, engages in

> mutilating hundreds of thousands of Vietnamese children with napalm, burning villages and rice fields at random, painting the valleys of that small Asian country red with human blood, leaving broken bodies in countless ditches and sending home half-men, mutilated mentally and physically (King, 1968, p. 213)

we have a grim and clear reminder that we must be wary of those who talk peace while they prepare for war.

We can make peace only through the affirmation of life and brotherhood, and this must take the form of action. War and violence are the negation of peace and justice. All the talk of peace in the world, all the justification of violence, will not revolutionize the social interaction of conflict.

What is the relation between means and ends? Martin Luther King, Jr. (1967, p. 71) believed that "the end is pre-existent in the means, and ultimately destructive means cannot bring about constructive ends." Advocates of nonviolence have claimed that peace is not a distant goal at which we can arrive through any means. The great ideals to be realized in the uncertain future have time and again served as justifications for the greatest horrors and injustices perpetrated in the present. The means are so important because they are here and now in the world of action, while the ideal ends exist only in people's minds, to be approached in the uncertain future.

Advocates of nonviolence believe that nonviolence is both moral and practical. Martin Luther King, Jr. believed that all life is interrelated, that whatever affects one directly affects all indirectly, that "If you harm me, you harm yourself." He has said that

> ... we cannot preserve self without being concerned about preserving other selves. The universe is so structured that things go awry if men are not diligent in their cultivation of the other-regarding dimension. (1968, p. 210)

The practical and the moral converge in peaceful and just means. This becomes increasingly apparent as the "network of mutuality" becomes more and more tightly woven through technological advancement of both a constructive and destructive nature. "We are in the fortunate position of having our deepest sense of morality coalesce with our self-interest" (King, 1968, p. 210).

The belief in the interrelatedness or unity of all life really can be said to underlie the concept of nonviolence. It is this interrelatedness, which I would argue is ever growing tighter, that is responsible for a convergence of morality and practicality. To the extent that life is interrelated, violence turns back upon itself; hatred turns back upon itself; and love turns back upon itself.

We often fail to see this when we look at conflict only in the short run. Was there not violence in the American Revolution? Were not the Nazis defeated through violence? Does not the United States now deter invasion through the threat of violence? Affirmative answers to these questions need not embarrass the nonviolent activist. When we step back from conflict and with historical perspective look at violence in the long run, a different picture emerges. Has not violence been responsible for the death of millions of people in this century alone? Does not nuclear weaponry place our world on the brink of destruction? Has war ended war and can it ever?

When one takes a long-run perspective, it is perhaps more apparent today than ever before that man is trapped by his own violence because he has not yet mastered the peaceful waging of conflict. We continuously live on the brink of war. Nuclear weapons aside, in less than three-quarters of a century we have seen the human destruction of World

Wars I and II, the Korean and Vietnam wars, the Pakistan Civil War, the Middle East conflict, the violence in Northern Ireland, the slaughter of the Armenians, Jews, Ibos, and the half-million "Communists" in Indonesia—the list is seemingly endless. Mankind must free itself from violence.

Let us ponder what truth there is in the words of Martin Luther King, Jr. (1968, p. 72):

> The ultimate weakness of violence is that it is a descending spiral, begetting the very thing it seeks to destroy. Instead of diminishing evil, it multiplies it. Through violence you may murder the liar, but you cannot murder the lie, nor establish the truth. Through violence you may murder the hater, but you do not murder hate. In fact, violence merely increases hate. So it goes. Returning violence for violence multiplies violence, adding deeper darkness to a night already devoid of stars. Darkness cannot drive out darkness: only light can do that. Hate cannot drive out hate: only love can do that.

In nonviolence, the moral and the practical converge. How to overcome injustice through intrinsically moral means is the challenge of mankind. Morality turns out to be a practical guide for our behavior when we are dealing with an uncertain future. We can be guided to a higher rationality only through morality. How strange the workings of life, that ancient moral premises—rationally developed—point the way to the survival of mankind. The increasing interdependence of human society makes it ever clearer that the good of the individual is contained in the good of all and that there is practicality in morality.

True peace is far more than, far different from, a lull between wars. Our leaders still persist in trying to convince us that the present war is the one that will bring enduring peace. But peace will come to mankind only when it learns to wage conflict peacefully. Peace as a distant goal is a meaningless delusion.

We must conceive of peace as an activity, not as an end-state. For too long, peace has been equated with the absence of conflict. This formulation of peace is inherent in the mistaken notion that war can end war. For without the development of nonviolent means, the next major conflict can only lead to war once again. Once we realize that conflict will always be with us, we can understand that *peace must be found in the means we use to wage conflict.*

Nonviolence must become a way of life. People must come to regard all human beings as their brothers and sisters. Nonviolence means that we do not violate anybody. It means that we do not exploit or oppress anybody. Nonviolence means that we regard life as too sacred to be destroyed for any reason. But beyond that, it means that we do not tolerate injustice anywhere or to anyone, that we do not turn our backs on the suffering of others. Nonviolence means active goodwill toward all people.

When we begin to take control of our own lives, when we begin to stand up to injustice to ourselves and refuse to be bribed and coerced into complicity with injustice to others, when we are able to say "I am somebody" and reserve our right to noncooperate with what we consider to be evil, not to be used or manipulated by others, then we not only become a social force in our own right but we begin to love ourselves. And the circle of love must be extended from ourselves beyond our immediate family, beyond our immediate circle of friends, beyond our nation, to all of humankind and perhaps eventually to all of life itself.

What is, however, of the most compelling urgency is the further creation and discovery of nonviolent alternatives. Those already known to us, some of which have been discussed in this book, should in no way be regarded as the only conceivable ones. The moral premises of nonviolence can serve only as the basis from which nonviolent alternatives can be rationally developed. "Thou shalt not kill" is not a strategy for waging conflict. It is a moral premise which, although accepted down through the ages, has not in itself saved us from the horrors of violence. It is only the human intellect, starting from that premise, proceeding from a belief in the sanctity of human life, that can create and discover new alternatives to violence.

Nonviolence goes beyond the rationality of weighing the immediate contingencies of strategies of death. It goes beyond mere proclamations of love and peace. Nonviolence is rational action based on love. It is *ahimsa*; it is *agapē*. It is rational, active love that abhors injustice and violence. It is a third alternative to those of ignoring injustice or creating injustice through violence. It seeks to forever push back the frontiers of the moral dilemma that leaves us with injustice on the one hand and violence on the other, by exploring new tactics, consistent with *ahimsa*, and capable of overcoming injustice.

The closer we can approximate the refusal to do or allow injustice, the more closely we have approached the ideal of nonviolence. One need not fully believe in the philosophy of nonviolence to grant that the creation and discovery of humane alternatives for the waging of conflict is a worthwhile endeavor. One need not be a pacifist in order to be interested in exploring the ways in which conflict can be waged nonviolently. Let the critics of nonviolence focus their attention on overcoming their own criticisms by participating in the task of improving the strategy and tactics of nonviolence, rather than allow their skepticism to turn them away from it. For as Martin Luther King, Jr. (1968, p. 223) said:

> We still have a choice today: nonviolent coexistence or violent coannihilation. This may well be mankind's last chance to choose between chaos and community.

Nonviolence must be studied now. Nonviolent action must be taken now. If it is our ignorance of nonviolent ways of resolving conflict that envelops our planet in violence, then we must strive to discover and demonstrate nonviolent alternatives.

The task of the further development of nonviolence in both theory and action awaits those dreamers among us who have visions of peoples of all religions, creeds, races, and nations dancing together in the streets of the world in joyous brotherhood. It awaits those who, having tremendous faith in the human mind and heart, overcome moments of despair and cynicism derived from looking at man as he is by lifting their gaze toward what man can be.

I believe that Gandhi and King were revolutionary social scientists who have pointed to a way out of the dark age of massive violence. It is easy to scoff at a strange idea. It is more difficult to accept its challenge. I believe that the question for us is not: Can nonviolence work? but: How can we make it work? I believe that the way of nonviolence is the way of peace and social justice. And I believe that we are capable of it.

Let us accept the challenge of Gandhi's truth and move toward brotherhood at last. What Martin Luther King, Jr. called "the nonviolent affirmation of the sacredness of human life" is morality in action. Let us choose life and affirm it.

*Occasionally in life one develops
a conviction so precious and
meaningful that he will stand on
it till the end. This is what I
have found in nonviolence.*

MARTIN LUTHER KING, Jr.

Bibliography

Abelson, R. and Miller, J. Negative persuasion via personal insult. *Journal of Experimental Social Psychology*, 1967, **3**, 321–333.

Adorno, T. W., Frenkel-Brunswik, E., Levinson, D. J., and Sanford, R. N. *The authoritarian personality.* New York: Harper & Row, 1950.

Alinsky, S. D. *Rules for radicals.* New York: Random House, 1971. Quotations used with permission from Random House, Inc.

Amir, Y. Contact hypothesis in ethnic relations. *Psychological Bulletin*, 1969, **71**, 319–342.

Arendt, H. *On violence.* New York: Harcourt, Brace & World, 1969.

Aronson, E. and Carlsmith, J. M. Effect of the severity of threat on the devaluation of forbidden behavior. *Journal of Abnormal and Social Psychology*, 1963, **66**, 584–589.

Baez, Joan, *Daybreak.* New York: Dial Press, 1968. Pp. 131–138.

Bandura, A., Ross, D., and Ross, S. A. Transmission of aggression through imitation of aggressive models. *Journal of Abnormal and Social Psychology*, 1961, **63**, 575–582.

Bandura, A., Ross, D., and Ross, S. A. Imitation of film-mediated aggressive models. *Journal of Abnormal and Social Psychology*, 1963, **66**, 3–11.

Barron, F. The psychology of imagination. *Scientific American*, 1958, **199**, 151–166.

Bem, D. J. *Beliefs, attitudes, and human affairs.* Belmont, California: Brooks/Cole, 1970.

Bennett, J. The resistance against the German occupation of Denmark 1940–1945. In A. Roberts (Ed.), *Civilian resistance as a national defense.* Harrisburg, Pa.: Stackpole Books, 1968.

Berkowitz, L. Some aspects of observed aggression. *Journal of Personality and Social Psychology*, 1965, **2**, 359–369.

Berkowitz, L. and LePage, A. Weapons as aggression-eliciting stimuli. *Journal of Personality and Social Psychology*, 1967, **7**, 202–207.

Berlyne, D. E. An experimental study of human curiosity. *British Journal of Psychology*, 1954, **45**, 256–265.

Berlyne, D. E. The influence of complexity and novelty in visual figures on orienting responses. *Journal of Experimental Psychology*, 1958, **55**, 289–296. (a)

Berlyne, D. E. Supplementary report: Complexity and orienting responses with longer exposures. *Journal of Experimental Psychology*, 1958, **56**, 183. (b)

271

Berlyne, D. E. *Conflict, arousal, and curiosity.* New York: McGraw-Hill, 1960.

Berlyne, D. E. Complexity and incongruity variables as determinants of exploratory choice and evaluative ratings. *Canadian Journal of Psychology,* 1963, **17,** 274–290.

Berlyne, D. E. *Structure and direction in thinking.* New York: Wiley, 1965.

Berlyne, D. E. Curiosity and exploration. *Science,* 1966, **153,** 25–33.

Berlyne, D. E. Novelty, complexity, and hedonic value. *Perception and Psychophysics,* 1970, **8,** 279–286.

Berlyne, D. E. and Frommer, F. D. Some determinants of the incidence and content of children's questions. *Child Development,* 1966, **37,** 177–189.

Berlyne, D. E. and Lawrence, G. H. Effects of complexity and incongruity variables on GSR, investigatory behavior, and verbally expressed preference. *Journal of General Psychology,* 1964, **71,** 21–45.

Berlyne, D. E., Ogilvie, J. C., and Parham, L. C. C. The dimensionality of visual complexity, interestingness, and pleasingness. *Canadian Journal of Psychology,* 1968, **22,** 376–387.

Bernard, V. W., Ottenberg, P., and Redl, F. Dehumanization. In N. Sanford and C. Comstock (Eds.), *Sanctions for evil.* San Francisco: Jossey-Bass, 1971. Quotation used with permission.

Berscheid, E. and Walster, E. H. *Interpersonal attraction.* Reading, Mass.: Addison-Wesley, 1969.

Blumenthal, M. D. Predicting attitudes toward violence. *Science,* 1972, **176,** 1296–1303.

Bondurant, J. V. *Conquest of violence: The Gandhian philosophy of conflict.* (Rev. ed.) Berkeley and Los Angeles: University of California Press, 1965. Originally published by the University of California Press; quotations reprinted by permission of the Regents of the University of California.

Bondurant, J. V. Satyagraha versus duragraha: The limits of symbolic violence. In G. Ramachandran and T. K. Mahadevan (Eds.), *Gandhi: His relevance for our times.* (Rev. ed.) Berkeley: World Without War Council, 1967.

Boserup, A. and Iverson, C. Demonstrations as a source of change. *Journal of Peace Research,* 1966, No. 4, 328–348.

Brehm, J. W. *A theory of psychological reactance.* New York: Academic Press, 1966.

Brehm, J. W. and Cohen, A. R. *Explorations in cognitive dissonance.* New York: Wiley, 1962.

Brinton, C. *The anatomy of revolution.* (Rev. ed.) New York: Prentice-Hall, 1952.

Brock, T. C. and Buss, A. H. Dissonance, aggression, and evaluation of pain. *Journal of Abnormal and Social Psychology,* 1962, **65,** 197–202.

Bruner, J. S. On perceptual readiness. *Psychological Review,* 1957, **64,** 123–152.

Burnstein, E. and Worchel, P. Arbitrariness of frustration and its consequences for aggression in a social situation. *Journal of Personality,* 1962, **30,** 528–541.

Burtt, E. A. *The metaphysical foundations of modern physical science.* (Rev. ed.) London: Routledge & Kegan Paul, 1932.

Cameron, J. M. On violence. *The New York Review of Books,* 1970, **XV,** No. 1, 24–32.

Carlsmith, J. M., Collins, B. E., and Helmreich, R. K. Studies in forced compliance: I. The effect of pressure for compliance on attitude change produced by face-to-face role playing and anonymous essay writing. *Journal of Personality and Social Psychology,* 1966, **4,** 1–13.

Carlson, E. R. Attitude change through modification of attitude structure. *Journal of Abnormal and Social Psychology,* 1956, **52,** 256–261.

Cartwright, D. and Zander, A. Power and influence in groups: Introduction. In D. Cartwright and A. Zander (Eds.), *Group dynamics*. (3rd ed.) New York: Harper & Row, 1968. Quotation used with permission.

Case, C. M. *Non-violent coercion*. New York and London: Century, 1923.

Chadwick, R. W. Power, control, social entropy, and the concept of causation in social science: A perspective for the individual. Presented at the Albany Symposium on Social Power, State University of New York at Albany, October, 1971.

Clark, K. B. The pathos of power: A psychological perspective. *American Psychologist*, 1971, **26**, 1047–1057.

Coch, L. and French, J. R. P., Jr. Overcoming resistance to change. *Human Relations*, 1948, **1**, 512–532.

Cohen, A. R. Social norms, arbitrariness of frustration, and status of the agent of frustration in the frustration-aggression hypothesis. *Journal of Abnormal and Social Psychology*, 1955, **51**, 222–226.

Collins, B. E. and Raven, B. H. Group structure: Attraction, coalitions, communication, and power. In G. Lindzey and E. Aronson (Eds.), *Handbook of social psychology*. Vol. 4. (2nd ed.) Reading, Mass.: Addison-Wesley, 1969.

Cooper, J. Effectiveness of students in the dissemination of political leaflets. In P. Zimbardo (Chm.), Freaks, hippies, and voters: The effects of deviant dress and appearance on political persuasion processes. Symposium presented at the meeting of the Eastern Psychological Association, New York, April 1971.

Coser, L. A. *The functions of social conflict*. London: The Free Press of Glencoe, Collier-Macmillan, 1956.

Crow, W. J. A study of strategic doctrines using the Inter-Nation Simulation. *Journal of Conflict Resolution*. 1963, **7**, 580–589.

Culbertson, F. M. Modification of an emotionally held attitude through role-playing. *Journal of Abnormal and Social Psychology*, 1957, **54**, 230–233.

Davidson, J. Cognitive familiarity and dissonance reduction. In L. Festinger (Ed.), *Conflict, decision, and dissonance*. Stanford, California: Stanford University Press, 1964.

Davis, K. E. and Jones, E. E. Changes in interpersonal perception as a means of reducing cognitive dissonance. *Journal of Abnormal and Social Psychology*, 1960, **61**, 402–410.

Day, H. and Berlyne, D. E. Human responses to complexity. Paper presented at the 27th Annual Meeting of the Canadian Psychological Association, Montreal, 1966.

de Jouvenel, B. *On power*. Boston: Beacon Press, 1962. (Originally published: Geneva: Les Editions du Cheval Ailé, 1945.) Copyright © 1948 by The Viking Press, Inc. Quotations reprinted by permission of The Viking Press, Inc.

Deming, B. On revolution and equilibrium. *Liberation Magazine*, Feb., 1968. (Also published in Deming, B. *Revolution and equilibrium*. New York: Grossman, 1971.) Quotations used with permission.

de Rivera, J. *The psychological dimension of foreign policy*. Columbus, Ohio: Merrill, 1968.

Desai, M. H. *A righteous struggle*. Ahmedabad, India: Navajivan Publishing House, 1951. Quotations used with permission.

Deutsch, M. Trust and suspicion. *Journal of Conflict Resolution*, 1958, **2**, 265–279.

Deutsch, M. The effect of motivational orientation upon trust and suspicion. *Human Relations*, 1960, **13**, 123–139.

Deutsch, M. and Collins, M. E. *Interracial housing: A psychological evaluation of a social experiment*. Minneapolis: University of Minnesota Press, 1951.

Deutsch, M., Epstein, Y., Canavan, D., and Gumpert, P. Strategies of inducing cooperation: An experimental study. *Journal of Conflict Resolution,* 1967, **11**, 345–360.

Diwakar, R. R. *Satyagraha: Its technique and history.* Bombay: Hind Kitabs, 1946.

Ebert, T. Non-violent resistance against Communist regimes? In A. Roberts (Ed.), *Civilian resistance as a national defense.* Harrisburg, Pa.: Stackpole Books, 1968. (a)

Ebert, T. Organization in civilian defense. In A. Roberts (Ed.), *Civilian resistance as a national defense.* Harrisburg, Pa.: Stackpole Books, 1968. (b)

Ehrlich, H. J. Attitudes, behavior, and the intervening variables. *American Sociologist,* Vol. 4, No. 1, Feb., 1969.

Erikson, E. H. *Gandhi's truth.* New York: Norton, 1969.

Etzioni, A. Kennedy's Russian experiment. *Psychology Today,* Dec., 1969, **3**, No. 7.

Feshbach, S. and Singer, R. D. *Television and aggression.* San Francisco: Jossey-Bass, 1971.

Festinger, L. An analysis of compliant behavior. In M. Sherif and M. O. Wilson (Eds.), *Group relations at the crossroads.* New York: Harper, 1953.

Festinger, L. *A theory of cognitive dissonance.* Evanston, Ill.: Row, Peterson, 1957.

Festinger, L. and Carlsmith, J. M. Cognitive consequences of forced compliance. *Journal of Abnormal and Social Psychology,* 1959, **58**, 203–211.

Frank, J. D. *Sanity and survival: Psychological aspects of war and peace.* New York: Vintage Books, 1967.

Frazier, T. R. An analysis of nonviolent coercion as used by the sit-in movement. *Phylon,* 1968, **29**, 27–40.

Freedman, J. L. and Sears, D. O. Selective exposure. In L. Berkowitz (Ed.), *Advances in experimental social psychology.* Vol. 2. New York and London: Academic Press, 1965.

French, J. R. P., Jr. and Raven, B. The bases of social power. In D. Cartwright and A. Zander (Eds.), *Group dynamics.* (3rd ed.) New York: Harper & Row, 1968. (Originally published: In D. Cartwright [Ed.], *Studies in social power.* Ann Arbor, Mich.: Institute for Social Research, 1959.)

French, J. R. P., Jr., Morrison, H. W., and Levinger, G. Coercive power and forces affecting conformity. *Journal of Abnormal and Social Psychology,* 1960, **61**, 93–101.

Gandhi, M. K. *Constructive Programme: Its meaning and place.* Ahmedabad, India: Navajivan Press, 1941. Quotations used with permission from the Navajivan Trust.

Gandhi, M. K. *Gandhi's autobiography: The story of my experiments with truth.* Washington, D.C.: Public Affairs Press, 1954. (a) Quotations used with permission.

Gandhi, M. K. *Satyagraha in South Africa.* Stanford, California: Academic Reprints, 1954. (b)

Gandhi, M. K. *Non-violent resistance.* New York: Schocken Books, 1961. (Originally published: Ahmedabad, India: Navajivan Publishing House, 1951.) Quotations used with permission from the Navajivan Trust.

Glass, D. C. Changes in liking as a means of reducing cognitive discrepancies between self-esteem and aggression. *Journal of Personality,* 1964, **32**, 531–549.

Gore, P. M. and Rotter, J. B. A personality correlate of social action. *Journal of Personality,* 1963, **31**, 58–64.

Gouldner, A. W. The norm of reciprocity: A preliminary statement. *American Sociological Review,* 1960, **25**, 161–178.

Green, J. A. Attitudinal and situational determinants of intended behavior toward blacks. *Journal of Personality and Social Psychology,* 1972, **22**, 13–17.

Greenwald, A. G. Cognitive learning, cognitive response to persuasion, and attitude change. In A. G. Greenwald, T. C. Brock and T. M. Ostrom (Eds.), *Psychological foundations of attitudes.* New York: Academic Press, 1968.

Greenwald, A. G. and Albert, R. D. Acceptance and recall of improvised arguments. *Journal of Personality and Social Psychology*, 1968, **8**, 31–34.

Greenwald, A. G. and Sakumura, J. S. Attitude and selective learning: Where are the phenomena of yesteryear? *Journal of Personality and Social Psychology*, 1967, **7**, 387–397.

Gregg, R. B. *The power of nonviolence.* (2nd rev. ed.) New York: Schocken Books, 1966. Quotations reprinted by permission of Schocken Books Inc. From *The power of nonviolence* by Richard B. Gregg. Copyright © 1935 by Richard B. Gregg. Second Revised Edition Copyright © 1959 by Richard B. Gregg.

Hartmann, D. P. Influence of symbolically modeled instrumental aggression and pain cues on aggressive behavior. *Journal of Personality and Social Psychology*, 1969, **11**, 280–288.

Hebb, D. O. On the nature of fear. *Psychological Review*, 1946, **53**, 259–276.

Hebb, D. O. Drives and the C. N. S. (conceptual nervous system). *Psychological Review*, 1955, **62**, 243–354.

Heider, F. and Simmel, M. An experimental study of apparent behavior. *American Journal of Psychology*, 1944, **57**, 243–259.

Hiller, E. T. *The strike.* Chicago: University of Chicago Press, 1928. Quotation used with permission.

Hinshaw, C. E. Non-violent resistance: A nation's way to peace. In M. Q. Sibley (Ed.), *The quiet battle*. Chicago: Quadrangle Books, 1963.

Hitler, A. *Mein Kampf.* New York: Reynal & Hitchcock, 1939. Edition published by arrangement with Houghton Mifflin. Quotations used with permission of Houghton Mifflin and Hutchinson Publishing Group Ltd. (United Kingdom publisher).

Horsburgh, H. J. N. *Non-violence and aggression: A study of Gandhi's moral equivalent of war.* London: Oxford University Press, 1968. Quotation used with permission.

Hovland, C. I. and Weiss, W. The influence of source credibility on communication effectiveness. *Public Opinion Quarterly*, 1951, **15**, 635–650.

Hovland, C. I., Lumsdaine, A. A., and Sheffield, F. D. *Experiments on mass communication.* Princeton, N. J.: Princeton University Press, 1949.

Hughan, J. W. Pacifism and invasion. In M. Q. Sibley (Ed.), *The quiet battle*. Chicago: Quadrangle Books, 1963.

Hyman, H. H. and Sheatsley, P. B. Attitudes toward desegregation. *Scientific American*, Dec., 1956, **195**, 35–39.

Hyman, H. H. and Sheatsley, P. B. Attitudes toward desegregation. *Scientific American*, July, 1964, **211**, 16–23.

Insko, C. A. One-sided versus two-sided communications and counter-communications. *Journal of Abnormal and Social Psychology*, 1962, **65**, 203–206.

Jameson, A. K. New way in Norway? In M. Q. Sibley (Ed.), *The quiet battle*. Chicago: Quadrangle Books, 1963.

Janis, I. L. Groupthink among policy makers. In N. Sanford and C. Comstock (Eds.), *Sanctions for evil*. San Francisco: Jossey-Bass, 1971.

Janis, I. L. and Gilmore, J. B. The influence of incentive conditions on the success of role playing in modifying attitudes. *Journal of Personality and Social Psychology*, 1965, **1**, 17–27.

Janis, I. L. and King, B. T. The influence of role-playing on opinion change. *Journal of Abnormal and Social Psychology*, 1954, **49**, 211–218.

Janis, I. L. and Mann, L. Effectiveness of emotional role-playing in modifying smoking habits and attitudes. *Journal of Experimental Research in Personality*, 1965, **1**, 84–90.

Janis, I. L. and Rausch, C. N. Selective interest in communications that could arouse decisional conflict: A field study of participants in the draft-resistance movement. *Journal of Personality and Social Psychology*, 1970, **14**, 46–54.

Jecker, J. and Landy, D. Liking a person as a function of doing him a favour. *Human Relations*, 1969, **22**, 371–378.

Kanouse, D. E. and Wiest, W. M. Some factors affecting choice in the Prisoner's Dilemma. *Journal of Conflict Resolution*, 1967, **11**, 206–213.

Katz, D. and Stotland, E. A preliminary statement to a theory of attitude structure and change. In S. Koch (Ed.), *Psychology: A study of a science*. Vol. 3: *Formulations of the person and the social context*. New York: McGraw-Hill, 1959.

Kauffmann, D. R. Incentive to perform counterattitudinal acts: Bribe or gold star? *Journal of Personality and Social Psychology*, 1971, **19**, 82–91.

Kaufmann, H. *Aggression and altruism*. New York: Holt, Rinehart & Winston, 1970.

Keating, J. P. and Brock, T. C. A myth about distraction. *American Scientist*, July–August, 1971, **59**, 416–419.

Kelman, H. C. Compliance, identification, and internalization: three processes of attitude change. *Journal of Conflict Resolution*, 1958, **2**, 51–60.

Kelman, H. C. Processes of opinion change. *Public Opinion Quarterly*, 1961, **25**, 57–78.

Kelman, H. C. The induction of action and attitude change. In S. Coopersmith (Ed.), *Personality research*. Copenhagen: Munksgaards, 1962. Quotations used with permission.

Kelman, H. C. *A time to speak: On human values and social research*. San Francisco: Jossey-Bass, 1968. Quotations used with permission.

Kelman, H. C. and Hovland, C. I. "Reinstatement" of the communicator in delayed measurement of opinion change. *Journal of Abnormal and Social Psychology*, 1953, **48**, 327–335.

Kelman, H. C. and Lawrence, L. H. Assignment of responsibility in the case of Lt. Calley: Preliminary report on a national survey. *Journal of Social Issues*, 1972, **28**, 177–212.

Kiesler, C. A. *The psychology of commitment*. New York and London: Academic Press, 1971.

King, B. T. and Janis, I. L. Comparison of the effectiveness of improvised versus non-improvised role-playing in producing opinion changes. *Human Relations*, 1956, **9**, 177–186.

King, M. L., Jr. *Stride toward freedom*. New York: Harper & Row, 1958. Quotations used with permission.

King, M. L., Jr. *The trumpet of conscience*. New York: Harper & Row, 1967. Quotations used with permission.

King, M. L., Jr. *Where do we go from here: chaos or community?* New York: Bantam Books, 1968. (Originally published: New York: Harper & Row, 1967.) Quotations used with permission.

King-Hall, S. *Defense in the Nuclear Age*. Nyack, New York: Fellowship Publications, 1959.

Koestler, A. Mahatma Gandhi—the yogi and the commissar. *The New York Times Magazine*, Oct. 5, 1969.

Koffka, K. *Principles of Gestalt psychology*. New York: Harcourt, Brace, 1935.

Köhler, W. *Gestalt psychology*. New York: Liveright, 1929.

Komorita, S. S. Cooperative choice in a Prisoner's Dilemma game. *Journal of Personality and Social Psychology*, 1965, **2**, 741–745.

Krech, D., Crutchfield, R. S., and Ballachey, E. L. *Individual in society*. New York: McGraw-Hill, 1962.

Kregarman, J. J. and Worchel, P. Arbitrariness of frustration and aggression. *Journal of Abnormal and Social Psychology*, 1961, **63**, 183–187.

Kuhn, T. S. *The structure of scientific revolutions.* Chicago and London: University of Chicago Press, 1962.

Kumarappa, B. Editor's note. In Gandhi, M. K. *Non-violent resistance.* New York: Schocken Books, 1961. (Originally published: Ahmedabad, India: Navajivan Press, 1951.) Quotation used with permission of Navajivan Trust.

Laidler, H. W. *Boycotts and the labor struggle.* New York: John Lane, 1913.

Lakey, G. R. The sociological mechanisms of non-violent action. *Peace Research Reviews*, 1968, Vol. II, No. 6.

Lave, L. B. Factors affecting cooperation in the Prisoner's Dilemma. *Behavioral Science*, 1965, **10**, 26–38.

Leeper, R. A study of a neglected portion of the field of learning—the development of sensory organization. *Journal of Genetic Psychology*, 1935, **46**, 41–75.

Lelyveld, J. The story of a soldier who refused to fire at Songmy. *The New York Times Magazine*, Dec. 14, 1969. Quotation used with permission.

Lerner, M. J. The desire for justice and reactions to victims. In J. Macaulay and L. Berkowitz (Eds.), *Altruism and helping behavior.* New York: Academic Press, 1970. Quotations used with permission.

Lerner, M. J. Observer's evaluation of a victim: Justice, guilt, and veridical perception. *Journal of Personality and Social Psychology*, 1971, **20**, 127–135.

Lerner, M. J. and Matthews, G. Reactions to the suffering of others under conditions of indirect responsibility. *Journal of Personality and Social Psychology*, 1967, **5**, 319–325.

Lerner, M. J. and Simmons, C. H. Observer's reaction to the "innocent victim": Compassion or rejection? *Journal of Personality and Social Psychology*, 1966, **4**, 203–210.

Levine, J. M. and Murphy, G. The learning and forgetting of controversial material. *Journal of Abnormal and Social Psychology*, 1943, **38**, 507–517.

Liddell Hart, B. H. *Deterrent or defense.* New York: Praeger, 1960.

Lifton, R. J. Existential evil. In N. Sanford and C. Comstock (Eds.), *Sanctions for evil.* San Francisco: Jossey-Bass, 1971.

Lincoln, A. and Levinger, G. Observers' evaluations of the victim and the attacker in an aggressive incident. *Journal of Personality and Social Psychology*, 1972, **22**, 202–210.

Linder, D. E., Cooper, J., and Jones, E. E. Decision freedom as a determinant of the role of incentive magnitude in attitude change. *Journal of Personality and Social Psychology*, 1967, **6**, 245–254.

Lowin, A. Approach and avoidance: Alternative modes of selective exposure to information. *Journal of Personality and Social Psychology*, 1967, **6**, 1–9.

Lowin, A. Further evidence for an approach-avoidance interpretation of selective exposure. *Journal of Experimental Social Psychology*, 1969, **5**, 265–271.

Lumsdaine, A. A. and Janis, I. L. Resistance to "counter-propaganda" produced by one-sided and two-sided "propaganda" presentations. *Public Opinion Quarterly*, 1953, **17**, 311–318.

Maccoby, E. E. The development of moral values and behavior in childhood. In J. A. Clausen (Ed.), *Socialization and society.* Boston: Little, Brown, 1968.

Mantell, D. M. The potential for violence in Germany. *Journal of Social Issues*, 1971, **27**, 101–112.

Matthiessen, P. *Sal si puedes: Cesar Chavez and the new American Revolution.* New York: Random House, 1969.

McGuire, W. J. The effectiveness of supportive and refutational defenses in immunizing and restoring beliefs against persuasion. *Sociometry*, 1961, **24**, 184–197.

McGuire, W. J. Inducing resistance to persuasion. In L. Berkowitz (Ed.), *Advances in experimental social psychology*. Vol. I. New York: Academic Press, 1964.

McGuire, W. J. and Papageorgis, D. The relative efficacy of various types of prior belief-defense in producing immunity against persuasion. *Journal of Abnormal and Social Psychology*, 1961, **62**, 327–337.

Meeker, R. and Shure, G. Pacifist bargaining tactics: Some "outsider" influences. *Journal of Conflict Resolution*, 1969, **13**, 487–493.

Merleau-Ponty, M. *Phenomenology of perception*. (Translated from the French by C. Smith.) New York: Humanities Press, 1962.

Michener, J. A. What to do about the Palestinian refugees? *The New York Times Magazine*, Sept. 27, 1970.

Milgram, S. Nationality and conformity. *Scientific American*, Dec., 1961, **205**, 45–51.

Milgram, S. Behavioral study of obedience. *Journal of Abnormal and Social Psychology*, 1963, **67**, 371–378.

Milgram, S. Liberating effects of group pressure. *Journal of Personality and Social Psychology*, 1965, **1**, 127–134. (a)

Milgram, S. Some conditions of obedience and disobedience to authority. *Human Relations*, 1965, **18**, 57–76. (b) Quotations used with permission.

Miller, W. R. *Nonviolence: A Christian interpretation*. New York: Association Press, 1964.

Mills, J. Opinion change as a function of the communicator's desire to influence and liking for the audience. *Journal of Experimental Social Psychology*, 1966, **2**, 152–159.

Minas, J. S., Scodel, A., Marlowe, D., and Rawson, H. Some descriptive aspects of two-person non-zero-sum games: II. *Journal of Conflict Resolution*, 1960, **4**, 193–197.

Munsinger, H. and Kessen, W. Uncertainty, structure, and preference. *Psychological Monographs*, 1964, **78** (Whole No. 586), 1–24.

Nader, R. *Unsafe at any speed*. New York: Grossman, 1965.

Naess, A. Nonmilitary defense. In Q. Wright, W. M. Evan, and M. Deutsch (Eds.), *Preventing World War III: Some proposals*. New York: Simon & Schuster, 1962.

Nanda, B. R. *Mahatma Gandhi: A biography*. Boston: Beacon Press, 1958. Quotations used with permission of Allen & Unwin Ltd.

Ofshe, R. The effectiveness of pacifist strategies: A theoretical approach. *Journal of Conflict Resolution*, 1971, **XV**, 261–269.

Oglesby, C. Vietnamese crucible: an essay on the meanings of the Cold War. In C. Oglesby and R. Shaull, *Containment and change*. New York: Macmillan, 1967.

Opton, E. M., Jr. It never happened and besides they deserved it. In N. Sanford and C. Comstock (Eds.), *Sanctions for evil*. San Francisco: Jossey-Bass, 1971. Quotations used with permission.

Orbison, W. D. Shape as a function of the vector field. *American Journal of Psychology*, 1939, **52**, 31–45.

Orne, M. T. On the social psychology of the psychological experiment. *American Psychologist*, 1962, **17**, 776–783.

Osgood, C. E. *Method and theory in experimental psychology*. New York: Oxford University Press, 1953.

Osgood, C. E. *An alternative to war or surrender*. Urbana, Ill.: University of Illinois Press, 1962.

Osterhouse, R. A. and Brock, T. C. Distraction increases yielding to propaganda by inhibiting counterarguing. *Journal of Personality and Social Psychology,* 1970, **15,** 344–358.

Page, M. M. and Scheidt, R. J. The elusive weapons effect: Demand awareness, evaluation apprehension, and slightly sophisticated subjects. *Journal of Personality and Social Psychology,* 1971, **20,** 304–318.

Papageorgis, D. and McGuire, W. J. The generality of immunity to persuasion produced by pre-exposure to weakened counterarguments. *Journal of Abnormal and Social Psychology,* 1961, **62,** 475–481.

Pastore, N. The role of arbitrariness in the frustration-aggression hypothesis. *Journal of Abnormal and Social Psychology,* 1952, **47,** 728–731.

Perloe, S. I., Olton, D. S., and Yaffe, D. L. The effect of nonviolent action on social attitudes. *Sociological Inquiry,* 1968, **38,** 13–22.

Pettigrew, T. F. Regional differences in anti-Negro prejudice. *Journal of Abnormal and Social Psychology,* 1959, **59,** 28–36.

Pettigrew, T. F. Social psychology and desegregation research. *American Psychologist,* 1961, **16,** 105–112.

Piaget, J. *The moral judgment of the child.* New York: Free Press, 1965.

Pierce, C. M. and West, L. J. Six years of sit-ins: Psychodynamic causes and effects. *International Journal of Social Psychiatry,* 1966, **12,** 29–34.

Pilisuk, M. and Skolnick, P. Inducing trust: A test of the Osgood proposal. *Journal of Personality and Social Psychology,* 1968, **8,** 121–133.

Powers, P. C. and Geen, R. G. Effects of the behavior and the perceived arousal of a model on instrumental aggression. *Journal of Personality and Social Psychology,* 1972, **23,** 175–183.

Rajendraprasad. *Satyagraha in Champaran.* (2nd rev. ed.) Ahmedabad, India: Navajivan Press, 1949.

Rapoport, A. and Chammah, A. M. *Prisoner's dilemma.* Ann Arbor, Mich.: University of Michigan Press, 1965.

Raven, B. H. Social influence and power. In I. D. Steiner and M. Fishbein (Eds.), *Current studies in social psychology.* New York: Holt, Rinehart & Winston, 1965.

Raven, B. H. and French, J. R. P., Jr. Legitimate power, coercive power and observability in social influence. *Sociometry,* 1958, **21,** 83–97.

Raven, B. H. and Kruglanski, A. W. Conflict and power. In P. Swingle (Ed.), *The structure of conflict.* New York and London: Academic Press, 1970.

Regan, J. W. Guilt, perceived injustice, and altruistic behavior. *Journal of Personality and Social Psychology,* 1971, **18,** 124–132.

Roberts, A. Civilian defense strategy. In A. Roberts (Ed.), *Civilian resistance as a national defense.* Harrisburg, Pa.: Stackpole Books, 1968. Quotations used with permission.

Rogers, R. W. and Thistlethwaite, D. L. An analysis of active and passive defenses in inducing resistance to persuasion. *Journal of Personality and Social Psychology,* 1969, **11,** 301–308.

Rokeach, M. *Beliefs, attitudes, and values.* San Francisco: Jossey-Bass, 1968.

Rokeach, M. Persuasion that persists. *Psychology Today,* Sept., 1971, **5,** No. 4.

Rokeach, M. and Kliejunas, P. Behavior as a function of attitude-toward-object and attitude-toward-situation. *Journal of Personality and Social Psychology,* 1972, **22,** 194–201.

Rokeach, M., Smith, P. W., and Evans, R. I. Two kinds of prejudice or one? In M. Rokeach, *The open and closed mind.* New York: Basic Books, 1960.

Rosenberg, M. J. Cognitive structure and attitudinal affect. *Journal of Abnormal and Social Psychology*, 1956, **53**, 367–373.

Rosenberg, M. J. Cognitive reorganization in response to the hypnotic reversal of attitudinal affect. *Journal of Personality*, 1960, **28**, 39–63.

Rosenberg, M. J. When dissonance fails: On eliminating evaluation apprehension from attitude measurement. *Journal of Personality and Social Psychology*, 1965, **1**, 28–43.

Rosenberg, M. J. Some limits of dissonance: toward a differentiated view of counter-attitudinal performance. In S. Feldman (Ed.), *Cognitive consistency*. New York and London: Academic Press, 1966.

Rosenberg, M. J. Hedonism, inauthenticity, and other goads toward expansion of a consistency theory. In R. P. Abelson, E. Aronson, W. J. McGuire, T. M. Newcomb, M. J. Rosenberg, and P. H. Tannenbaum (Eds.), *Theories of cognitive consistency: A sourcebook*. Chicago: Rand McNally, 1968.

Rothaus, P. and Worchel, P. The inhibition of aggression under non-arbitrary frustration. *Journal of Personality*, 1960, **28**, 108–117.

Rubin, E. *Visuell wahrgenommene Figuren*. Copenhagen: Gyldendalske, 1921.

Rubin, E. Figure and ground. In D. C. Beardslee and M. Wertheimer (Eds.), *Readings in perception*. Princeton, N.J.: Van Nostrand, 1958.

Sampson, E. E. *Social psychology and contemporary society*. New York: Wiley, 1971.

Sanford, N. and Comstock, C. Sanctions for evil. In N. Sanford and C. Comstock (Eds.), *Sanctions for evil*. San Francisco: Jossey-Bass, 1971. Quotations used with permission.

Scholmer, J. Vorkuta: Strike in a concentration camp. In M. Q. Sibley (Ed.), *The quiet battle*. Chicago: Quadrangle Books, 1963.

Scodel, A., Minas, J. S., Ratoosh, P., and Lipetz, M. Some descriptive aspects of two-person non-zero-sum games. I. *Journal of Conflict Resolution*, 1959, **3**, 114–119.

Sears, D. O. Biased indoctrination and selectivity of exposure to new information. *Sociometry*, 1965, **28**, 363–376.

Sharp, G. *Gandhi wields the weapon of moral power*. Ahmedabad, India: Navajivan Press, 1960.

Sharp, G. Tyranny could not quell them. In M. Q. Sibley (Ed.), *The quiet battle*. Chicago: Quadrangle Books, 1963.

Sharp, G. The technique of non-violent action. In A. Roberts (Ed.), *Civilian resistance as a national defense*. Harrisburg, Pa.: Stackpole Books, 1968. Quotations used with permission.

Sharp, G. *Exploring nonviolent alternatives*. Boston: Porter Sargent, 1970.

Sharp, G. *The politics of nonviolent action*. Boston: Porter Sargent, 1973.

Sheatsley, P. B. White attitudes toward the Negro. *Daedalus*, 1966, **95**, 217–238. Quotation reprinted by permission of *Daedalus*, Journal of the American Academy of Arts and Sciences, Boston, Mass. Winter 1966, *The Negro American-2*.

Sherif, M. A preliminary experimental study of inter-group relations. In J. H. Rohrer and M. Sherif (Eds.), *Social psychology at the crossroads*. New York: Harper & Row, 1951.

Sherif, M. *In common predicament*. Boston: Houghton Mifflin, 1966. Quotations used with permission.

Sherif, M. and Sherif, C. W. *Groups in harmony and tension*. New York: Harper & Row, 1953.

Sherif, M. and Sherif, C. W. *An outline of social psychology*. (Rev. ed.) New York: Harper & Row, 1956. Quotations used with permission.

Sherif, M. and Sherif, C. W. *Social psychology*. New York: Harper & Row, 1969.

Shridharani, K. *War without violence.* New York: Harcourt, Brace, 1939. (Also published in revised and updated form: Bombay: Bharatiya Vidya Bhavan, 1962.) Quotations used with permission.

Shure, G. H., Meeker, R. J., and Hansford, E. H. The effectiveness of pacifist strategies in bargaining games. *Journal of Conflict Resolution,* 1965, **9,** 106–117.

Simmons, C. H. and Lerner, M. J. Altruism as a search for justice. *Journal of Personality and Social Psychology,* 1968, **9,** 216–225.

Skodvin, M. Norwegian non-violent resistance during the German occupation. In A. Roberts (Ed.), *Civilian resistance as a national defense.* Harrisburg, Pa.: Stackpole Books, 1968.

Smith, M. B., Bruner, J. S., and White, R. W. *Opinions and personality.* New York: Wiley, 1956.

Solomon, F. and Fishman, J. R. The psychosocial meaning of nonviolence in student civil rights activities. *Psychiatry,* 1964, **27,** 91–99. (a)

Solomon, F. and Fishman, J. R. Youth and peace: A psychosocial study of student peace demonstrators in Washington, D.C. *Journal of Social Issues,* 1964, **XX,** No. 4, 54–73. (b)

Solomon, F., Walker, W. L., O'Connor, G. J., and Fishman, J. R. Civil rights activity and reduction in crime among Negroes. *Archives of General Psychiatry,* 1965, **12,** 227–236.

Solomon, L. The influence of some types of power relationships and game strategies upon the development of interpersonal trust. *Journal of Abnormal and Social Psychology,* 1960, **61,** 223–230.

Stagner, R. *Psychological aspects of international conflict.* Belmont, California: Brooks/Cole, 1967.

Stanford, P. A model, clockwork-orange prison. *The New York Times Magazine,* Sept. 17, 1972.

Stotland, E., Katz, D., and Patchen, M. The reduction of prejudice through the arousal of self-insight. *Journal of Personality,* 1959, **27,** 507–531.

Tannenbaum, P. H. Initial attitude toward source and concept as factors in attitude change through communication. *Public Opinion Quarterly,* 1956, **20,** 413–425.

Tannenbaum, P. H. The congruity principle revisited: Studies in the reduction, induction and generalization of persuasion. In L. Berkowitz (Ed.), *Advances in experimental social psychology.* Vol. 3. New York: Academic Press, 1967.

Tannenbaum, P. H., Macaulay, J. R., and Norris, E. L. The principle of congruity and reduction of persuasion. *Journal of Personality and Social Psychology,* 1966, **3,** 233–238.

Thoreau, H. D. Civil disobedience. In O. Thomas (Ed.), *Henry David Thoreau: Walden and civil disobedience.* New York: Norton, 1966. Quotations used with permission.

Turiel, E. Developmental processes in the child's moral thinking. In P. H. Mussen, J. Langer, and M. Covington (Eds.), *Trends and issues in developmental psychology.* New York: Holt, Rinehart & Winston, 1969.

Ulrich, P. and Ammons, R. B. Voluntary control over perceived dimensionality (perspective) of three-dimensional objects. *Proceedings of the Montana Academy of Sciences,* 1959, **19,** 169–173.

Von Eschen, D., Kirk, J., and Pinard, M. The disintegration of the Negro non-violent movement. *Journal of Peace Research,* 1969, No. 3, 215–234.

Walker, E. L. and Heyns, R. W. *An anatomy for conformity.* Belmont, California: Brooks/Cole, 1967.

Walster, E. H., Berscheid, E., and Walster, G. W. The exploited: Justice or justification? In J. Macaulay and L. Berkowitz (Eds.), *Altruism and helping behavior.* New York: Academic Press, 1970.

Walster, E. and Prestholdt, P. The effect of misjudging another: Overcompensation or dissonance reduction? *Journal of Experimental Social Psychology*, 1966, **2**, 85–97.

Walters, R. H., Thomas, E. L., and Acker, C. W. Enhancement of punitive behavior by audiovisual displays. *Science*, 1962, **136**, 872–873.

Waly, P. and Cook, S. Attitude as a determinant of learning and memory: A failure to confirm. *Journal of Personality and Social Psychology*, 1966, **4**, 280–288.

Watson, G. *Social psychology: Issues and insights.* Philadelphia and New York: Lippincott, 1966.

Watts, W. A. Relative persistence of opinion change induced by active compared to passive participation. *Journal of Personality and Social Psychology*, 1967, **5**, 4–15.

Weintraub, D. J. and Walker, E. L. *Perception.* Belmont, California: Brooks/Cole, 1966.

Weiss, W. Opinion congruence with a negative source on one issue as a factor influencing agreement on another issue. *Journal of Abnormal and Social Psychology*, 1957, **54**, 180–186.

Werner, H. *Comparative psychology of mental development.* (Rev. ed.) New York: International Universities Press, 1948.

White, R. K. Misperception and the Vietnam War. *Journal of Social Issues*, 1966, 22, No. 3.

Wicker, A. W. Attitudes versus actions: The relationship of verbal and overt behavioral responses to attitude objects. *Journal of Social Issues*, 1969, **25**, No. 4, 41–78.

Wicker, A. W. An examination of the "other variables" explanation of attitude-behavior inconsistency. *Journal of Personality and Social Psychology*, 1971, **19**, 18–30.

Wilson, W. Cooperation and the cooperativeness of the other player. *Journal of Conflict Resolution*, 1969, **13**, 110–117.

Woodruff, H. and DiVesta, F. The relationship between values, concepts, and attitudes. *Educational and Psychological Measurement*, 1948, **8**, 645–660.

Worchel, S. and Brehm, J. W. Effect of threats to attitudinal freedom as a function of agreement with the communicator. *Journal of Personality and Social Psychology*, 1970, **14**, 18–22.

Young, P. T. *Motivation and emotion.* New York and London: Wiley, 1961.

Zajonc, R. B. Attitudinal effects of mere exposure. *Journal of Personality and Social Psychology Monograph Supplement*, 1968, **9**, 1–27.

Author Index

Subject Index

Agapē, 206, 268
Aggression
  in Arab–Israeli conflict, 39
  defined, 3–4
  as interpretation, 39, 42
  in Vietnam War, 42
Ahimsa, 16, 150, 157, 190n, 248n, 257, 268
  defined, 14–15
Ahmedabad textile workers' campaign,
  158–159, 163, 188n, 189n, 220, 222
Amritsar massacre, 173
Appeal to conscience, 50, 131–132, 143
Arab–Israeli conflict, 39–41, 109–110, 111,
  267
  and dehumanization, 200
  and Six-Day War, 39–40
Attitude
  and behavior, 71–80, 81n, 223, 226
  components of, 67, 81n
  defined, 67
  motivational bases of, 68–69
  stability of, 69–71, 75, 76, 90–91, 92–98,
  111n
Attitude change, 58, 70–71, 73–80, 81n,
  83–108, 111n, 115, 128–132, 134, 141,
  191, 222–228, 236, 248n
Attitudinal vacuity, 102–105, 109, 111n,
  227

Belief system(s), 53n
  of Arabs, 39–40

change of, 47, 49–50
  as construct, 35–36, 49, 193
  Hitler's, 43–44
  of Israelis, 39–40
  and new information, 45–52, 124–125,
  149, 194
Boycott, 153, 154, 166, 167, 183, 184, 189n.
  See also Montgomery bus boycott;
  Noncooperation

Cambodian invasion, 184
Catonsville Nine, 183, 185, 186
Champaran campaign, 83–85, 111n, 163,
  214
Civil disobedience. *See* Disobedience,
  civil
Civil rights movement, 114, 115, 128–135,
  141–143, 144–146, 150, 155, 167, 168,
  171, 172, 173, 180–181, 240, 246, 252
Cognitive consistency, 44–52, 81n, 248n
Cognitive construction, 34–41
Cognitive dissonance, 44–52, 73–75, 111n,
  121, 123–125, 127, 146–147n, 248n
Cognitive uncertainty, 118, 122
Conflict
  and attitude change, 222–228
  and dehumanization, 199–207
  deterioration of, 192–199, 205
  and friendship, 219–222, 228, 232
  and game mentality, 17–18, 21, 22, 193
  and games, 19–26

Noncooperation (*continued*)
and coercion, 165–167, 186
and constructive work, 162–169
and democracy, 169–172
in foreign policy, 259–263
as form of coercive power, 59–60, 80, 143, 150–151, 159, 218, 219, 227
as form of reward power, 61
forms of, 153–155
and interdependence, 240–247, 248n
moral and practical bases of, 150–153
and organization, 152–153, 154, 168, 174–176, 187–189n, 219
and personal touch method, 221
protest characteristics of, 177, 181–182
and psychological resistance, 207, 208–210, 223, 224
and revolution, 175
and self-determination, 155–162
sit-in as, 180–182
with totalitarianism and invasion, 172–180
and violence, 146
Nonviolence
and the atom bomb, 1
and attitude change, 222–228
and constructive work, 162–169
criticisms of, 251–259
and democracy, 169–172
and friendship, 219–222
and independence, 241–247
and interdependence, 238–247
and means and ends, 251–269 (*see also* Means and ends)
and noncooperation, 149–187
and organization, 152–153, 174, 253
and peace, 263–269
and persuasion, 83–87, 105, 110–111
as a philosophy of action, 5, 14–19
and power, 25, 26, 55–56, 59–60, 61, 64, 65, 66, 79, 80
and the power of information, 83–111
preventive, in foreign policy, 259–263
and protest, 113–146
and psychological effects on participants, 133–135
and reducing psychological resistance, 204–210

and resistance against totalitarianism
and invasion, 172–180
and self-determination, 155–162
and self-suffering, 135–144
and superordinate goals, 228–238
and trusting behavior, 210–219
Nonviolent campaign, stages of, 26, 113, 150, 153. *See also* Nonviolence
Nonviolent intervention and obstruction, 182–186
Nonviolent protest. *See* Protest, nonviolent
Northern Ireland conflict, 68–69, 200, 267
Norwegian resistance against Nazi occupation, 174, 246
Novelty, 118–120, 122–123, 124, 125, 127, 147–148n, 182
Nuclear arms race, 122–123, 215–218, 236–237

Obedience, 151, 156, 182, 242
and dehumanization, 201–204
and legitimate power, 63–65, 156, 169
and violence, 10–14, 201–204

Peace, 263–269
Pentagon Papers, 9, 169–170
Perceptual facts
defined, 34
interpretation of, 37–41, 42, 46, 48–49, 65–66, 81n, 87–88, 110–111, 193, 194, 195
and stereotypes, 36–37
Perceptual organization, 28–34, 35, 38, 53n, 87
Personal touch method, 220–221, 222
Persuasion
and attitudinal vacuity, 102–105
and credibility, 95, 101
defined, 49
and distraction, 92
and information, 66–67, 83–108, 149
and inoculation, 93–96, 104, 111n
nonviolent, 83–87, 110
and psychological resistance, 89–90, 99–101
and rationalization, 105–108
and role-playing, 90–91, 95–96, 111n

TITLES IN THE PERGAMON GENERAL PSYCHOLOGY SERIES